MY SECRETS FOR BETTER COOKING

Madame Benoit

My Secrets for Better Cooking

 Les éditions Héritage inc.

PRODUCTION
Director: Bernard Benoit
Assistant: Ginette Guétat
Editorial consultant: Michelle Robertson

ART AND DESIGN
Director: Dufour et Fille, Design
Illustrations: Christine Dufour

PHOTOGRAPHY
Director: Paul Casavant

Données de catalogage avant publication (Canada)

Benoit, Jehane, 1904-1987

    My secrets for better cooking

    Issued also in French under title:
    Mes secrets de la bonne cuisine

    ISBN 2-7625-6057-8 (v. 1)

    1. Cookery. I. Benoit, Bernard II. Guétat, Ginette.
    III. Robertson, Michelle. IV. Title.

    TX651.B4613   1990   641.5   C90-096619-X

Copyright© 1990 Les Éditions Héritage Inc.
All rights reserved

Legal deposit: 4th quarter 1990
National Library of Canada

ISBN: 2-7625-6057-8   Printed in Canada

LES ÉDITIONS HÉRITAGE INC.
300, Arran, Saint-Lambert, Québec J4R 1K5
(514) 875-0327

Contents

Introduction

IN THE PAST few decades our living patterns have changed drastically. In today's world, food is moved from country to country rapidly; food processing and preservation techniques are highly developed; refrigeration and freezing are universal; and there are many mechanical and electrical kitchen aids, such as the blender, the mixer, the food processor, the electric frypan, coffee makers, and convection and microwave ovens. The result of all this is that we are much more capable of exploiting the natural flavors of a great many basic foods, including some once considered the specialties of a short season or imported exotics impossible for the average family to sample.

As for the future, no doubt there is much to come that we, at this point, can only imagine. Certainly there will be more cooking aids and new methods of food preparation. Soon everyone will be cooking with microwave ovens. This will mean almost instant cooking with little water, fat or other medium required.

Another change is increased informality. Mealtime is no longer a solumn occasion, but a time for togetherness. Even when entertaining, this trend is in force. Though we still sometimes have formal dinners or luncheons, we are more apt to invite our guests for a picnic, a barbecue or for a buffet meal.

While our grandparents ate large meals with many courses, the trend today is toward meals that are both satisfying and nutritionally sound without being fattening. In fact, a knowledge of nutrition is something every homemaker needs.

To provide the daily food three generations ago, the housewife spent most of the day in the kitchen, but today's homemaker has a great many more things to do than her mother or grandmother ever dreamed of and this applies not only to the woman who goes out to work. In the face of all this, one may well ask how it is possible to provide calm, happy, gracious dining for one's family and friends.

One thing that will not change is the need to understand the basic techniques that facilitate every kind of cooking. My own experience has taught me that people with the will and the desire to learn and practice the fundamentals of good cooking — and these include how to shop for food as well as how to prepare it — have an inestimable advantage over those who, through ignorance or lack of interest, function haphazardly. Unfortunately, everyone cannot become an expert cook, but almost everyone can acquire a modest knowledge of food preparation. One basic recipe, thoroughtly understood, will enable even a fair cook to create variations without the help of any cookbook.

Another unchanging fact is that food is more than something to satisfy hunger. Good food can appeal to all five senses. The smell of good cooking never fails to stimulate the desire to taste; its fragrance seems to prickle our taste buds. Think for a moment of the smell of homemade bread fresh from the oven, or the delicious aroma of frying bacon or freshly ground coffee, or the subtle perfume of strawberries still warm from the sun. A hundred other fragrances could be conjured up, but let these suffice to prove the point. Food has its own perfume, which is an invitation to taste and enjoyment.

The sounds issuing from a busy kitchen — like the sizzle of chops, the rattle of a lid being lifted to taste a sauce, the clink of ice against glass — create in those who hear them a pleasant anticipation of the approaching meal. The sight of colorful food well arranged on a platter, even such a small touch as a sprig of green parsley on a mound of creamy mashed potatoes, seem to increase the appetite. Taste and touch are enhanced by contrasts, so the imaginative cook makes sure to combine foods with a variety of textures to please the tongue and palate.

An important thing to learn is what to mix with what, and how, because this broadens one's scope and frees one from the obligation of slavishly following the specific steps of particular recipes. With this sort of knowledge a cook can surpass even some of the great culinary masters. Most dishes are a combination of several ingredients that, when cooked together, enhance the taste of both themselves and each other. By varying the combinations, you are constantly able to create new dishes. This is the way to develop your own very definite personality as a cook, and you can become a truly creative artists in your cuisine.

Cooking is creative and should be treated as an art as well as a science. Both art and science begin in the food store, where you must know what to look for and how to receive the best value for every cent you spend, and they continue in the way you work with the food you have purchased and the way you finally present it at the table.

It is my hope that this book will teach you a great deal about the creative and artistic craft of cooking. You will be surprised when you discover how easy it is to produce meals with a touch of elegance. You will find here many of my personal notes on all aspects of food. I have recorded these notes from my own experiences in shopping, cooking, arranging menus, feeding my family and entertaining my friends. And I've added some of the information I discovered through my constant curiosity about food.

ALL OF MY SPECIAL SECRETS
I HAVE MARKED WITH THE
SYMBOL ⚷ .

I am convinced that there is no such thing as a cookbook containing entirely new and original recipes, since cooking of one sort or another has been going on since (Mère) Eve took her first bite of that apple. Therefore, I make no claim that this is a book of novelties. It is not meant to be a book of recipes, but an explanation of basic techniques and a brief survey of some fields of knowledge that will help you to understand foods and cooking much better.

The recipes and ideas you will find here are based on things I have learned as a food specialist and nutritionist, teacher, writer, broadcaster and, most important, wife, mother and hostess. While some of the recipes are quite specific and are meant to be followed exactly — at least for the first few times you make them — most of the recipes in this book are "patterns" or basic guides. You will use them to give you a start, and you will adapt the basic pattern to your own tastes and needs by choosing a different liquid or herb, or changing the proportions of the ingredients, and so on. My sincere wish is to stimulate you to experiment with food — in shopping for it, in cooking it, in serving it to your family and friends.

Jehane Benoit

CHAPTER 1

Nutrition: the key to health

FOOD MARKETS today offer such variety that it is sometimes difficult to select foods wisely as well as economically. To provide essential nourishment, you must serve foods providing adequate amounts of protein, carbohydrate and fat, plus vitamins and minerals; so you must understand the body's requirements and know what foods best fulfil them.

When we consider that the study of foods and their nutritive values is one of our more recent sciences, it is surprising to discover how much is already known. Chemical analysis of foods was relatively unknown before the beginning of the 20th century. To begin with, foods were analyzed only for their calories and for their fat, protein and carbohydrate content. Later work led to the discovery of other food ingredients: vitamins, minerals, amino acids that play an important role in growth and the maintenance of health. Scientists working in this field continue to add to our knowledge of nutrition.

A healthy body is the basic requirement for a good life as well as a long one, and you will learn from reading this section how you can improve your general health and feel more energetic by providing your body with the dietary materials it needs.

NOURISHMENT VALUES

The dietary needs of our bodies fall into three main categories: proteins, the "building blocks" we use for growth and repair and which help form antibodies to fight infection; carbohydrates, which supply fuel; and fats, which also have high caloric value and which store in the body certain essential vitamins and minerals until they can be used. In addition, we need to ensure that the protein, carbohydrates and fats we eat provide the vitamins and minerals that help the body function successfully. Some foods are more valuable contributors of vitamins and minerals than others.

Protein

By absorbing and using protein, the body creates bones, muscles, nerves, skin, hair and much more. In fact, almost half of the solid matter of the body is protein.

Plants manufacture protein by combining the energy of the sun with the nitrogen and moisture of the soil and the carbon dioxide in the air. Some animals, those that are ruminants, or cud-chewers, can create protein from the plants they eat. The human body, however, cannot itself manufacture protein, but must acquire it from the foods it digests. Once taken in, these proteins are broken down into smaller units and rearranged to form the special and distinct proteins the body needs.

Because of its similarity to human protein, animal protein such as that found in lean meat, fish, poultry, eggs, milk and cheese is of more value to us than the "poorer" vegetable proteins found in flours, cereals, beans, peas and peanut butter. By themselves, these poorer proteins cannot be used for repair or growth, so it is important to eat some animal protein every day.

Protein needs alter throughout life: an older person, one who is no longer growing but who is merely repairing existing tissues, needs less protein than do children, adolescents, pregnant women and nursing mothers.

When planning meals for your family, remember that fish and the cheaper cuts of meat provide as much protein as more expensive cuts of meat. All cheeses except cream cheese contain a good deal of protein. Throughout this book you will find suggestions for filling your family's protein needs as easily and as inexpensively as possible.

Carbohydrates

Starches and sugars comprise the food group known as carbohydrates. There are smaller amounts of carbohydrates in fruits, vegetables and milk, but the major proportion of our carbohydrate intake comes from bread and other baked goods, cereals, rice, macaroni and highly sweetened foods.

Sugar, a pure carbohydrate, is our poorest food, containing only its energy value and no proteins, vitamins or minerals at all. Sugar supplies us only with calories, and we usually obtain enough of these from other more nutritious foods so we cannot afford to overindulge in highly sweetened items.

Our bodies need carbohydrates not for their energy value alone, but also in order to use fats efficiently. Some diseases, such as diabetes, develop when the body is unable to handle the carbohydrates it takes in.

Fats

Is fat needed in our daily diet? Absolutely. High in calories, fat is the body's most concentrated source of energy. It is necessary for the utilization of protein and carbohydrates and is the storehouse for certain fat soluble vitamins.

Many claims have been made in recent years about the benefits of "polyunsaturated" fats and oils. An "unsaturated" fat is one that has some of its molecular "arms" free to join with other materials in the body. Unsaturated fats are more readily absorbed and can carry around other nutrients more easily than can saturated fats, which have no free "arms". Vegetable oils such as soya or sunflower oil have much more unsaturated fat than animal fats such as butter and lard.

Beware of "hidden" fats in foods. Recognizable fat, that found on meat, or in the form of butter, lard, drippings or shortening is not the only fat we eat. A glass of whole milk contains 159 calories, of which 81 come from fat. Of the 181 calories in 1.5 ounces (45 g) of Cheddar cheese, 135 come from fat. Only about 30% of our total consumption of calories should come from fats, yet this figure is now, on average, 40%.

Vitamins

Vitamins are organic substances contained in food. They do not provide energy, nor do they themselves serve as building material the way proteins do, but they are necessary to keep the body's metabolic "equation" balanced. Some are produced in the body, but we must acquire the major portion from the foods we eat. These are the most important ones, and their sources:

VITAMIN A
Keeps skin and mucous membranes healthy and resistant to infection; protects against night blindness; aids normal bone and tooth development. It is fat soluble and stable at cooking temperatures.

Best sources: Liver, yellow vegetables and fruits, green vegetables (the darker the colour the better), whole or homogenized milk, cream, butter, margarine, eggs, cheese (except cottage or skim-milk cheeses).

VITAMIN B1 (thiamin)

Maintains normal growth and appetite; helps change food substances into energy for work and heat. It is water soluble; stable in heat but not light.
Best sources: Whole-grain cereals, wheat germ, lean pork, liver, kidney, heart, potatoes, peas, green lima beans, asparagus.

VITAMIN B2 (riboflavin)

Helps cells use oxygen, keeps vision clear and skin smooth. Maintains healthy nerve and gastrointestinal tissues. Water soluble, it is stable in heat but not light.
Best sources: Milk, eggs, liver, heart, kidney, spinach, mushrooms. Other fruits, vegetables and meats add smaller amounts.

VITAMIN C (ascorbic acid)

Helps strengthen the walls of blood vessels; helps our bodies resist infection; aids healing. Helps maintain healthy teeth and gums. Water soluble, it is easily lost to boiling water and is light sensitive.
Best sources: Vitamin C cannot be stored in the body, so it is important to eat at least one of the following every day:
1 orange
½ grapefruit
4 ounces (113 ml) orange or grapefruit juice
(fresh, frozen, canned)
4 ounces (113 ml) vitaminized apple juice
8 ounces (225 ml) tomato juice, or fresh or canned tomatoes
1 serving of cantaloupe, strawberries, raspberries, or cabbage salad.

VITAMIN D

Assists the absorption of calcium and phosphorus and builds strong bones and teeth. Lack of this vitamin results in rickets, a disease characterized by stunted growth, soft bones and poorly developed and defective teeth. It is fat soluble and stable at cooking temperatures.
Best sources: The only common foods naturally high in Vitamin D are salmon, sardines, tuna and herring. Some milk and margarine is fortified with Vitamin D and will say so on the label. During the summer, our bodies can absorb Vitamin D from the direct rays of the sun.

OTHER VITAMINS

Some other vitamins have been discovered and labeled E, F, G, K and so on. Research on these and their essential roles in human nutrition continues. We do not as yet know the minimum daily requirement of these vitamins, but it appears they can be supplied by the foods in a well-balanced diet.

Lack of a particular vitamin in the human diet can lead to poor health, even in extreme cases to deficiency diseases or death. Remember the old adage "an ounce of prevention is worth a pound of cure." If you provide well-balanced meals for your family, you will usually supply an adequate amount of vitamins. While synthetic vitamins can be administered, the natural vitamins in foods are more readily used by the body, especially in the case of fat-soluble vitamins A and D. Also, an overdose of vitamins in pill form is a possibility to be guarded against. This is particularly significant with Vitamin D, which can be stored in the body with resulting toxicity. High doses of Vitamin C can cause kidney and bladder problems.

Minerals

Minerals are chemical elements that are necessary constitutients of all body cells and fluids. Their most obvious function is to provide strength and rigidity to bones and teeth. In addition, they participate in muscle contraction, nerve responses and other processes. In addition to the vitamin and calorie content of the foods we eat, we ought to know which foods supply the most essential minerals; iron, iodine, calcium, phosphorus. If your diet is well balanced, the other minerals probably will be present in sufficient quantity.

IRON

Maintains the red-cell count in blood. Too little hemoglobin (red protein) leads to low vitality and poor health.
Best sources: Liver, kidney, heart, red meat, poultry, eggs, enriched white flour or bread, whole-grain and special baby cereals, fruits and vegetables, particularly cooked greens, peas and mature beans.

IODINE

Regulates growth and rate of metabolism by aiding in the function of the thyroid gland.
Best sources: All table salt in Canada must be iodized. The amounts of iodized salt normally used will supply the body's total requirement. Seafoods are high in iodine content.

CALCIUM

Helps maintain muscular tissues and helps build and maintain strong bones and teeth. Promotes healthy nerve function and normal blood clotting.
Best sources: Milk, cheese, leafy vegetables, dried legumes, fruits, meats.

PHOSPHORUS

Helps build and maintain strong bones and teeth.
Best sources: Meats, fish, poultry, dried legumes, eggs, nuts, root vegetables.

Other minerals are found in small quantities in foods, and research on their place in human nutrition is still being explored.

THE SEVEN BASIC FOOD GROUPS

Foods are classified roughly into seven groups, and for best meal planning you should include food from each of these groups every day. They will help you to arrange an energy-giving menu plan.

GROUP I

Calcium foods; milk or other dairy products.

Two servings every day.

Milk may be whole, 2%, skim or buttermilk; or it may be evaporated or dried.

On the basis of calcium content, the following alternates may be used for 1 cup (250 ml) of milk: Cheddar cheese, 1 ounce (28 g); cream cheese, 4 ounces (113 g); cottage cheese, 12 ounces (340 g); ice cream, 2 to 3 large scoops.

GROUP II

Fruits and vegetables high in Vitamin C.

Two servings every day.

Grapefruit, fresh, and grapefruit juice	Pineaple, raw
Lemons	Strawberries, raw
Limes	Cabbage, raw
Oranges, fresh, and orange juice	Green pepper, raw
	Salad greens, raw
Tangerines	Tomatoes, fresh or canned
Cantaloupe	Tomato juice

GROUP III

Vegetables high in Vitamin A.
Leafy, green, yellow vegetables, raw, cooked, canned, frozen;

one or more servings every day.

Asparagus, fresh	Mustard greens
Beans, green or wax or lima	Peas, green
	Peppers, green and red
Broccoli	
Brussels sprouts	Carrots
Cabbage	Pumpkins
Endives, green	Rutabaga (yellow turnips)
Escarole, green	
Kale	Squashes, all kinds
Lettuce	

GROUPE IV

Other vegetables and fruits.
Potatoes and other vegetables and fruits; raw, cooked, canned, frozen;

two or more servings every day.

Potatoes	Avocado
Sweet potatoes	Bananas
Beets	Berries
Jerusalem artichokes	Cherries
Parsnips	Cranberries
Radishes	Currants
Salsify	Dates
Turnips, white	Figs
Artichokes, French or globe	Grapes
	Pears
Cauliflower	Peaches
Celery	Pineapple, canned
Corn	Pineapple juice, canned
Eggplant	Plums
Leeks	Prunes
Mushrooms	Raisins
Onions, all types	Rhubarb
Sauerkraut	Watermelon
Apples	
Apricots	

GROUPE V

Bread and cereals
Whole-grain or enriched breads and cereals;
serve some every day.

Whole-wheat bread
Dark rye bread
Enriched white bread
Oatmeal bread
Cornmeal
Rolls or biscuits made with whole-wheat or enriched flour
Crackers made with enriched or soy flour

Enriched, whole-wheat, other whole-grain flour used in cooking
Whole-wheat cereal
Rolled-oat cereal
Brown rice
Other cereals of whole grains, or enriched

GROUP VI

The protein group
Meat, fish, poultry, dried legumes, fresh, cured, canned or frozen;

one serving every day, if possible.

Beef
Veal
Lamb
Pork (except bacon and salt pork)
Lunch meats

Organ meats, such as liver, heart, kidneys, brains, tongue, sweetbreads
Poultry, such as chicken, duck, goose, turkey
Fish and shellfish
Dried beans and peas

Two or more servings a week of the following:
Lentils
Soybeans, soybean flour or grits

Nuts of all kinds
Peanut butter

Serve at least 4 eggs every week to each member of your family, unless there is a problem with high serum cholesterol or a history of heart disease. They may be served as egg dishes or as ingredients in other preparations.

GROUP VII

Butter and margarine

Serve some every day.

Foods not found in the basic seven groups

There are other foods not listed in the basic seven groups. The foods listed below give energy. They may be eaten *in addition to, but not instead of,* the basic seven. First serve your family what is essential, then treat them to any of these if you wish.

Bacon
Dripping
Lard or shortening
Suet
Poultry fat
Salad dressing
Salad oil
Honey
Jam
Jellies
Molasses
Syrup

Cakes
Cookies
Pastries
Candy
Chocolate
Cocoa
Cornstarch
Macaroni
Noodles
Spaghetti
Rice, polished

CANADA'S FOOD GUIDE

Now that you have had an introduction to the food elements we need, you will see the logic behind the balanced diet suggested in Canada's Food Guide, following, which gives daily servings for your family as recommended by Health and Welfare Canada.

Canada's Food Guide divides the food we eat into four basic groups; milk and milk products; meat, fish, poultry and alternates; breads and cereals; fruits and vegetables. It's important to choose different kinds of food from within each group in appropriate numbers of servings and portion sizes.

Needs vary with age, sex and activity. To control weight, balance energy intake from foods with energy output from physical activity. Foods selected according to the Food Guide can supply 1,000 to 4,000 Calories (4,000 to 6,000 kilojoules) of energy a day. For additional energy, increase the number and size of servings from the various food groups and/or add other foods.

Select and prepare foods with limited amounts of fat, sugar and salt. If alcohol is consumed, use limited amounts.

MILK AND MILK PRODUCTS

Children up to 11 years, 2-3 servings a day; adolescents, 3-4 servings; pregnant and nursing women, 3-4 servings; adults, 2 servings.

Skim, 2%, buttermilk, reconstituted dry or evaporated milk may be used as a beverage or as the main ingredient in other foods. Cheese may also be chosen.

Some examples of one serving: 1 cup (250 ml), ¾ cup (175 ml) yogurt, 1½ ounces (45 g) Cheddar or process cheese.

MEAT, FISH, POULTRY AND ALTERENATIVES

For everyone, 2 servings a day.

Some examples of one serving: 2 to 3 ounces (60 to 90 g) cooked lean meat, fish, poultry or liver; 4 tablespoons (60 ml) peanut butter; 1 cup (250 ml) cooked dried peas, beans or lentils; ½ cup (125 ml) nuts or seeds; 2 ounces (60 g) Cheddar cheese; 2 eggs.

BREADS AND CEREALS

For everyone, 3 to 5 servings a day.

These may be whole grain or enriched. Whole grain products are recommended.

Some examples of one serving: 1 slice bread; ½ cup (125 ml) cooked cereal; ¾ cup (175 ml) ready-to-eat cereal; 1 roll or muffin; ½ to ¾ cup (125 to 175 ml) cooked rice, macaroni, spaghetti or noodles; ½ hamburger or wiener bun.

FRUITS AND VEGETABLES

For everyone, 4 to 5 servings a day.

Choose a variety of both vegetables and fruits, cooked, raw or their juices. Include at least two vegetables and include yellow, green or green leafy vegetables.

Some examples of one serving: ½ cup (125 ml) vegetables or fruits fresh, frozen or canned; ½ cup (125 ml) juice fresh, frozen or canned; 1 medium-size potato, carrot, tomato, peach, apple, orange or banana.

CALORIES

WHAT ARE CALORIES?

Different foods satisfy different bodily requirements, but almost everything we eat has the quality of providing energy. A Calorie (or kilocalorie) is the name we give to the amount of heat, or energy, needed to raise the temperature of 1 kilogram of water 1 degree centigrade. We use this measure to estimate the energy potential of foods we eat. So when we speak of the caloric value of a certain amount of a specified food, we mean the amount of energy, or heat, this portion provides.

Portions of food identical in weight do not necessarily have the same caloric content. For example:

    1 ounce (28 g) of orange juice has 15 Calories;
    1 ounce (28 g) of sugar has 102 Calories;
    1 ounce (28 g) of salad oil has 254 Calories.

Similarly, portions identical in calorie count may differ vastly in the amount of nutrition each provides.

As the body exercises it uses up energy, the amount varying with the type of work done; but even when the body is immobile, or sleeping, the very process of staying alive (through breathing, digesting, etc.) consumes calories. The energy loss is replaced through the calorie content of the food we eat. Body weight, height, size, age, activity all of these factors together determine just how many Calories we need. This list showing the Calorie content of some foods is from a longer list published by Health and Welfare Canada under the title Nutrient Value Of Some Common Foods.

1- Calcium foods

Calories in Some Milk Products

Cheese, Camembert	1.5 oz (45 g)	135 Cal.
Cheese, Cheddar	1.5 oz (45 g)	181 Cal.
Cream, table 18% bF,	1 cup (250 ml)	467 Cal.
Cream, whipping 35% bF,	1 cup (250 ml)	822 Cal.
Ice cream 10% bF,	1 cup (250 ml)	284 Cal.
Milk 2% bF,	1 cup (250 ml)	128 Cal.
Milk 3.3% bF,	1 cup (250 ml)	150 Cal.
Yogurt, natural 1.5% bF,	1 cup (250 ml)	158 Cal.

2- Foods High in Vitamin C

Calories in Some Fruits and Vegetables

Cabbage, red, chopped	½ cup (125 ml)	10 Cal.
Cantaloupe	½ medium (267 gr)	93 Cal.
Grapefruit, pink or red	½ medium (123 gr)	37 Cal.
Grapefruit juice, fresh	½ cup (125 ml)	51 Cal.
Lemon	1 medium (84 gr)	24 Cal.
Orange	1 medium (131 gr)	62 Cal.
Orange juice, fresh	½ cup (125 ml)	59 Cal.
Pineapple, fresh, cubed	½ cup (125 ml)	40 Cal.
Rasberries, fresh	½ cup (125 ml)	32 Cal.
Strawberries, fresh	½ cup (125 ml)	24 Cal.
Tomato	1 medium (123 gr)	23 Cal.

3- Vegetables High in Vitamin A

Calories in Some Leafy, Green and Yellow Vegetables

Asparagus, cooked, cut	1 cup (250 ml)	48 Cal.
Beans, green or wax, cooked	1 cup (250 ml)	46 Cal.
Beans, lima, cooked	1 cup (250 ml)	221 Cal.
Broccoli, cooked	1 cup (250 ml)	48 Cal.
Brussels Sprouts, cooked	1 cup (250 ml)	64 Cal.
Carrots, minced	1 cup (250 ml)	50 Cal.
Lettuce, iceberg	1 leaf	3 Cal.
Peas, green, cooked	1 cup (250 ml)	132 Cal.
Rutabaga, cooked, cubed	1 cup (250 ml)	53 Cal.

4- Calories in Some Other Vegetables and Fruits

Apple, unpeeled	1 medium	100 Cal.
Apricots, canned whole in syrup	1 cup (250 ml)	227 Cal.
Avocado	1	306 Cal.
Banana	1	105 Cal.
Beets, cooked, diced	1 cup (250 ml)	56 Cal.
Cauliflower, cooked	1 cup (250 ml)	36 Cal.
Celery	1 Stalk	6 Cal.
Corn cob, cooked	1	83 Cal.
Cranberry sauce, sweetened	1 cup (250 ml)	442 Cal.
Dates, seedless, chopped	1 cup (250 ml)	517 Cal.
Eggplant, cooked, diced	1 cup (250 ml)	48 Cal.
Fig,dry	1	48 Cal.
Grapes	1 cup (250 ml)	120 Cal.
Mushrooms	1 cup (250 ml)	19 Cal.
Onions, sliced	1 cup (250 ml)	57 Cal.
Parsnips, cooked, sliced	1 cup (250 ml)	134 Cal.
Peach, peeled	1 medium	37 Cal.
Pear, unpeeled	1 medium	100 Cal.
Pineapple, canned in syrup sliced	1 slice	50 Cal.
Pineapple juice	1 cup (250 ml)	148 Cal.
Plum	1 medium	36 Cal.
Potato, peeled, raw	1 (135 gr)	116 Cal.
Potato, unpeeled, microwaved	1	128 Cal.

Potato salad	½ cup (132 gr)	189 Cal.
Prunes, cooked, unsweetened	1 cup (250 ml)	240 Cal.
Raisins	1 cup (250 ml)	522 Cal.
Rhubarb, diced	1 cup (250 ml)	27 Cal.
Sauerkraut, canned	1 cup (250 ml)	47 Cal.
Sweet potato, cooked, mashed	½ cup (173 gr)	181 Cal.
Turnip, white, cooked,mashed	1 cup (250 ml)	44 Cal.
Watermelon	1 slice (368 gr)	118 Cal.

5- Calories in Bread and Cereals

Cornmeal	½ cup (125 ml)	266 Cal.
Muffins, bran	1	104 Cal.
Oatmeal Bread	1 slice	65 Cal.
Rice, brown	1 cup (250 ml)	214 Cal.
Rice, instant with butter	1 cup (250 ml)	255 Cal.
Rice Krispies	½ cup (125 ml)	66 Cal.
Rice, long grain	1 cup (250 ml)	179 Cal.
Rolled Oat Cereal	½ cup (125 ml)	77 Cal.
Rye Bread, dark	1 slice	79 Cal.
Wheat Flour, all purpose	1 cup (250 ml)	484 Cal.
White Bread, enriched	1 slice	76 Cal.
Whole Wheat Cereal	½ cup (125 ml)	68 Cal.
Whole Wheat Flour	1 cup (250 ml)	423 Cal.
Whole Wheat Bread 100%	1 slice	61 Cal.

6- Calories in Some Protein Foods

Beef, ground, fried, well done	3 oz (90 gr)	188 Cal.
Beef liver, fried	2¾ oz (86 gr)	187 Cal.
Beef, sirloin steak, broiled	3 oz (90 gr)	188 Cal.
Blood sausage	1 oz (30 gr)	47 Cal.
Chicken, roast	3 oz (90 gr)	154 Cal.
Dried Beans, Peas, cooked	1 cup (250 ml)	250 Cal.
Haddock, fried in bread crumbs	4 oz (120 gr)	185 Cal.
Ham, cooked	1 oz (30 gr)	49 Cal.
Hamburger, regular	2 oz (60 gr)	245 Cal.
Lake trout, broiled	3 oz (90 gr)	201 Cal.
Lamb chops, broiled, lean fat	4 oz (118 gr)	424 Cal.
Lamb chops, broiled, no fat	2¾ oz (86 gr)	164 Cal.
Lobster, canned	⅔ cup (150 ml)	87 Cal.
Nuts, many kinds	½ cup (125 ml)	450 Cal.
Oysters, raw	9 small (90 gr)	59 Cal.
Peanut Butter	1 tbsp (15 ml)	95 Cal.
Pork chop, loin, lean fat	2¾ oz (86 gr)	263 Cal.
Pork chop, loin, lean	2¼ oz (72 gr)	159 Cal.
Pork roast, loin, lean	3 oz (90 gr)	148 Cal.
Salmon, broiled in butter	3 oz (90 gr)	167 Cal.
Sausage, beef and pork	1 oz (30 gr)	59 Cal.
Scallops, steamed	7 (90 gr)	101 Cal.
Shrimps, fried in butter	11 (90 gr)	200 Cal.
Sole, roasted, lemon, no fat	3 oz (90 gr)	85 Cal.
Turkey, roast	3 oz (90 gr)	160 Cal.
Veal, liver, fried	3 oz (90 gr)	248 Cal.
Veal, loin chops, broiled	3 oz (90 gr)	215 Cal.

7- Calories in Butter and Some Other Fats

Butter	1 tbsp (15 ml)	100 Cal.
Butter	1 cup (250 ml)	1720 Cal.
Lard, pure	1 tbsp (15 ml)	117 Cal.
Margarine	1 tbsp (15 ml)	100 Cal.
Margarine	1 cup (250 ml)	1720 Cal.
Mayonnaise, 65% oil	1 tbsp (15 ml)	102 Cal.
Oil: peanut, corn, olive	1 tbsp (15 ml)	124 Cal.
Salad dressing, various	1 tbsp (15 ml)	25-77 Cal.
Shortening, vegetable oil	1 tbsp (15 ml)	117 Cal.

8- Calories in Some Others Foods

Cake, White, no icing	1 piece	313 Cal.
Cake, White, with icing	1 piece	401 Cal.
Cake, Sponge	1 piece	131 Cal.
Cake mix, white	1 piece	249 Cal.
Cake, Fruit	1 piece	227 Cal.
Chocolate Milk	1 oz (30 gr)	156 Cal.
Chocolate Eclair	1	239 Cal.
Cookies, sweetened, various	2	100-139 Cal.
Egg Noodles	1 cup (250 ml)	211 Cal.
Honey	1 tbsp (15 ml)	64 Cal.
Jams (various)	1 tbsp (15 ml)	54 Cal.
Macaroni, spaghetti, cooked	1 cup (250 ml)	164 Cal.
Maple Syrup	1 tbsp (15 ml)	50 Cal.
Molasses	1 tbsp (15 ml)	45 Cal.
Pie (various)	1 slice	331-428 Cal.
Sugar, white	1 tbsp (15 ml)	50 Cal.
Sugar, brown	1 tbsp (15 ml)	34 Cal.

9- Calories in Some Composite Meals

Beef, sandwich, fast food	1	345 Cal.
Chicken à la King	1 cup (250 ml)	495 Cal.
Chop Suey with meat or chicken	1 cup (250 ml)	317 Cal.
Fish, sandwich, with cheese	1	420 Cal.
Hamburger, regular	2 oz (60 gr)	245 Cal.
Hamburger, with cheese	2 oz (60 gr)	300 Cal.
Macaroni and cheese	1 cup (250 ml)	454 Cal.
Pizza, cheese	1 slice	153 Cal.
Tourtière	1 slice	482 Cal.

Cholesterol Content in Various Foods

HIGHEST

Butter	Organ meats (liver)
Cream	Potato Salad
Eggs	Quiche Lorraine
	Whipping Cream (35% cream)

MODERATELY HIGH depending on portions

Cheese	Poultry
Fish	Rich pastry
Meat	Shellfish

MODERATELY LOW

Milk	Soup
Salad	Dressing, Yogurt

NONE or LOWEST

Bread	Margarine
Dry Beans, Nuts	Pasta
Breakfast cereals	Potatoes
Flour, grains	Sweets
All fruits	All vegetables, legumes

HOW MUCH IS ENOUGH?

Being overweight is recognized as a hazard to health. It increases the tendency to diseases such as diabetes, gallstones, heart disease, high blood pressure and stroke. And when your diet supplies more calories than your body requires, you will gain weight. The following plans, based on Canada's Food Guide, vary the amounts of food for overweight or underweight conditions without omitting any of the important food groups. *But don't make a drastic change in your diet without consulting your doctor.*

Normal pattern

BREAKFAST: citrus fruit or juice; whole-grain cereal with milk; other protein food, if desired; toast with butter or fortified margarine; beverage, milk for children.

DINNER: (at noon or at night) meat, fish, or poultry; potato; other vegetable(s); bread (if desired); fruit or fruit dessert; beverage milk, for children.

SUPPER OR LUNCH: cheese, egg, or other protein food; vegetable; bread with butter or fortified margarine; dessert; beverage, milk.

To lose weight

Follow the normal pattern, but

FOR BREAKFAST
Omit: sugar and cream on cereal and in beverages; cereal, or eat only a small serving (have a soft-cooked egg instead); bread alternates such as pancakes, doughnuts; jam, jelly, syrup, marmalade.

FOR DINNER
Eat: lean meats and fish; fresh fruits instead of canned or dried fruits.
Omit: gravy; cream and sugar.

FOR SUPPER OR LUNCH
Eat: clear soups instead of cream soups; skim-milk cheeses (they are labeled as such); lemon juice or vinegar on salads instead of salad dressing; fresh fruits for dessert instead of rich puddings, pies, cakes, sundaes; skim milk or buttermilk.
Omit: fried foods, or rich creamed dishes; cookies, cake; gravy.
Do not: eat large servings or second helpings; eat between meals; omit any meal (three regular meals should still be eaten); drink soft drinks, beer, liquor.

To gain weight

FOR BREAKFAST
Eat: sugar and cream on cereals; bacon or extra protein food; extra bread and butter; jam, jelly, syrup, or marmalade; cream in beverage.

FOR DINNER
Eat: cream soup if desired; bread and butter; gravy or butter on potatoes; butter on vegetables; cookies or cake with the fruit dessert; milk as a beverage.

FOR SUPPER OR LUNCH
Eat: richer main dishes (creamed dishes, extra butter, etc.); mayonnaise or French dessings on salads; extra bread and butter; richer desserts; beverage of half milk and half cream.
Do: eat generous servings; eat between meals as long as it does not spoil your appetite at mealtime.

How To Economize

You can use the listing of the seven basic food groups profitably by studying each group and figuring out for yourself which foods you can serve together in an interesting fashion without stinting on essential nutrition. As a wise shopper you will have a fairly good idea of the prices of these foods, and with a little ingenuity you will be able to balance those that are expensive against those that are less expensive. A little experience is all you need, and before you know it you will be amazed at how easy it will be to economize on your food costs at the same time as you are keeping your family satisfied and healthy.

Buy the cheaper foods in each nutritive group more generously and buy the more expensive sparingly. Let me give you a few simple examples.

In Group I, milk and other dairy products, make use of buttermilk and dried milk. Both are cheaper and therefore more economical to use than whole milk. Powdered skim milk can be used in cooking and baking, as well as for a beverage.

In Group II, fruits high in Vitamin C, make use of tomatoes in the summer when they can be bought fresh cheaply, but use canned tomatoes at other times of the year. Buy citrus fruits and the other fruits as they become most plentiful, and are therefore at their cheapest.

In Groups III and IV, make the most use of potatoes, cabbage, carrots, turnips, parsnips and squash, which are available during the winter months and are filling and nutritious. Use canned corn when the short season for fresh corn is over.

Study the other groups and tick off those foods that are the most reasonably priced, and use those more frequently than the others. Always remember to vary the way you serve them so they won't become dull or boring.

Dividing your money among different kinds of food

This is an important consideration, and it is more a matter of judgment and your own good intelligence than a question of rules. A family's needs and tastes vary as much as foods prices.

Take as an example three foods: oranges, grapefruit and tomatoes. They are equally nutritious, but the seasons and the production can change the prices. It is not difficult to see that buying grapefruit when it is most expensive would be spending too much for the same nourishment as you could get out of either tomatoes or oranges. Depending on your family's taste and need, the tomatoes may be a far better nutrition buy than the oranges.

There may be differences among varieties of the same food that could make you choose one over another, a choice that could affect your spending as well as your planning for good nutrition. Consider as an example the type of oranges you buy. Thin-skinned oranges, heavy for their size, are good for juice, but navel oranges are better to slice or to eat out of hand. Loose-skinned oranges are better to section, and they make a good fruit for the lunch box. The right fruit for the purpose will be more economical.

Here is a brief guide that was given to me many years ago by a famous food scientist. These notes have been a great help to me and I pass them on in the hope that they will be equally helpful to you.

MILK: Spend enough to get a least 1 cup (250 ml) for each adult per day, 2 to 4 cups (500 ml to 1 l) for cooking. If you use skim milk or buttermilk, make up the needed supply of fat (which contains Vitamin A) with butter.

FRUITS AND VEGETABLES: Spend at least one-fifth of your food money on these, with emphasis on green and yellow vegetables as well as on potatoes and inexpensive seasonal fruits.

MEAT: Keep the cost down to one-fourth or one-fifth of the money you spend for food. Although meat is important, it is relatively the most expensive of the basic foods. Watch carefully how you buy it. To economize, serve meat one day and another protein food in place of it the next day.

CHAPTER 2

Good cooking starts with good shopping

FEEDING your family properly can never be reduced to merely turning switches, opening packages, thawing and heating, or adding water and baking. This is the sort of thing many advertisers want you to believe, but it is not so. It takes knowledge to select the food that will keep your family healthy and to be able to get all that your dollar should buy. Preparing meals requires planning, and your planning begins before you enter your food store.

WHY FOOD COSTS FLUCTUATE

1. *Age and occupation.* Naturally, those who do manual labor or who participate in athletics burn up more energy and require more food than those with sedentary jobs and less active lifestyles. Younger children eat less than adolescents, older people less than young people or middle-aged adults, and after the age of 12, girls eat less than boys.

2. *Family size.* "Average" figures for food budgeting are based on a 3- to 5-person family. If the family is larger than this, food costs per person drop about 10% because more foods can be bought in quantity and greater savings result. For a person living alone, a rule-of-thumb adjustment is to increase the per-person food costs 20% to 35%; for a family of two, costs rise 10% above the per-person average.

3. *Weather.* Produce grown outdoors is at the mercy of the elements, so a bumper crop can lower prices, while a drought or an unseasonable cold spell can raise them.

4. *Geography.* Where you live influences how much you pay for certain foods; locally produced food is less expensive than food that must be transported great distances.

5. *Hidden costs.* Often, more than half the retail price of a food goes for some service that adds to its costs: processing, packaging, transportation, advertising, wholesalers' and retailers' profits.

6. *Consumer demand.* Consumers want and buy new foods and more convenient packaging. The price we pay for foods also pays the cost of creating, developing and testing new recipes and new products.

Your food bills may be higher than you'd like, but do not see the budget picture as grimmer than it really is. Not all the money you spend in the supermarket pays for foods; 15% to 20% of your supermarket bill may go for such non-food items as paper goods, cleaning materials, health and beauty aids.

MAKE A PATTERN FOR YOUR DAILY MEALS

Make a menu pattern that suits the tastes and habits of your family while keeping in mind considerations of nutrition and budget. Here's an example of a pattern.

BREAKFAST: fruits or juice; eggs or cereal; bacon or other meat; bread; beverage.

LUNCH: meat or cheese dish with bread and greens; dessert; beverage.

DINNER: meat, poultry or fish; potatoes or a substitute; vegetable other than potatoes; bread; dessert; beverage.

Once the pattern for your meals is well established, proceed in the following manner, starting with breakfast:

Fruits. List the number of fruits or juices that will be needed for the week. Then consider, will some be used at lunch, or for the lunch box? Be aware of which fruits are in season and buy these rather than some rare exotic ones; you will pay less and still have variety.

Eggs. Decide how many you will need for a week's breakfasts; decide how many for lunch or lunch box; how many for cooking and baking. When you have worked out the quantity, add 3 to 6 more to be kept on hand for unexpected uses.

Bacon. Determine whether it is more economical to use bacon only once or twice a week for breakfast, or whether it will be practical to use it as well as part of a lunch or light dinner menu. This will depend on your budget and eating habits. Then work out the amount needed for the week.

Cereal. A slow-cooking cereal is the tastiest and the least costly. When prepared the night before, it can be easily reheated in the morning. Also, it has more nourishment than ready-to-serve cereals. **○━►** Add 2 to 4 teaspoons (10 to 20 ml) of powdered skim milk to each 1 cup (250 ml) of water used for cooking dry cereals; this will add nourishment without altering the flavor. Ready-to-serve cereals are sometimes preferred. Plan on serving both, and work out the amount you will need.

Bread and beverage. The use of these varies from one family to the next. Consider your family's tastes here, but don't forget that a family that has a large proportion of bread in its diet must get a large proportion of nutrition from it, so try to use whole-grain or enriched breads as much as possible.

O— Remember — always serve a hearty breakfast; it can be the cheapest meal of the day, but it should be no less nutritious than the more expensive meals. This meal, which follows a long fast, has to make up for the hours without food.

Using this example of a way to plan a week's breakfasts, proceed in a similar manner with your other meals.

We have been talking of serious matters: food value, food quality, price, but you must remember that you and your family must also derive pleasure from the food you put on the table. So **guard against slipping into a "Food Rut".** You're in a rut when you are buying the same food week after week and cooking and serving it with little or no variation. This is a deadly habit, because it invariably means that you are spending good money on good food and valuable time preparing it, then finding that it all adds up to little or nothing.

O— It is especially easy to fall into this rut if you use too many packaged, canned or frozen items; packers must maintain uniform standards, and while this gives good quality to the food, it also results in a sameness of flavor and style. Using seasonal foods will help you to avoid this. Another way is to use a different herb or spice to accent a familiar food in a new way. You will find many suggestions to help you later on in the section on herbs and spices. You do not need to buy expensive items; you can learn to make interesting, tasty dishes from inexpensive ingredients.

Here are some pointers to consider while you are planning your menus for the week.

1. O— Review your menus and try to use less costly foods to supply your family's nutritional needs.

2. O— Avoid waste and leftovers. If you have six members in the family, don't cook enough for seven. A five-year-old boy doesn't eat as much as an adult, so plan accordingly.

3. O— If your family is large enough so that substantial savings can result, plan to freeze or can fresh fruits and vegetables at home.

4. O— Entertain more simply if you find that lavish hospitality destroys your food budget. Plan a dessert party or a light supper rather than an elaborate sit-down dinner.

5. O— Casserole meals may save work and fuel, but check the cost of the ingredients; sometimes the extras called for raise the price per serving to that of a steak dinner.

6. O— Margarine and butter have the same nutritional value, except that some margarine is enriched with Vitamin D. Some brands of margarine are much less expensive than butter.

7. O— Skim-milk powder reconstituted to fluid skim-milk will reduce your milk bill by approximately two-thirds. The nutritional value of this milk is almost exactly that of whole milk; the loss of Vitamin A (from the lower fat content in skim milk) can be made up by serving more green and yellow vegetables or other foods rich in Vitamin A. If your family does not enjoy the flavor of skim milk, try mixing it with whole milk to economize.

FITTING NUTRITION REQUIREMENTS INTO YOUR BUDGET

Naturally, consumers are concerned not only with the *amount they spend on food, but the value* they get. A family that spends a great deal on food is not necessarily well nourished. Price is not necessarily the most important factor when shopping. Some foods are cheap at almost any reasonable price because they supply so much nutrition, whereas some "cheap" foods may not be worth the price spent on them.

One example of good value for your shopping dollar is dairy products. A group of city families spent 14% of their food money on milk, cheese, and ice cream. This bought approximately 15% of the calories, 22% of the protein, 65% of the calcium, and 44% of the riboflavin (Vitamin B.) needed for good human nutrition. It is a real bargain to obtain much more than 14% of your requirements of some of the essential nutrients for 14% of your food money.

You must plan carefully to ensure that your food money is well spent, and this planning requires a knowledge of just what quantities of various foods your family needs. It is not sufficient merely to understand why our bodies need certain foods; it is also important to know specifically the amount of each item you must purchase. To assist you, here are three charts showing how much of each kind of food is required by each of several age groups, male and female. The three charts are organized around low, moderate, and liberal budgets.

Only you can decide, after a few weeks of examining your food expenditures carefully, which plan best suits your budget. First try the moderate plan and if, after a few weeks, you realize you can afford (and want) to spend more than you have been on food, organize your meals around the liberal plan; if you have been spending more than you can afford, switch to the low-cost plan, reducing the quantities of higher-priced protein and fruits on your shopping list.

To adapt the food plan of your choice to your own family, simply list the quantities necessary for the types that fit the members of your household and determine, according to the food plan you have selected, how much of each food your family needs for one week. The amounts are for persons of "average" weight and height.

The next step is to plan your week's menus, deciding which foods you want to buy in each category. The season of the year, the amount of time you have for food preparation and your family's preferences will all influence your decisions, as will the choice of food plan. For example, the low-cost plan allows less for fruits, so fruit desserts cannot be served often. But grain products can be the basis for dessert, as rice pudding or shortcake, with a little fruit added for contrasting texture and flavor.

WEEKLY FOOD PLANS FOR

Low cost budgets

FAMILY MEMBERS	MILK, CHEESE ICE CREAM	MEAT, POULTRY FISH	DRY BEANS PEAS NUTS	FLOUR, CEREAL BAKED GOODS
	QUARTS (Litres)	LB OZ (kg, gr)	LB OZ (kg, gr)	LB OZ (kg, gr)
Children	5 Quarts (5.7 L)	1 lb 8 oz (680 gr)	0 lb 2 oz (57 gr)	2 lb 0 oz (900 gr)
Teenagers	7 Quarts (8 L)	2 lb 8 oz (1 kg 130 gr)	0 lb 6 oz (170 gr)	4 lb 4 oz (1 kg 930 gr)
Women	3½ Quarts (4 L)	2 lb 8 oz (1 kg 130 gr)	0 lb 4 oz (113 gr)	2 lb 8 oz (1 kg 130 gr)
Pregnant women	7 Quarts (8 L)	2 lb 8 oz (1 kg 130 gr)	0 lb 4 oz (113 gr)	2 lb 8 oz (1 kg 130 gr)
Lactating women	10 Quarts (11 L)	3 lb 4 oz (1 kg 470 gr)	0 lb 4 oz (113 gr)	3 lb 0 oz (1 kg 360 gr)
Men	3½ Quarts (4 L)	3 lb 8 oz (1 kg 590 gr)	0 lb 6 oz (170 gr)	3 lb 12 oz (1 kg 700 gr)

FAMILY MEMBERS	EGGS	CITRUS FRUIT TOMATOES	DARK GREEN AND DEEP YELLOW VEGETABLES	POTATOES
	NO.	LB OZ (kg, gr)	LB OZ (kg, gr)	LB OZ (kg, gr)
Children	5	1 lb 12 oz (790 gr)	0 lb 4 oz (113 gr)	1 lb 4 oz (570 gr)
Teenagers	6	2 lb 8 oz (1 kg 130 gr)	0 lb 12 oz (340 gr)	3 lb 4 oz (1 kg 470 gr)
Women	5	2 lb 0 oz (900 gr)	0 lb 12 oz (340 gr)	1 lb 8 oz (680 gr)
Pregnant women	7	3 lb 8 oz (1 kg 590 gr)	1 lb 8 oz (680 gr)	2 lb 0 oz (900 gr)
Lactating women	7	4 lb 8 oz (2 kg 40 gr)	1 lb 8 oz (680 gr)	3 lb 4 oz (1 kg 470 gr)
Men	6	2 lb 4 oz (1 kg 20 gr)	0 lb 12 oz (340 gr)	3 lb 0 oz (1 kg 360 gr)

FAMILY MEMBERS	OTHER VEGETABLES AND FRUIT	FATS OILS	SUGAR SWEETS
	LB OZ (kg, gr)	LB OZ (ml)	LB OZ (kg, gr)
Children	3 lb 4 oz (1 kg 470 gr)	0 lb 6 oz (170 ml)	0 lb 6 oz (170 gr)
Teenagers	5 lb 4 oz (2 kg 380 gr)	0 lb 12 oz (340 ml)	0 lb 12 oz (340 gr)
Women	4 lb 8 oz (2 kg 40 gr)	0 lb 4 oz (113 ml)	0 lb 10 oz (280 gr)
Pregnant women	5 lb 0 oz (2 kg 270 gr)	0 lb 6 oz (170 ml)	0 lb 8 oz (230 gr)
Lactating women	5 lb 8 oz (2 kg 500 gr)	0 lb 8 oz (228 ml)	0 lb 10 oz (280 gr)
Men	5 lb 0 oz (2 kg 270 gr)	0 lb 10 oz (285 ml)	0 lb 12 oz (340 gr)

Moderate cost budgets

FAMILY MEMBERS	MILK, CHEESE ICE CREAM	MEAT, POULTRY FISH	DRY BEANS PEAS NUTS	FLOUR, CEREAL BAKED GOODS
	QUARTS (Litres)	LB OZ (kg, gr)	LB OZ (kg, gr)	LB OZ (kg, gr)
Children	6 Quarts (7 L)	2 lb 4 oz (1 kg 20 gr)	0 lb 1 oz (28 gr)	1 lb 12 oz (790 gr)
Teenagers	7 Quarts (8 L)	4 lb 12 oz (2 kg 50 gr)	0 lb 4 oz (113 gr)	4 lb 0 oz (1 kg 815 gr)
Women	3½ Quarts (4 L)	4 lb 4 oz (1 kg 930 gr)	0 lb 2 oz (57 gr)	2 lb 0 oz (900 gr)
Pregnant women	7 Quarts (8 L)	4 lb 4 oz (1 kg 930 gr)	0 lb 2 oz (57 gr)	2 lb 4 oz (1 kg 20 gr)
Lactating women	10 Quarts (11 L)	5 lb 0 oz (2 kg 270 gr)	0 lb 2 oz (57 gr)	2 lb 12 oz (1 kg 250 gr)
Men	3½ Quarts (4 L)	5 lb 4 oz (2 kg 380 gr)	0 lb 4 oz (113 gr)	3 lb 8 oz (1 kg 590 gr)

FAMILY MEMBERS	EGGS	CITRUS FRUIT TOMATOES	DARK GREEN AND DEEP YELLOW VEGETABLES	POTATOES
	NO.	LB OZ (kg, gr)	LB OZ (kg, gr)	LB OZ (kg, gr)
Children	6	2 lb 0 oz (900 gr)	0 lb 4 oz (113 gr)	1 lb 0 oz (454 gr)
Teenagers	7	2 lb 12 oz (1 kg 250 gr)	0 lb 12 oz (340 gr)	3 lb 0 oz (1 kg 360 gr)
Women	6	2 lb 8 oz (1 kg 130 gr)	0 lb 12 oz (340 gr)	1 lb 4 oz (570 gr)
Pregnant women	7	3 lb 8 oz (1 kg 590 gr)	1 lb 8 oz (680 gr)	1 lb 8 oz (680 gr)
Lactating women	7	5 lb 0 oz (2 kg 270 gr)	1 lb 8 oz (680 gr)	2 lb 12 oz (1 kg 250 gr)
Men	7	2 lb 12 oz (1 kg 250 gr)	0 lb 12 oz (340 gr)	2 lb 8 oz (1 kg 130 gr)

FAMILY MEMBERS	OTHER VEGETABLES AND FRUIT	FATS OILS	SUGAR SWEETS
	LB OZ (kg, gr)	LB OZ (ml)	LB OZ (kg, gr)
Children	4 lb 0 oz (1 kg 815 gr)	0 lb 6 oz (170 ml)	0 lb 10 oz (280 gr)
Teenagers	6 lb 0 oz (2 kg 720 gr)	0 lb 14 oz (398 ml)	1 lb 0 oz (454 gr)
Women	5 lb 4 oz (2 kg 380 gr)	0 lb 8 oz (228 ml)	0 lb 12 oz (340 gr)
Pregnant women	5 lb 12 oz (2 kg 610 gr)	0 lb 8 oz (228 ml)	0 lb 12 oz (340 gr)
Lactating women	6 lb 4 oz (2 kg 835 gr)	0 lb 12 oz (340 ml)	0 lb 12 oz (340 gr)
Men	5 lb 12 oz (2 kg 610 gr)	0 lb 14 oz (398 ml)	1 lb 0 oz (454 gr)

Liberal cost budgets

FAMILY MEMBERS	MILK, CHEESE ICE CREAM	MEAT, POULTRY FISH	DRY BEANS PEAS NUTS	FLOUR, CEREAL BAKED GOODS
	QUARTS (Litres)	LB OZ (kg, gr)	LB OZ (kg, gr)	LB OZ (kg, gr)
Children	6 Quarts (7 L)	3 lb 0 oz (1 kg 360 gr)	0 lb 1 oz (28 gr)	1 lb 8 oz (680 gr)
Teenagers	7 Quarts (8 L)	5 lb 8 oz (2 kg 500 gr)	0 lb 4 oz (113 gr)	4 lb 0 oz (1 kg 815 gr)
Women	4 Quarts (4.5 litres)	4 lb 12 oz (2 kg 150 gr)	0 lb 1 oz (28 gr)	1 lb 12 oz (790 gr)
Pregnant women	7 Quarts (8 L)	4 lb 12 oz (2 kg 150 gr)	0 lb 1 oz (28 gr)	2 lb 0 oz (900 gr)
Lactating women	10 Quarts (11 L)	5 lb 12 oz (2 kg 610 gr)	0 lb 2 oz (57 gr)	2 lb 12 oz (1 kg 250 gr)
Men	4 Quarts (4.5 litres)	5 lb 8 oz (2 kg 500 gr)	0 lb 4 oz (113 gr)	3 lb 8 oz (1 kg 590 gr)

FAMILY MEMBERS	EGGS	CITRUS FRUIT TOMATOES	DARK GREEN AND DEEP YELLOW VEGETABLES	POTATOES
	NO. (kg, gr)	LB OZ (kg, gr)	LB OZ (kg, gr)	LB OZ
Children	7	2 lb 4 oz (1 kg 20 gr)	0 lb 8 oz (228 gr)	0 lb 12 oz (340 gr)
Teenagers	7	3 lb 4 oz (1 kg 470 gr)	0 lb 12 oz (340 gr)	3 lb 0 oz (1 kg 360 gr)
Women	6	3 lb 0 oz (1 kg 360 gr)	0 lb 12 oz (340 gr)	1 lb 0 oz (454 gr)
Pregnant women	7	4 lb 8 oz (2 kg 40 gr)	1 lb 8 oz (680 gr)	1 lb 4 oz (570 gr)
Lactating women	7	5 lb 8 oz (2 kg 500 gr)	1 lb 8 oz (680 gr)	2 lb 8 oz (1 kg 130 gr)
Men	7	3 lb 0 oz (1 kg 360 gr)	0 lb 12 oz (340 gr)	2 lb 4 oz (1 kg 20 gr)

FAMILY MEMBERS	OTHER VEGETABLES AND FRUIT	FATS OILS	SUGAR SWEETS
	LB OZ (kg, gr)	LB OZ (ml)	LB OZ (kg, gr)
Children	4 lb 8 oz (2 kg 40 gr)	0 lb 8 oz (228 ml)	0 lb 12 oz (340 gr)
Teenagers	6 lb 8 oz (2 kg 950 gr)	0 lb 14 oz (398 ml)	1 lb 4 oz (570 gr)
Women	6 lb 0 oz (2 kg 720 gr)	0 lb 8 oz (228 ml)	1 lb 0 oz (454 gr)
Pregnant women	6 lb 4 oz (2 kg 835 gr)	0 lb 8 oz (228 ml)	1 lb 0 oz (454 gr)
Lactating women	6 lb 4 oz (2 kg 835 gr)	0 lb 12 oz (340 ml)	1 lb 2 oz (510 gr)
Men	6 lb 8 oz (2 kg 950 gr)	0 lb 14 oz (398 ml)	1 lb 4 oz (570 gr)

WHERE SHOULD YOU SHOP?

Many families get into the habit of shopping at only one or two stores. This habit is largely influenced by proximity and convenience. Actually, you will broaden your experience considerably by shopping around a bit and comparing prices, quality of food and service.

If, for instance, you are the sort of person who likes to ask questions and get suggestions, you should search out a store that will best satisfy you on these counts. This may not apply to all your shopping, but there may be certain foods, like cheeses or breads, about which you do want special information.

You might want a store with a wide variety of some particular food, to give you greater choice. However, if you are in a hurry, you might be content to shop where the variety is limited as long as you know the particular things you need will be available.

You may like to shop in a store where prices and weight are well displayed and easily readable; you will probably find self-service quicker and more convenient. If you are the type of pereson who still wants assistance from sales clerks, self-service stores will just frustrate you and make your marketing a chore.

Generally speaking, you will find the lowest prices in self-service stores, since trained clerks who give customers individual assistance cost the management more, and these higher operating costs are added to the price of food. Self-service does leave you free to study and reflect on the information on labels and the weights and prices of different cuts of meat. Another point in favor of supermarkets is that they enable you to make a lot of your shopping decisions at home, since they all have detailed newspaper advertisements featureing their best buys and specials.

Don't be a lazy shopper. It is important for you to be curious about all foods, their origins, and their uses. Occasionally, take time to visit specialty shops where you can look and learn. You will be truly amazed at how many interesting ideas you will get and how many exciting foods this will enable you to bring to your table.

Here are some suggestions to help you shop.

1. Learn to recognize good quality in fresh foods. Before picking up a "bargain" in fresh fruits or vegetables, check their condition carefully. Perfect produce would not be reduced to "seconds". Make sure that vegetables have not dried out. Buy spotted or bruised fruits only if you know you can use them soon after purchase so they will neither spoil nor lose their food value. Buy fresh produce in season, it will be lower in price and better flavored.

2. Fancy packaging adds to food costs. Choose simple containers over elaborate jars, reusable canisters, etc., unless the price per unit for the same quality is the same or lower for the special package.

3. Know the different grades of canned fruits, vegetables and meats, and learn which foods retain good nutritive value, colour and flavour when canned.

4. Suit the style of food to your purposes. Standard or Choice canned goods, government graded, are just as nutritious as the more expensive Fancy fruits and vegetables and should be used when uniform appearance is not important. For instance, low-grade sliced peaches are good for pie, even if not attractive as a plate of fruit. Broken olives are fine when used in salads or sandwiches or sauces, even if they are not appealing to use as appetizers.

5. Read labels and observe carefully to learn the different forms in which some foods are available. Find out the difference in price, quantity and cost between fresh, frozen and canned products of the same variety.

6. 0⟶ Study bread labels before you buy. Choose bread for weight and food value, not by size of loaf. Look for bread that is whole-grain or enriched and that contains milk.

7. 0⟶ Buy packaged cereals or any other packaged food by weight, not by the size of the package. To compare prices, first look for the weights listed on the labels, and note the prices. Then figure costs for an ounce (or gram).

8. 0⟶ Ready-to-serve cereals in multi-packs of small boxes may cost two or three times more per ounce (or gram) than the same cereal in a larger box. Sugar-coated ready-to-serve cereals cost more per unit than many common unsweetened ones, and furnish more calories but less food value.

9. 0⟶ Dried fruits give 8 or more servings per pound (18 or more servings per kilogram); canned fruits, which contain more water, may give fewer servings. Compare costs per portion.

10. 0⟶ "Day-old" pastries and bread may be a good buy, especially if your bread supply is never wholly consumed in one day anyway. Buying day-old baked goods and freezing them until you use them may lower your bread costs as much as 50%. Supermarkets usually have day-old bakery products available in the morning.

11. 0⟶ Buy in quantity if you pay a lower price per unit; if you have adequate storage space for the food; and if you can use all you buy before it can spoil or lose some of its nutritive value. For instance, you may be able to buy a large piece of meat at a lower price per pound (or kilogram). If you can cut this up and freeze what you don't plan to use immediately, this may save you money.

12. 0⟶ The cost of national advertising, packaging and promotion often makes brand-name products much more expensive than the same foods marketed under the store's own brands. Supermarkets often feature their own labels at prices below those of comparable national brands. Watch for the best values. Study food advertisements and compare; don't just read the words.

13. 0⟶ Trading stamps, games and contests cost you money, unless you are sure that the prices at stores that offer them are no higher than at stores without such gimmicks.

14. 0⟶ Remember your family's preferences in food. A supermarket bargain will turn out to be a waste if no one in the family will eat it.

15. 0⟶ Snack foods are expensive for the food value they provide. Low-calorie fresh fruits and vegetables are more practical "nibbles." Remember that pure fruit juices give better nutritional value per dollar than soft drinks. Spend money first on foods that provide the most nutrition at the lowest cost; then, if money permits, buy the extras.

16. 0⟶ If you have a low food budget, choose foods with little or no waste, or make sure the waste you pay for can be put to use in some way. For instance, the bones in meat can be used to make a substantial soup that will make the main course of another family meal. When used in this way, bones cease to be a waste. But meat that contains a lot of fat or gristle that has to be discarded is waste and costs money. Judge your purchases by the cost per serving rather than the cost per pound (or kilogram).

17. 0⟶ Make a shopping list based on your week's menu and keep a pad and pencil in the kitchen to add whatever staples you may need. Always know how much you need, so you won't buy too much or too little of an item. The buying guide on portions and quantities will help you. Consult it. When you get to the market, stick to your shopping list.

Avoid impulse buying unless you see something you need at a real saving from its regular price.

18. 0━┳ Ask questions. Don't hesitate to ask for information from a clerk when you are not sure of what you want to buy. This is one way you learn.

19. 0━┳ Keep records of your food purchases, both the amount you buy and the price you've paid. Study your notes after 3 or 4 weeks, and you may find areas where you have done exceptionally well. You will be able to use these findings in future buying and they will prove invaluable.

Eventually, these steps to good shopping will become so automatic that this record-keeping can be discontinued.

CONVENIENCE FOODS

What are convenience foods? They are foods that come to us either partly prepared or fully prepared, baked, canned, dehydrated, frozen, etc. They are very often a saving grace, but you have to realize that you have to pay for all this service, so convenience foods are relatively the most expensive foods to buy.

If your budget is limited, it is not wise to depend on convenience foods. However, if you study them from the point of view of prices, portions and flavors, as well as the servings they supply, it will be simple to decide which you can afford on your budget and how often you can buy them.

Since convenience foods are so expensive, we must look into their virtues. First, of course, they save work. Yes, but remember, someone else has done the work for you, the peeling, coring, chopping, mincing, mixing, sifting, grating, mashing, kneading and, in many instances, the browning, frying, boiling, baking, simmering and sautéing. They have also saved you from washing up the pots and pans, the spoons and bowls, etc. You will have to pay for this.

The chief saving is in time. A beef stew that would take 30 minutes to prepare and perhaps hours to simmer while you kept vigil over it, takes only a couple of minutes to remove from a can and heat on the stove. However, there is a drawback, the personal touch is not there.

A dinner that might take you 45 minutes to prepare from scratch may take only a few minutes to warm in the oven when it's packed on an aluminum tray as a TV dinner. But when you compare the cost, you will discover you would have more food for less money if you took the time to do it yourself.

Convenience foods are easier to carry home from the market and they usually are less bulky to store. No doubt, sometimes this aspect has to be given due consideration. As a rule, produce bought fresh will need to be bought in greater quantity than processed produce because so much of it is discarded as peels, seeds, husks, etc.

Some convenience foods are actually cheaper than fresh foods, because they are more compact to ship and store and because they have a longer shelf life. These relatively less-expensive convenience foods include frozen lima beans, canned cherries, devil's-food cake mix and instant coffee. Convenience foods that are much more expensive than their homemade counterparts are baked ready-to-serve yeast rolls, frozen chicken and turkey dinners and precooked rice.

Your food budget must strike a balance between time and energy on the one hand and money on the other. You will need to compare the time, work and space saved with the time and work you would spend if you made the whole dish or the whole dinner from the necessary ingredients. But you must also compare the quality, quantity and flavor of the prepared food with the food you could cook yourself with a dash or so of imagination. Perhaps you can afford to use one in place of the other for certain occasions, but a diet made up primarily of convenience foods would be very dull fare indeed.

HOW TO BUY MEAT

On average, one out of every three dollars spent for food is spent on meat. The reason is that meat, because of its richness of flavor, seems to best satisfy the appetite particularly through long periods of cold weather.

Many homemakers still favour large roasts that provide cold meat for several other meals. The price of meat today makes this expensive. Don't be discouraged, however. You can give your family wholesome nourishing meals without spending a third of your food budget on meat.

Muscle meats, the most popular, are a poor source of several important vitamins. This is not so of organ meats such as heart, kidney, sweetbreads and, most important of all, liver; ironically, these are the meats that are most often discarded.

Many homemakers should spend less money than they do for meat and more for fresh fruits and vegetables. In any case, when you do serve meat it should be supplemented by foods that furnish carbohydrates, vitamins, cellulose and minerals. You will have no shortage of protein if you provide 1 serving of meat per day to each member of your family. If you cannot afford to do this or you don't want to serve that much meat, you can provide adequate protein through other foods such as fish or cheese.

HOW MUCH MEAT SHOULD YOU BUY?

In general, 1 pound (500 gr) of meat provides 3 servings, but when there is little bone and little or no other waste, 1 pound (500 gr) may serve 4 people. When buying meat for stew, meat pie, etc., where the dish contains vegetables as well, 1 pound (500 gr) of meat is sufficient for 4 or 5 servings. Use the following as a buying guideline:

1 lb (500 gr) beef round steak
    = 3 or 4 servings
1 lb (500 gr) liver
    = 4 or 5 servings
4 lbs (1 kg 815 gr) leg of lamb
    = 10 to 12 servings
1 lb (500 gr) lamb or veal chops
    = about 3 chops, usually 3 servings
2 lbs (1 kg) beef pot roast
    = 8 servings
2 lbs (1 kg) pork spareribs
    = 4 servings
2 lbs (1 kg) ham
    = 6 to 8 servings

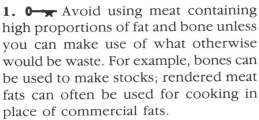

How to save money on meat purchases

1. 0━┱ Avoid using meat containing high proportions of fat and bone unless you can make use of what otherwise would be waste. For example, bones can be used to make stocks; rendered meat fats can often be used for cooking in place of commercial fats.

However, keep in mind that some meats that may not appear to be wasteful may contain fat in large quantities. For instance, it takes about 10 slices of crisp side bacon to equal the protein in 1 serving of cooked ground beef, because bacon is largely fat.

2. 0━┱ Learn to estimate the cost per pound (or kilogram) of the meat that is actually eaten as against the price paid per pound (or kilogram) for the whole piece of meat, including waste. A higher-priced cut may be less costly to serve than a cheaper one, depending on the percentage of fat, bone and gristle in each. Meaty, less tender cuts from the shoulder and flank of beef, lamb and pork are usually good buys, but cuts such as beef short ribs, lamb neck and pigs' feet, unless sold very cheaply, are usually uneconomical.

Meats such as liver, heart and kidney are economical because of the high nutritional value and total absence of waste. Beef, chicken and pork liver cost much less than calf's liver and have similar food value. Use organ meats judiciously and in small portions because of their high cholesterol content.

3. 0—⚷ Meat prices depend mostly on supply and demand. Beef is available all year and is the most popular meat in Canada, since it provides so many different cuts at a wide range of prices. Pork is most plentiful and therefore most economical to buy in the fall and winter months, veal in the spring, and Canadian lamb from September to December. Frozen meat of all varieties is available year round.

4. 0—⚷ Some sliced meats may be more economical to buy in a large piece and sliced at home. Bacon is an example, although this is not easy to slice at home. Some butchers will slice it for you without adding to the price. You can save money by buying bologna in bulk and slicing it at home. For lunch-box sandwiches, an inexpensive roast of beef cooked at home, chilled and sliced thin may make more economical sandwiches than store-bought sliced luncheon meats, and it provides good nourishment with much less fat than the prepared meats.

5. 0—⚷ To save money, serve combination dishes of meat mixed with other ingredients in preparations such as stews, meat pies and meat macaroni. These are especially successful with ground meat. The ''meat extenders'' you use, rice, macaroni, spaghetti, skim-milk powder, bread crumbs, not only stretch the expensive meat ingredient but add food value other than protein and improve the texture of the dish. The usual amount of extender per pound (500 gr) of ground meat is:

½ cup (125 ml) skim-milk powder
½ cup (125 ml) dry bread crumbs
1 cup (250 ml) fresh bread crumbs
¾ cup (190 ml) rolled oats
½ cup (125 ml) cornmeal

6. 0—⚷ Leftover meat goes further as a sandwich filling when it is ground and combined with chopped raw cabbage, onions, carrots or celery.

7. 0—⚷ You can prepare successful dishes with tough cuts of meat if you learn how to cook in a Dutch oven or a casserole. Long slow cooking is the way to tenderize. You can accomplish this in less time in a pressure cooker.

8. 0—⚷ If you use eggs as a protein substitute for meat, you should remember that it takes 3 medium-size eggs to replace the amount of protein in a good serving of meat.

9. 0—⚷ When buying a large roast, be sure to plan dinner menus for the week ahead that make use of the roast by varying your cooking and cutting methods.

HOW TO BUY POULTRY

Poultry includes chicken, turkey, duck, goose, squab, cornish hens, partridge and quail. Chickens are sold according to their age as broilers, fryers, roasters, fowls or hens, and capons.

Their selection:

Broilers (about 3 months old)
  1 to 2 lbs (500 gr to 1 kg)
Fryers (3 to 6 months old)
  2½ to 3½ lbs (1.1 to 1.6 kg)
Roasters
  3½ to 5 lbs (1.6 to 2.3 kg)
Fowls or hens
  4 to 5 lbs (1.8 to 2.3 kg)
Capons
  6 to 9 lbs (2.7 to 4 kg)
Turkeys
  8 to 20 lbs (12 to 14 lbs / 5.4
  to 6.4 kg best size)

From 50 to 60 per cent of the live weight of poultry is edible meat. This makes poultry more expensive per pound (or kilogram) of edible meat than it appears from the purchase price per unit. Nevertheless, poultry is a good buy for protein, and it is often a bargain. Instead of buying cut-up chicken, you can save a few cents per pound (or kilogram) by cutting up whole poultry at home.

Watch for special sales. Be aware of the months in which the supply of any given poultry is at its peak; that's when its price is the lowest. But note that most poultry is now available all year round.

HOW TO BUY FISH

Fish is one of the oldest foods used by man. While we do not eat as much fish in this country as do people in many parts of the world, the fish in our waters offer an abundant source of food. Domestic fisheries occupy a place of great economic importance in the Canadian food industry.

The chief nutrient in fish is protein, a complete protein that makes it interchangeable with meat in the diet.

The price of fresh fish varies with the distance from the source of supply and with the seasons. Nowadays, portions of the catch are frozen, and well-organized transportation makes it possible for fish to be marketed in excellent condition at great distances from the source of supply. When shopping for fresh fish, take a good look at the eyes. They should be bright, full and clear. When you touch the flesh of a scaled fish with your finger, no impression should remain. Fresh fish is not slimy. **O—➤** Take advantage of this protein-rich food as a mean of varying your family's diet. And don't overlook the fact that it is not only a good health food, but it is also quick to prepare.

How much fish should you buy?

Fish servings are generally based on ⅓ to ½ pound (150 to 250 gr) of cooked fish per person. To provide this amount, buy ⅓ pound (150 gr) per person of fresh or frozen fillets, sticks or steaks; ½ pound (250 gr) of fresh or frozen dressed fish; and 1 pound (500 gr) of fresh or frozen whole fish. Since fillets, fresh or frozen, are 100 per cent edible, steaks 85 per cent edible, and dressed fish 45 per cent edible, it is often cheapest to buy fillets, even though the price may be higher per unit.

How much shellfish should you buy?

Shellfish is high in cholesterol but it is nutritious and low in calories. In general, 1 pound (500 gr) of completely shelled and cleaned shellfish will provide 4 to 6 servings. If you are buying them uncooked and still in their shells, you must allow more. For an average 6 servings:

4 to 6 pounds (1.8 to 2.7 kg) live lobster (about 6 small lobsters) or 1 to 2 pounds (500 gr to 1 kg) shelled cooked lobster meat
1 pound (500 gr) scallops (These are completely shelled and there is no waste.)
2 pounds (1 kg) uncooked unshelled shrimps
1 to 1½ pounds (500 to 750 gr) cooked crabmeat

HOW TO BUY CHEESE

Cheese is one of the oldest known prepared foods. Despite this, we still know relatively little about it. There are more than a thousand varieties of cheese, all of which use milk as a base. The milk of cows, goats and sheep is used, sometimes the whole milk, sometimes only the skim milk or the fatty portion. Herbs, bacterial cultures, colouring, etc., are added to produce cheeses of different taste and appearance.

Supermarket refrigerators are full of many general-purpose processed cheeses. These come in any number of types, bearing as many different labels. They are generally rindless, pre-cut, sliced and packaged.

Supermarkets, along with specialized cheese shops and delicatessens, also offer a wide variety of natural cheeses from all over the world. With such a wide range of types from which to choose, a little daring is all you need to discover the ones that will please you and your family. And this is important, because eating the same few favourites week in and week out can become dull and might lead to a complete lack of interest in this vital food.

Cheese contains high concentrations of protein and fat; 1 pound (500 gr) equals in food value approximately 1 gallon (4.5 l) of milk. On the basis of calcium content, 1 ounce (30 gr) of Cheddar cheese, 4 ounces (120 gr) of cream-type cheese, or 12 ounces (340 gr) of cottage cheese are the equivalent of 1 cup (250 ml) of milk. Learn to think of cheese primarily as a diet staple, rather than merely as an addition to apple pie, or as a last course after a heavy meal.

Generally speaking cheese can be divided into three classes soft, semi-soft and hard. Each class contains hundreds of different cheeses. Learning about cheese can become a personal adventure. The best way to begin is to buy a small quantity of a cheese that is new to you. Find out where it comes from and what type it is. Make a note of the name.

Read the label, and ask the cheese man for more detailed information. Note the shape, the flavour, the texture and, most of all, watch your family's reaction. In this way, before you realize it you may find yourself a real connoisseur. For more on cheese see Chapter 18, Vol. III.

HOW TO BUY FRESH FRUITS AND VEGETABLES

If you have ever gathered fruits and vegetables at their peak from your own garden, you may never find any in stores that suit you perfectly. But you have the advantage of knowing what perfect produce should look like. A city homemaker has to learn this, and you may make some unfortunate purchases while learning. These suggestions may help to prevent mistakes.

First, I want to say again that fresh produce bought in season is cheaper because more of it is available, and it is also more nutritious. For example, tomatoes vine-ripened outdoors in the sun of summer have twice as much Vitamin C as winter hothouse tomatoes. If you can buy local produce, so much the better. Local fruits and vegetables have had less time to travel with less risk of bruising and of drying and losing vitamins. And, of course, if you don't have to pay for trucking and elaborate packing as well, you will save money.

In general, avoid fruits or vegetables that have cracks, bruises and soft spots and those that appear to be drippy or mushy. Good fruits are heavy for their size and firm. Leafy vegetables should be crisp and glossy, with their green color fresh and bright. The leaves of root vegetables such as carrots, beets and parsnips should also be green and crisp; if they are limp and droopy, you can be sure the roots have been out of the ground for some time and that there has been some drying out. Of course, you may never see the leaves of these vegetables, for they may be trimmed and packed in plastic. In that case, be sure the vegetables do not look wet, for even one spoiled carrot or potato or onion can spoil the rest. In any case, even one bad vegetable is just that much less than you paid for.

When I say that produce should be firm, I don't mean the rock hardness of green unripe fruits or vegetables. Unripe produce has already suffered vitamin loss because it has been picked too soon. Then a trip from somewhere may harm it further. There is a point at which tomatoes, melons, avocados, etc., may be picked and still continue to ripen until a satisfactory if not ideal state is reached. But if picked sooner than this, the fruit may never ripen, but just change color and dry a little. It may be edible but it will not be luscious. If you are a new shopper, ask the greengrocer to help you. Sometimes a green tomato may look perfect, but when it ripens it will develop spoiled areas, so it is really hard to tell no matter how experienced a shopper you are. If you buy unripe tomatoes or melons, they will ripen best at room temperature, but not on a hot window sill. If you attempt to ripen tomatoes in the refrigerator, they become watery and more subject to decay.

It is possible to have overripe produce that is not spoiled. This is easier to detect. In the case of melons, you may hear the seeds move and liquid sloshing around in the centre. With some vegetables, such as squashes and pumpkins, the skin will be very hard, almost too hard to pierce with a knife, and there will be some loss of weight through drying in the centre. You will seldom hear seeds move, however; they are too firmly netted.

You have heard many a joke about the shopper pinching the apples or pears. Of course, you shouldn't pinch them; press gently with a finger. A ripe peach, pear, plum, melon, tomato or avocado should yield just a little to gentle pressure while still feeling firm. It will soon be easy for you to recognize ripeness in tree fruits and melons by their smell. Only fully ripe fruit has the fragrance that gives us

an added dimension of pleasure in serving them.

As for peas and beans and such, of course they must have good colour and feel crisp; pea pods should not be splitting. If the seeds inside snap beans are very developed, the pods will be dry and tough. Unless you plan to use them for shell beans, avoid them.

To help with your planning, the chart on pages 44 and 45 lists the percentage of the crop that is available each month for the produce listed. The largest figure indicates when the vegetable or fruit is most plentiful and cheapest. Of course some will never be cheap, and the entire crop for the year may be small, but this will at least give you an idea of the best times to buy.

Remember that all imported produce is more costly, for instance, citrus fruits. But this is a good example of food that is cheap at any price, because it is the best source of Vitamin C. To equal the Vitamin C in 1 orange you would need to eat several fresh tomatoes or a great deal of cabbage. Also, some years crops are very small because of weather, plant pests, etc. In those years the percentage may be the same but the amount available will be small and the price higher.

Buying guide
By learning to compare the weight of an item as purchased with the number of servings it will yield, you will find it as easy to cook for many as it is to cook for two. It is merely a matter of adding and subtracting. Check the items on your shopping list against this chart. Jot down next to the items any information you feel important for you to know.

FOOD	NUMBER OF SERVINGS	EQUIVALENTS & COMMENTS
Almonds, shelled 1 lb (500 gr)	20 (12 nuts each serving)	6 oz (170 gr) whole almonds = 1 cup (250 ml)
Almonds, in shell 1 lb (500 gr)	8 servings	6 to 8 oz (170 to 225 gr) nutmeats
Apples, fresh 1 lb (500 gr)	3 (1 whole apple each serving)	3 cups (750 ml) pared and sliced 2½ cups (625 ml) cubed
Apples, dried 8 oz (225 gr)	18 servings	2 cups (500 ml) uncooked 5 cups (1.25 L) cooked
Apricots, fresh 1 lb (500 gr)	5 (2 apricots each serving)	8 to 12 apricots
Apricots, dried 1 lb (500 gr)	16 servings	3 cups (750 ml) uncooked 5 cups (1.25 L) cooked
Asparagus, fresh 1 lb (500 gr)	3 (5 to 6 stalks each serving)	16 to 20 stalks
Asparagus, canned (No. 2)	5 to 7 servings	
Bacon, 1 lb (500 gr)	8 (3 slices each serving)	25 thin slices
Bananas, 1 lb (500 gr)	3 servings	3 bananas
Bananas, sliced 1 lb (500 gr)	5 servings	2½ cups (625 ml)
Bananas, mashed 1 lb (500 gr)		2 cups (500 ml)
Barley, whole 1 lb (500 gr)	8 servings	
Barley, pearl 1 lb (500 gr)	8 servings	
Beans, dried 1 lb (500 gr)	8 servings	6 cups (1.5 L) cooked
Beef, ground 1 lb (500 gr)	4 servings	5 servings with stretcher added
Beef, porterhouse, 1 lb (500 gr)	2 servings	
Beef, round, 1 lb (500 gr)	3 to 4 servings	
Beef, sirloin, 1 lb (500 gr)	2 servings	
Beef, stewing 1 lb (500 gr)	4 servings	
Beets, 1 lb (500 gr)	4 servings	3 to 5 beets, 2 cups (500 ml) diced
Blueberries, 1 pint (500 ml)	4 servings	
Brazil nuts, in shell, 1 lb (500 gr)	12 to 15 (10 nuts each serving)	½ lb (250 gr) nutmeats
Bread, 1 lb (500 gr)	6 to 8 servings	12 to 16 slices
Bread stuffing, 8 oz (225 gr)		3 cups (750 ml) enough to stuff 5-lb (2.3 kg) chicken

Broccoli, 1 lb (500 gr)	3 servings	
Brussels sprouts 1 lb (500 gr)	5 servings	
Butter, 1 lb (500 gr)	48 (⅓ oz (10 gr) square each serving)	2 cups (500 ml)
Cabbage, raw, 1 lb (500 gr)	10 to 12 servings	4 cups (1 L) shredded
Cabbage, cooked (1 lb/500 gr raw)	4 (½ cup (125 ml) each serving)	
Carrots, 1 lb (500 gr)	4 (½ cup (125 ml) each serving)	2½ cups (625 ml) diced or shredded
Cauliflower 1 lb (500 gr)	4 servings	
Celery, 1 lb (500 gr)	4 servings	1 medium-sized head, or 2 cups (500 ml) diced
Cheese, Cheddar 1 lb (500 gr)	20 (1-inch (2.5 cm) cube each serving)	8 oz (225 gr) = 2 cups (500 ml) grated
Cheese, cottage 1 lb (500 gr)	4 (½ cup (125 ml) each serving)	2 cups (500 ml)
Cherries, 1 lb (500 gr)	4 servings	2 cups (500 ml) pitted
Chicken, small broiler	2 servings	
Chicken, large broiler	4 servings	
Chicken, roaster or capon, per lb (500 gr)	2 servings	
Chinese cabbage, 1 lb (500 gr)	10 to 12 servings	4 cups (1 L) shredded
Chinese cabbage, cooked, (1 lb / 500 gr raw)	4 (½ cup (125 ml) each serving)	
Chocolate, unsweetened, 8 oz (225 gr)		8 squares, 1 oz (30 gr) each
Chocolate unsweetened, grated		1 square grated = ½ cup (125 ml)
Cocoa unsweetened 8 oz (225 gr)	30 (1 cup (250 ml) hot cocoa each serving)	2 cups (500 ml)
Coconut, 3½ oz (100 gr)		1⅓ cups (330 ml)
Coffee, ground all types, 1 lb (500 gr)	40 to 45 servings	5 cups (1.25 L)
Coffee, instant, 2 oz (60 gr)	25 servings	1 cup (250 ml)
Corn, ears, 12 medium	5 to 6 servings	3 cups (750 ml) cut kernels
Cornflakes, 15 oz (425 gr)	18 (1 cup (250 ml) each serving)	16 to 20 cups (4 to 5 L) average volume
Crackers, graham 1 lb (500 gr)		66 crackers 15 crackers crushed = 1 cup (250 ml)
Crackers, soda, 3½ oz (15 gr)		33 crackers 22 crackers crushed = 1 cup (250 ml)
Cranberries fresh, 1 lb (500 gr)	4 to 6 servings	4¾ cups (1.2 L) = 3 to 3½ cups (750 to 875 ml) cooked

FOOD	NUMBER OF SERVINGS	EQUIVALENTS & COMMENTS
Cream, table (15%) pint (500 ml)	15 to 18 for coffee	
Currants, dried 11 oz (310 gr)		2 cups (500 ml)
Dates, 1 lb (500 gr)		2⅔ cups (660 ml)
Eggplant, medium-sized	5 to 6 servings	2 to 2½ cups (500 to 625 ml) diced
Figs, dried, 1 lb (500 gr)	7 servings	2¾ cups (690 ml) cut up
Filberts, shelled, 1 lb (500 gr)	25 (10 nuts each serving)	
Fish (any type) boneless, 1 lb (500 gr)	3 servings	
Flour all-purpose 1 lb (500 gr)	4 cups (1 L) sifted	
Flour, cake, 1 lb (500 gr)		4½ cups (1.125 L) sifted
Flour, whole-wheat or graham, 1 lb (500 gr)		3½ cups (875 ml) unsifted
Gelatin, unflavored, 1 envelope		1 tablespoon (15 ml) (approx.). enough to set 2 cups (500 ml) liquid
Grapefruit, 1 medium-sized	2 servings	1 lb (500 gr)
Grapefruit juice		¾ cups (190 ml) per grapefruit
Grapefruit sections		1¼ cups (310 ml) per grapefruit
Grapes, Concord, 1 lb (500 gr)		1 qt. (1 L) whole 2¾ cups (690 ml) halved and seeded
Green beans fresh 1 lb (500 gr)	4 servings	2 to 3 cups (500 to 750 ml) diced or slivered
Ham, cooked 1 lb (500 gr)	4 (1 slice each serving)	
Honey, 1 lb (500 gr)		1½ cups (375 ml)
Ice cream, 1 quart (1 L)	6 to 8 servings	
Lemons, juice from 1 lemon		3 tablespoons (50 ml) juice
Lemons, grated rind of 1 lemon		2 tablespoons (30 ml) rind
Liver, 1 lb (500 gr)	4 to 5 servings	4 to 5 slices
Macaroni, 1 lb (500 gr)	6 to 8 servings	1 cup (250 ml) uncooked = 2 cups (500 ml) cooked
Marshmallows		10 miniatures = 1 large ¼ lb (115 gr) = 16 large
Mixed peels, 1 lb (500 gr)		2½ cups (625 ml)
Molasses, 1 lb (500 gr)		1⅓ cups (330 ml)
Mushrooms, fresh ½ lb (250 gr)	2 to 3 servings	15 to 20 small mushrooms

Noodles, 1 lb (500 gr)	4 to 6 servings	
Onions, 1 lb (500 gr)	3 to 4 servings	3 large onions
Oranges, juice from 1 orange		½ cup (125 ml) juice
Oranges, grated rind of 1 orange		3 tablespoons (50 ml) rind
Parsnips, 1 lb (500 gr)	4 servings	4 medium-sized parsnips
Peaches, fresh 1 lb (500 gr)	3 to 4 servings	3 to 4 peaches
Peanuts in shell, 1 lb (500 gr)	25 (10 nuts each serving)	⅔ lb (280 gr) nutmeats
Pears, fresh, 1 lb (500 gr)	3 servings	3 large pears
Pecans, in shell, 1 lb (500 gr)	20 (10 nuts each serving)	½ lb (250 gr) nutmeats = 2 cups (500 ml)
Plums, prune fresh, 1 lb (500 gr)	5 (4 plums each serving)	20 plums
Plums, red or green, fresh, 1 lb (500 gr)	5 servings	5 plums
Potatoes, sweet, 1 lb (500 gr)	3 to 4 servings	2 to 3 large potatoes
Potatoes, white 1 lb (500 gr)	3 to 4 servings	3 large or 6 to 8 small potatoes
Prunes, dried, 1 lb (500 gr)	12 servings	2½ cups (625 ml) uncooked 4 cups (1 L) cooked
Raisins, 11 oz (310 gr)		2 cups (500 ml)
Rice, raw, 1 lb (500 gr)	10 to 12 portions	6 cups (1.5 L) cooked rice
Spaghetti, 1 lb (500 gr)	4 to 6 servings	
Spinach, fresh, 1 lb (500 gr)	2 servings	
Sugar, granulated 1 lb (500 gr)		2¼ cups (560 ml)
Sugar, fruit		2⅓ cups (580 ml)
Sugar, icing		4 to 4½ cups (1 to 1.125 L) sifted
Sugar, brown		2¼ cups (560 ml) packed
Tea, loose ¼ lb (115 gr)	75 cups	1 teaspoon (2 ml) per cup
Tomatoes, fresh 1 lb (500 gr)	3 servings	2 to 3 medium-sized tomatoes
Turnips, 1 lb (500 gr)	4 servings	3 cups (750 ml) mashed 2 to 2½ cups (500 to 625 ml) diced
Walnuts, in shell 1 lb (500 gr)	15 to 18 (10 nuts each serving)	½ lb (250 gr) nutmeats

SEASONAL GUIDE FOR FRESH FRUITS AND VEGETABLES
This chart shows you when fruits and vegetables are at their peak of production, which is also when they are cheapest. Monthly availability is expressed as a percentage of total annual supply.

	JAN. %	FEB. %	MAR. %	APRIL %	MAY %
Apples	9	9	9	7	7
Apricots	-	-	-	-	-
Artichokes	10	9	12	18	12
Asparagus	-	1	19	34	25
Avocados	9	13	9	12	9
Bananas	7	7	9	9	10
Beans, wax	4	5	5	4	7
Beets	6	5	7	6	5
Blueberries	-	-	-	-	2
Broccoli	12	13	11	11	8
Brussels sprouts	18	12	2	1	1
Cabbage	8	8	8	9	10
Cantaloupes	-	-	3	5	13
Carrots	8	8	11	9	9
Cauliflower	5	6	8	5	5
Celery	9	8	8	9	9
Cherries	-	-	-	-	2
Chicory	8	8	10	10	10
Corn	-	-	1	2	9
Cranberries	3	1	1	-	-
Cucumbers	3	3	5	7	10
Eggplant	6	5	7	7	7
Endive	19	13	10	12	9
Escarole	17	11	11	12	11
Garlic	10	7	10	11	6
Grapes (table)	4	3	4	3	2
Grapefruit	10	11	13	11	9
Honeydew melons	3	8	11	12	11
Lemons	8	7	9	7	9
Lettuce	8	7	8	9	11
Limes	2	2	1	1	7
Mushrooms	8	9	9	9	9
Onions	7	7	10	7	9
Oranges	8	10	11	9	10
Parsley	8	6	14	11	6
Parsnips	9	9	8	7	5
Peaches	-	-	-	-	-
Pears	3	3	5	3	2
Peppers	6	5	7	6	7
Pineapples	7	8	19	23	16
Plums-prunes	-	-	-	-	1
Potatoes	8	8	9	9	10
Pumpkins	-	-	-	-	-
Radishes	5	4	5	7	10
Rhubarb	6	15	16	16	21
Shallots	6	6	7	9	11
Spinach	12	12	12	9	9
Squash	8	6	4	2	2
Strawberries	-	-	3	7	25
Sweet potatoes	10	10	11	8	5
Tangelos	23	13	-	-	-
Tangerines	4	1	1	-	-
Tomatoes	6	7	9	8	11
Turnips	10	10	11	8	6
Watermelons	-	-	2	4	18

JUNE %	JULY %	AUG. %	SEPT. %	OCT. %	NOV. %	DEC. %
3	2	4	12	16	12	10
7	48	45	-	-	-	
3	-	-	2	4	15	15
20	1	-	-	-	-	-
2	6	6	8	7	11	8
10	9	9	8	8	8	6
11	15	19	9	9	7	5
8	12	14	13	9	8	7
12	24	46	16	-	-	-
3	1	3	6	9	11	12
1	-	3	9	16	13	24
8	8	8	8	9	8	8
22	21	21	11	3	1	-
8	5	7	8	9	9	9
7	7	10	15	16	10	6
8	7	8	7	8	8	11
19	71	7	1	-	-	-
9	10	10	-	1	8	15
13	12	39	18	3	2	1
-	-	-	18	22	19	36
14	14	16	11	6	6	5
5	5	18	15	10	8	7
5	4	3	2	2	8	12
5	4	4	3	4	8	10
12	10	3	13	9	6	3
5	7	11	19	24	10	8
6	4	3	4	9	11	9
8	9	16	12	6	3	1
10	10	9	7	8	7	9
10	9	9	7	7	8	7
7	48	10	10	3	4	5
8	5	6	6	9	12	10
7	6	9	12	10	9	7
8	7	7	8	7	7	8
6	8	8	7	7	8	11
2	1	4	12	18	13	12
14	24	37	24	1	-	-
1	5	24	28	14	8	4
8	7	13	14	10	10	7
7	3	2	2	3	4	6
16	16	35	30	2	-	-
9	8	7	8	8	9	7
-	-	-	11	75	14	-
17	16	12	7	6	5	6
21	5	-	-	-	-	-
14	11	9	7	6	6	8
8	5	8	5	5	7	8
1	1	9	17	22	16	12
35	20	5	3	2	-	-
5	2	4	8	13	9	15
-	-	-	-	8	35	21
-	-	-	-	-	38	56
10	10	13	8	7	5	6
3	3	6	10	12	12	9
30	28	16	2	-	-	-

CHAPTER 3

The kitchen:
Where the action is

A FAMILY'S KITCHEN is where the action is. It is more than just a place to prepare three meals a day. Often it is where the children entertain their friends, and where the family gathers to see "what's cooking." So although it must be truly efficient, it should also be a place that is a pleasure to work in, a place for informality and hospitality.

Good lighting is a must. Try to arrange things so that you get lots of sunshine during the day, or at least bright daylight. It can be very depressing to work in a gloomy or badly lighted place.

An efficient kitchen should also be colourful and interesting. Don't hesitate to furnish it comfortably and attractively. A kitchen does not need to look like an industrial laboratory. Hang a favourite picture on the wall. Keep a green plant or two there, and in the spring a flowering plant. You'll be surprised how these little touches will help to relieve the tension you sometimes feel when you are faced with getting "another meal" ready.

Crisp salads, creamy sauces, hot muffins, tasty stews, perfect roasts and everything else you cook or prepare depend for their success upon the kind of equipment you use. **The proper tools and utensils will give you better results and cut down on the time you spend in preparation. So choose wisely.**

You need ample storage space for utensils, dishes, condiments and for canned, bottled and packaged foods as well; in other words, all the things a good cook needs at her fingertips. Kitchen drawers and cabinets are too often overcrowded with nonessentials. This means that a lot of time is wasted rummaging around trying to find the important things you need and use most often. Take stock of what you have and begin by parting with those pieces of equipment that you never use. Then organize so that the things you use regularly are close at hand. It will save you time and energy if you can store equipment close to where you'll use it; for instance, your electric appliances should be handy to an electrical outlet; your chopping block should be handy to the sink and to your garbage disposal. Decide where things should be placed or stored for your greatest convenience. You may not choose the perfect arrangement at first, so be flexible until you have given your new system a good trial. No kitchen is ever exactly as you want it by accident; a well-equipped and convenient kitchen requires thoughful planning and loving care.

If you are a new homemaker, the following lists may seem impossibly long, and equipping your kitchen may seem impossibly expensive. But you don't have to buy everything at once. Start with the essentials, then add things that would be convenient to have; later still, treat yourself to a few luxuries.

Another important point is that what is essential to one cook may not be essential to another. This depends so much on your family and its eating preferences. If you like vegetables and fish as often as possible, you will need modest-sized saucepans for the first and fairly large steamers or baking dishes for the second. If your family eats a lot of meat, you will need roasting and broiling pans and good carving boards and knives. If stews and casseroles are preferred, you will need heavy and sturdy pots and pans to withstand long, slow cooking. Of course, the sizes of the utensils depend on the number of servings you require. Remember, it is not economical to cook more food than your family needs.

POTS AND PANS

One very common mistake a lot of people make, especially those equipping their first kitchen, is to buy matched sets of pots and pans. When it comes to actual cooking, most cooks soon discover that assorted ware is much more suitable. Become acquainted with the different types on the market and find out which are best for you.

Stainless steel
This falls into the expensive category, but it is practically indestructible and so easy to clean and shine. Some stainless-steel pans have copper bottoms, which look fine but require work to keep clean. It may be better to buy pots with aluminum or laminated-steel bottoms, which you will find indicated on the label or on the pan itself. Use stainless-steel pots for vegetables, soups, stews and fruits.

Aluminium
This is the best material for all-around use. It does require quite a bit of care, though, to keep clean and shiny. I find the constant use of a steel-wool soap pad is the best, as well as the easiest. All you have to do to keep your pan constantly neat is give it a little buff with a soap pad every time it is washed. A heavy-duty aluminum frying pan is the very best for pan-cooking and sautéing, and for cooking white meats and variety meats, because it gives even heat distribution. You will find a cover for the frying pan useful.

Enamelware
This term is applied to a lightweight pan made of a thin layer of glass fused onto metal. These pans tend to crack, chip and discolour easily, and some heat distribution is very spotty. If you already have some in your kitchen, use them to melt fat or use as the top part of a double boiler, placed in a pan of hot water, to melt small quantities of chocolate.

Porcelain enamelware
This is made of porcelain enamel applied over cast iron. It combines bright colors, sturdiness and good heat control for foods that require long slow cooking. The best is porcelain applied to both the inside and outside of the cast iron. Good-quality pots and pans of this type are on the expensive side, like stainless steel, but with careful handling they will last a lifetime. The use of this heavy ware is the secret of many of the great recipes of classic cuisines. It is perfect for casserole cooking. There are so many attractive ones available in different sizes, many of them attractive enough to be brought from the stove to the table.

Cast iron
This is still the dependable, low-priced, sturdy ware that our forebears cooked with. As they have no wooden parts, they can be used on top of the stove as well as in the oven.

Before using a new cast-iron pan, it must be seasoned. Spread melted lard, shortening, or salad oil on the inside of the utensil, as well as on the cover. Then place it on a sheet of heavy aluminum foil in a 200°F (95°C) oven for 3 hours, brushing the sides and cover occasionally with more fat. When it is cured, turn the heat off. When the utensil has cooled, wipe off the excess fat with paper towels. Wash it in warm water with no soap, and put it back in the warm oven to dry thoroughly. ⚬⟶☞ This procedure can also be used for cast-iron pots that have rusted. Wash them well before seasoning. Every time a cast-iron utensil is washed after use, dry it completely, over low heat or in a warm oven, before storing. Do not cover tightly when storing, as humidity trapped inside may cause rusting. This is perfect ware to pan-broil steaks, chops, etc. It is also excellent to use for frying bacon, pancakes, eggs and many other things.

Copper

All copper utensils are very expensive, and they require a lot of work to keep clean. However, if soufflés, meringues and the like are on your list of accomplishments, the most indispensable luxury you can have is a large, tin-lined, copper bowl for beating egg whites.

Teflon

This is a most serviceable type of ware that allows cooking without fat because of the coating applied to its surface. It is also very easy to clean, though its delicate surface must be protected against scratches. That's why Teflon-coated utensils or wooden spoons are used when turning or stirring anything in a Teflon pan. They really excel as omelet pans.

Pyrex

Watching the pot boil or the cake bake became possible with this heatproof and flameproof glass. It is especially useful when you want to see how things are getting on. For instance, when using a Pyrex pie dish, you can tell if the crust is getting too brown on the botton and adjust the oven heat accordingly. But it cannot be moved from hot to cold with safety, and it is fragile, like all glass.

Pyroceram

This is a wonder of the modern world. It is a special ceramic that can be stored in the freezer or refrigerator and can be taken from either and put in a hot oven or onto a hot element. And it goes from the stove to the table. The manufacturers have been extremely clever in making this ware in all sizes and so attractive that it is suitable with any type of table setting. It is most useful for all types of slow cooking. A few basic pieces are indispensable and should be a part of every kitchen.

Earthenware

Casseroles, marmites and ramekins of red clay are an ancient kind of cooking ware that was once used almost universally. It is still made and used extensively in France, and special sizes and shapes are available for special purposes. It is fragile and can be used for stove-top cooking only with the greatest care. If you plan to cook certain classics of the provincial French cuisine, such as cassoulet or tian, an earthenware pot of the right shape is a good choice, but it is better to choose a less-fragile ware for top-of-the-stove cooking.

If you find it hard to determine what size or type of pot or pan to buy, check the following list as an aid.

TOP-OF-STOVE UTENSILS

1 large covered pan, 6- to 10-quart (7 to 11 L) size, for meat, soup, spaghetti or food for a large party.

1 double boiler, the 2-quart (2 L) size is the best, but they come smaller or larger. The bottom part can always be used as an extra saucepan.

2 saucepans, 1-quart (1 L) size; this is the size that is most used for all types of small jobs. One at least should be stainless steel.

1 saucepan, 2-quart (2 L) size; this should be stainless steel or porcelain enamelware.

2 frying pans; I would suggest the 10-inch (25 cm) size, with a cover, in porcelain enamelware or heavy aluminium. This kind of pan is often called a sauteuse, which means a pan for sautéing (frying in very little fat). For the second pan, choose the 7- or 8-inch (17 or 20 cm) size in cast iron, Pyroceram or Teflon.

1 cast-iron Dutch oven, although a 2-quart (2 L) saucepan of porcelain enamelware with a cover can be used instead.

1 tea kettle. Choose the 2- or 3-quart (2 or 3 L) size and make sure it can be cleaned inside. (Many prefer to use an electric tea kettle.)

1 or 2 teapots. Choose two sizes, one small or medium, the other large. They should be either earthenware or, if you prefer something a little more elegant, porcelain. But don't make tea in a metal pot whatever you do; any lover of tea will tell you that metal alters the fine, delicate flavor of tea.

1 or 2 coffee makers. Here you have a wide choice. Personally, I prefer filtered drip coffee because it is the most digestible. Whatever your choice, however, shop around to make sure you find the one that's right for you. They come in all sizes and types, of course. If you have retained the good habit of making coffee from milled coffee rather than instant, choose a 2- to 3-cup size to suit small daily needs and a larger size to use when the entire family is gathered, or when you have guests.

3 or 4 assorted pieces of Pyroceram ware in different sizes to suit your needs. Get all of these with covers. Of course, they can be used on top of the stove, in the oven, in the microwave and in the broiler.

OVEN AND BROILER UTENSILS

1 large shallow roasting pan, with no cover. The best sizes are 12 to 15 inches (30 to 38 cm) long by 10 to 12 inches (25 to 30 cm) wide and 2 to 3 inches (5 to 7.5 cm) deep. The best are porcelain enamelware; the next best, stainless steel.

1 broiler pan with a rack. Ovens often are equipped with these, but a small-size one as an extra is very practical.

1 porcelain enamelware casserole in the 2-quart (2 L) size. Choose something elegant enough to bring to the table. This can be most useful, but is not really essential to start with, unless you are cooking for a large family. However, it is an ideal utensil to use for braising a large piece of meat. You can use this on top of the stove as well as in the oven.

2 cookie sheets or baking sheets. At least one should be Teflon-coated.

2 pie pans; you could have both 9-inch (23 cm) size, or one 9-inch (23 cm) and the other 8-inch (20 cm) size.

2 square cake pans, 8 by 8 by 2 inches (20 by 20 by 5 cm); these can be either Teflon-coated or plain.

3 round cake pans, 8 by 1½ inches (8 by 4 cm), Teflon-coated.

2 loaf pans, 9 by 5 by 3 inches (23 by 13 by 8 cm), 1. Pyroceram and 1 Teflon-coated aluminium.

2 bread pans, 10 by 5 by 3 inches (25 by 13 by 8 cm) Teflon-coated.

1 jelly-roll pan, 11 by 7 by 2 inches (28 by 18 by 5 cm) or 12 by 8 by 2 inches (30 by 20 by 5 cm), Teflon-coated.

2 cake racks, 1 large, 1 small.

1 tube pan; 10 by 4 inches (25 by 10 cm) is the most practical size.

1 muffin or cupcake pan. These come with depressions of 1½, 2½ and 3 inches (4, 6 and 8 cm). The 2½-inch (6 cm) size is the best all-around size and the most practical. Teflon ware is almost a must for muffins or cupcakes, for they unmold with ease every time.

6 custard cups. These come in different sizes, but the 6-ounce (170ml) size is the most practical. You will use them for many things besides custard.

1 springform pan. This consists of a rim and insets, with a clamp or a spring to open the rim. They sometimes come with a flat bottom inset and a tube inset. The usual size is 9 by 3 inches (23 by 8 cm). These are very useful for Torten, angel-food and cheesecake, as well as for other fancy cakes and desserts.

Oven-to-table servers; the number and size depend on your preferences and needs.

Assorted small fancy molds, again dependent on your needs.

Ring molds that range in capacity from 3 ⅓ to 11 cups (830 ml to 2.75 L) or 1- to 3-quart (1 to 3 L) sizes, the size is usually marked on the molds. Use for molding desserts, jellied foods, cakes, etc.

WHEN A PAN OR MOLD IS THE WRONG SIZE

Often a recipe calls for a mold or pan of a size you do not have. The following suggestions will help you solve the problem.

O—☞ If the volume is the important factor in the receipe -for instance, if the directions say, "pour the gelatin into a 3-cup (750 ml) mold," or "bake in a 2-quart (2 L) casserole", you can use any other container of any shape, as long as it holds the same volume. To determine this, fill a standard 8-ounce (250 ml) measuring cup with water and pour it into the pan. Continue to do this until the pan is full. If it holds 4 cups (1 L) of water, it will be the equivalent of 1-quart (1 L) casserole, and so on.

O—☞ If a baking recipe specifies a pan measuring 13 by 9 by 2 inches (33 by 23 by 5 cm) it is the surface area that is important and not the shape of the pan. For this you will have to do a little arithmetic. Measure the width and the length of the pan you have and multiply these figures to determine the area in square inches (or centimetres). Do the same for the measurements given in the recipe. A pan 13 by 9 inches o(33 by 23 cm) will have a surface area of 117 square inches (759 square centimeters). A pan 12 by 10 inches (30 by 25 cm) may look quite different, but its surface area is almost the same — 120 square inches (750 square centimeters). If you have only small pans, use two or more of them to get the same surface area. Determining the specified 2-inch (5 cm) depth is not as important; the pan could be deeper, although it should not be shallower. It is the surface area that counts.

Here is another way to solve the problem. O—☞ Cake batters should never fill a pan more than two-thirds full. If you do not have a pan large enough to contain all the batter and still leave one-third of the depth empty, fill the pan to the proper level and make cupcakes with what is left over.

O—☞ When the recipe calls for a 9- to 10-inch (23 to 25 cm) tube pan, the batter can be baked in a flat pan 13 by 9 by 2 inches (33 by 23 by 5 cm).

If you don't know the size of your pie pan, measure with a ruler from the inside edge to the opposite side. To measure the depth, be sure to measure perpendicularly, not following the sloping sides. You can measure the volume of a pie pan just as you do any other baking pan, with cups of water. A 9-inch (23 cm) pie pan 1½ to 2 inches (4 to 5 cm) deep holds about 4 cups (1 L) of filling. An 8-inch (20 cm) pie pan holds about 3 cups (750 ml).

O—☞ When a recipe calls for a casserole with a cover and you have none, use any heavy baking pan that is the right size and make a cover of heavy-duty foil.

MICROWAVE OVEN UTENSILS

Microwave cooking opens new possibilities in convenience and flexibility in terms of cooking containers. New microwave accessories are constantly being introduced, but don't feel you have to buy a whole set of microwave cooking equipment. You will be surprised by how many conventional cooking utensils are suitable for microwave cooking.

Glass, ceramic and china

Most utensils made from these materials are excellent for use in the microwave oven. Heat-resistant glassware, unless it has metallic trim or decoration, can almost always be used. However, be careful about using delicate glassware, since it can crack -not from microwave energy but from the heat of the food. Here are a few heat-resistant glass or ceramic cookware items — many of them

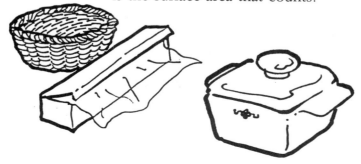

staples of conventional cooking — that are invaluable in microwave cookery: measuring cups, custard cups, loaf dishes, covered casserole dishes, cake dishes, pie plates, mixing bowls and large bowls with covers.

Browning dish and grill

These microwave cooking utensils help to give microwaved meat a pleasing color.

Browning dishes and grills have a special dielectric coating on the underside that is activated by preheating them, empty and uncovered, in the microwave oven. You don't remove them from the oven after preheating; simply place in the dish the food you want to brown, pressing down on it with the fork to make perfect contact with the bottom of the dish. Browning dishes come in two sizes — 8 by 8 by 2 inches (20 by 20 by 5 cm), 6 cups (1.5 L); and 9.5 by 9.5 by 2 inches (24 by 24 by 5 cm), 10 cups (2.5 L). The grill is 8 by 8 inches (20 by 20 cm).

Cooking bags

Cooking bags designed to withstand boiling, freezing or conventional heating are safe to use in a microwave oven. Make six small slits in the top of the bag to allow steam to escape. It is best to use a piece of cotton string, a nylon tie or a strip cut from the open end of the bag to close the bag.

Plastic wrap

When your microwave cooking dish doesn't have a lid, plastic wrap can be used. It may become disfigured over an extended cooking time, but its efficiency won't by affected. When you use plastic wrap as a casserole dish cover, fold back a small section of it from the edge of the dish to allow some steam to escape.

Paper

Paper napkins, waxed paper, paper towels, freezer wrap and paper cups and plates are all handy utensils for microwave cooking. Use them for foods with short cooking times and low fat content. Avoid wax-coated paper goods, since the wax may melt onto the food at high temperatures. But a sheet of waxed paper works well to prevent spattering. Disposable polyester-coated paperboard pans are sturdy; they come in a variety of sizes and are ideal for microwaving.

Straw and wicker

Straw and wicker baskets can be used in the microwave oven for short periods of time to warm food, especially rolls or bread.

Frozen dinner trays

Frozen dinner trays can be used in the microwave oven, but only if the container is no more than ¾ inch (2 cm) high.

KNIVES

These are among the most neglected tools in the kitchen, although they are used constantly. They are often poor in quality, dull or not the proper kind for the work they are expected to do. There is a knife for every job. The variety available is endless. But you can get a perfect starter set consisting of 6 knives. If you are not willing or able to pay for a good-quality set, buy one good knife at a time as you can afford them, or as the need arises. Cheap knives are a waste of money.

Knives with a scalloped edge have become popular with practical cooks. Originally designed for slicing crumbly bread and cake, they are now made in many sizes and shapes for use in paring, cutting and even carving. Although this knife stays sharp much longer than a straight type, the teeth that project beyond the cutting edge do wear down.

The knife requires an occasional sharpening with a butcher's steel on the flat side of the blade, and eventually will need regrinding by an expert.

A good-quality knife made of hard steel is expensive, but it will last a lifetime if well cared for. ☞ It is a good idea to have a good long butcher's steel with which to sharpen knives. Keep your knives sharp by frequent honing on the steel. To do this press the knife edge against the steel at a 20° angle, then draw the knife across from the handle, starting at the top of the steel to the tip of the knife. Do this several times. Repeat on the other side.

Starter set of knives

Chef's knife. This is one of the most used knives. It is often referred to as a French chef's knife, a butcher knife or a general-purpose knife. It is used to chop, mince and cut at all angles. The blade size ranges from 7 to 14 inches (18 to 35 cm). The best buy is the 10-inch (25 cm) size, as it can do the work of both a small or large type and is easy to manipulate.

Carving knife. The best kind has a straight blade 8½ to 9 inches (21 to 23 cm) long with plain or scalloped edges.

Slicer. This can have a straight blade with a slightly turned-up point or it can be completely straight. It is usually 4½ to 5 inches (11 to 12 cm) long. The scalloped edge is very practical here, as this knife is perfect to cut tomatoes, citrus fruits, hard-cooked eggs or cucumbers into thin, even slices.

Utility knife. This usually has a 5-inch (13 cm) blade with a concave ground edge; it is available plain or scalloped. Use this to peel and pare vegetables and fruits and to slice through tough-skinned vegetables.

Small slicing and scraping knife. The most useful size has a 4-inch (10 cm) blade with a slightly scalloped edge.

Bread knife. The scalloped-edged types can slice a loaf of bread wafer-thin, whereas those with serrated edges tend to tear rather than cut.

If you do not know the difference between a scalloped edge and a serrated edge, ask a sales clerk to show you one of each the next time you are shopping. Scalloped-edged knives have been made from a high-carbon steel formula and have been heat tempered. This makes them more expensive, but they are worth the money.

1. Chef's knife
2. Carving knife
3. Bread knife
4. Butcher's steel
5. Small slicing and scraping knife
6. Slicer
7. Utility knife

Other essential tools

In addition to pots and pans and knives, you will need certain other small tools. Purchased one at a time, they are not costly. Do not try to economize by buying cheap tools. They will prove to be a poor investment; they may bend, break, rust or come apart at the joint of blade and handle. Cheap tools are always a waste of money.

1 set of large sturdy salt and pepper shakers.

1 set of canisters. Buy airtight ones for storage of such staples as flour, salt and sugar.

1 set of measuring spoons. Choose good quality for accurate measurement.

2 sets of measuring cups. For dry ingredients, buy 4 graduated metal cups that nest inside each other. When using these, fill to the brim. Buy glass measuring cups for the other set to use for liquid ingredients. The rims of these are above the 1-cup (250 ml) line to prevent spilling, but accurate measurement can be assured by holding the measuring line at eye level.

1 set of mixing bowls. Get either stainless steel, which is expensive but will last a lifetime, or a good-quality plastic or polyethylene, which is light in weight.

1 set of wooden spoons. Get 3 or 4 spoons in graduated sizes. You will find these are indispensable, and they do not scratch the bottoms of your pots and pans.

1 large 2-pronged fork. Get this in stainless steel with a sturdy handle.

1 slotted spoon. This is used to remove foods from hot liquids such as fresh fruits or vegetables you have put into boiling water to skin, cooked vegetables, eggs or food that may have released sandy particles in the cooking liquid, such as spinach or fresh mussels.

1 vegetable peeler. Even one of good quality is inexpensive. It is indispensable.

2 metal spatulas. Choose a short squatty spatula with a flexible blade that can double as a butter spreader and sandwich maker, and a long narrow one for lifting cookies from the baking sheet and many other purposes.

2 or 3 rubber scrapers. Like short-bladed spatulas, these are useful for scraping any mixture out of a bowl because they bend around the inside and collect every bit of the mixture.

1 pair of metal tongs. To turn steak and other meats.

1 pancake turner. The short wide type is best. The Teflon-coated kind can play a double role, since they can be used on Teflon-coated pans as well as others. This is stiffer than a spatula; use it to turn fish cakes, eggplant slices and the like.

1 potato masher. Stainless steel is best. You will use this not only for potatoes, but also to make applesauce and cranberry sauce, to mash fruits for jam and jellies, and to mash other vegetables.

2 French wire whisks or whips or beaters. Buy one medium-sized and one large. Use for making hollandaise, mayonnaise, meringues, even for blending the ingredients of a simple salad dressing. The wooden-handled type with a double row of piano wires is the very best.

1 egg beater. Buy a top-quality beater with smooth, heavy-duty bearings and stainless-steel blades. Cheap beaters do not last and never work efficiently.

1 soup ladle. A small sauce ladle is also very useful.

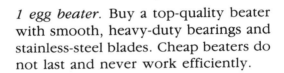

2 cutting boards. Buy a large one for meat, and a smaller one for cheese or vegetables.

1 pair of kitchen scissors or shears. These will help you in countless ways — cutting herbs, especially chives and parsley; cutting up dried fruits such as dates or figs; opening plastic bags of food; cutting pizza.

1 apple corer. Choose a sturdy one. They can scoop round pieces from any firm fruit or vegetable.

1 set of graters. The best have four grater sizes.

2 strainers. Choose one for tea and the other large enough to double as a small colander. Later you may want to have other sizes of strainers and a large colander.

2 funnels. These should be in plastic, so no metallic taste mars the flavor of the liquid you pour into them. Get a small one and a medium-sized one.

1 corkscrew. Choose one that really works; many on the market are worthless.

1 bottle opener. Get one with a sturdy handle.

1 punch opener for cans.

1 meat thermometre. This is essential, especially if you are a new cook; it will help you prepare successful roasts from the start. Also, it is essential if you plan to cook frozen meats.

1 candy (or frying) thermometre. This is important if you plan to make candy or do a lot of deep frying.

1 microwave oven thermometre. Do not use a conventional mercury thermometre in a microwave oven.

When you start to bake, you will need to add a few more items.

1 flour sifter. These are used less and less because of the no-sifting flour now available, but you will need regular flour for many recipes. A 1-cup (250 ml) sifter should be adequate. Place it over the measuring cup to save time.

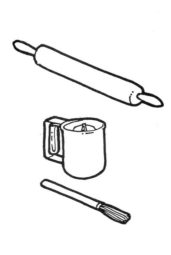

1 rolling pin. Choose one made of wood or Teflon-coated. Add a pastry cloth if you wish.

1 pastry brush. Personally, I prefer a small paint brush, 1 inch (2.5 cm) wide.

Small appliances

Some small appliances are invaluable because they save so much time and labour. They may be hand-operated or electrically powered.

A can opener. Quality is essential. In a hand type, choose one with a sturdy handle, or get a good-quality hand-operated wall type. A can opener should be cleaned often and oiled occasionally. There are electric can openers too.

A fruit juicer. Choose a good reamer that fits over a cup to catch the juice. A hand reamer can be just as good as any electric juicer unless you use large quantities of juice daily.

A food mill. A medium-sized mill is a most useful kitchen tool to purée vegetables for soups or fruits for sauces. There are also larger and smaller mills. A similar appliance is a ricer, but the mill is easier and quicker to operate for a variety of vegetables and fruits.

An electric hand mixer. If you do not have a large electric mixer, this will serve well, although it is heavy to hold for a long time. A large electric mixer is very useful if you make cakes or need to stir up heavy mixtures.

A food grinder. Some electric mixers have a grinder attachment. This will grind meat, vegetables, nuts — almost anything you can think of. An old-fashioned hand grinder is just as effective, but not as easy to use.

Scales. These are handy, especially if you enjoy making international dishes or if you are a dieter who must measure food by weight. There are several types and sizes. Choose one marked in ounces, pounds, grams and kilograms.

Few luxuries

These items do not belong on a master list of essentials. However, if you have developed a genuine interest in cooking, you may have a yearning for some of them. Study their use before you buy. Some elaborate and expensive kitchen equipment is seldom used, and it would be foolish to spend the money and clutter up your cupboard space with something you won't use very often.

Boxwood spatula and spoons. Spatulas and spoons made from French boxwood, a fine, hard-grained wood, are light and smooth. Their flexibility lets you feel the consistency and texture of the ingredients you stir with them.

Chopping or butcher's block. A larger, thicker and sturdier board than the cutting boards listed earlier. Price varies according to size and quality. You don't have to get the biggest or the best, but do make sure that the wood is thick and the board is heavy so it will not slide around when used.

Meat hammer. This is a double-headed hammer made of metal or hard plastic with blunt teeth on one side and grooves on the other. Pounding meat with it breaks up the fibres while spreading the meat into a thin layer. You prepare meat to make *scaloppini* or *schnitzel* in this manner.

Electric frying pan. Many cooks never use this appliance, while others say they wouldn't be without one and use it several times a week. Whether this item would be useful depends on the sort of cooking you do. Some cooks find it convenient as a thermostatically controlled utensil for cooking at the table, or as a chafing dish.

Electric coffee grinder. This item should not be classed as a luxury if you make fresh coffee every day. A cup of coffee is at its best only when it has been made with freshly ground beans. Keep your grinder clean; use it every day and you will relish every cup of coffee you make.

Blender. This may come with two speeds -slow and fast — or with with several. An electric blender is certainly not essential, but it is a great joy to use. Among other things, it can help you produce something special out of leftovers. And it takes the tediousness out of many preparations by doing the job quickly and efficiently. A good blender is expensive but well worth the price if it is used for more than the preparation of the odd fancy drink.

Food processor. This is a blender, chopper, grinder, mixer, slicer, shredder and whipper in one. It is expensive, but it is so useful it can hardly be considered a luxury.

Electric hot tray. A hot tray of good quality will keep hot food just right for 2 to 3 hours if necessary and can be a tremendous help when entertaining. You can set food on it long before guests or family arrive for dinner.

Portable food heater. These propane fueled table heaters with adjustable flame are wonderful for an elegant fondue party and can be used for many other things.

A garbage-disposal unit in the sink is extremely handy. The location of your home and your plumbing arrangements will determine if this is practical.

REFRIGERATOR AND FREEZER

When you shop for a refrigerator or freezer, save yourself time and money by first deciding what you want and need. Consider the following points:

How much storage space do you need? This is determined by how large your family is, how often you shop and the kind of food you buy. Since no one has ever had too much refrigerator space, get one as large as room and budget will allow.

If you have a freezer or intend to buy one, take advantage of the extra fresh-food capacity in an "all-refrigerator" refrigerator.

What types are available? Refrigerators with single doors include conventional types, "all-refrigerator" refrigerators and compact refrigerators. Two-door combinations include those with a separate freezer at the top, at the bottom or at the side. When deciding which you want, consider the convenience of use, freezer-refrigerator proportion, and the shelf arrangement that will work best for you.

Freezers may be the chest-type or upright, small or large. Some upright freezers are designed to match an "all-refrigerator" refrigerator. All these types are also available as built-in units.

What features do you want?

0— *Shelf arrangement:* Shelves vary in flexibility. They may adjust up or down, a little bit or in a great variety of combinations. They may slide, glide or swing out.

Special storage areas: Look for an abundance of compartmentalized storage areas if you want ease in organizing. Super-chilled drawers are great for more-than-one-day storage of fresh meats. Some are used as an extra crisper drawer. Doors may have compartmentalized storage, adjustable shelves, even a vegetable crisper.

Freezer storage features are important, too. Think of the frozen foods you use most. Can you store these so they are convenient to reach?

Ice making: Many refrigerator-freezer combinations now include automatic ice makers. Other refrigerators have trays with special ice-removal features.

"Fast cold recovery". This feature lets you maintain a uniform cold temperature inside, no matter how often the door is opened.

What styling do you want?
The large variety of decorator designs for refrigerators now runs the gamut. Their kaleidoscope of colours includes greens, reds, blues, copper tones, beiges, brushed chrome, and wood grains. Trim, square lines give a built-in look, and you can get wood-grained finishes to match your cabinets.

What size? Measure the kitchen space available so you can choose a refrigerator of the correct size. Refrigerators are available in many dimensions: even the side-by-side combination comes as narrow as 33 inches (84 cm) and as wide as 48 inches (122 cm).

And while you're at it, don't overlook the compact refreshment refrigerators or freezers; they're a wonderful convenience for the family room or den.

As for the freezer, when buying one for the first time it will not be easy to judge the best size. It has been said that a freezer can never be too big. But, if you use a freezer only to make meal planning a little easier, by storing only enough frozen food for 2 or 3 days and keeping a few emergency items, it is more economical to buy a large refrigerator with a good frozen-food compartment. The investment in a freezer is not economical under such circumstances.

For more about the freezer and how to use it, see the chapter on Freezing Foods

Efficient refrigerator use
Since a refrigerator is a large investment, you will want to get the best use from it. It also is one appliance that is plugged in all the time, so savings on power costs are worth knowing about. Here are some ideas:

1. Place the refrigerator in the coolest part of your kitchen. Air should be able to circulate around it freely.
2. Be sure the outside door, hinges and door catch work properly; otherwise warm air can enter.

3. Don't open your refrigerator any more often or for any longer than necessary.

4. Avoid turning your freezer to the coldest setting.

5. Turn your control down to "low" or "economy" when you go away for several days.

6. If your refrigerator isn't frost free, defrost it when frost around the freezing unit is ¼ inch (6 mm) thick. The coils will then continue to work at maximum efficiency.

7. Maintain circulation of air inside the refrigerator. Do not line the shelves with waxed paper or foil, despite the temptation to avoid drips in this manner. Air circulates best through the open grid of the shelves, and lining them reduces the efficiency of the cooling mechanism.

8. Do not use your refrigerator as pantry space. Chill canned goods only when you want them cold for serving.

9. Never put liquids or moist foods in uncovered. The refrigerator will dry them out, and their moisture will freeze into ice that covers the refrigerator coils.

10. Don't put hot food or dishes into the refrigerator. Allow them to cool to room temperature first, or if speed is essential, set the dish in a bowl of ice cubes.

As you continue to use your kitchen you will think of other pieces of equipment, other handy tools, that you will want. Your family's food tastes and habits will determine whether the new utensil is an extravagance or a useful work saver. Remember that you need electrical outlets, and that for any new item you will need storage space close to where you use it.

THE CUPBOARD

When properly stocked with the right items, your cupboards can save you money as well as wear and tear.

Study the following list and then look at your own cupboards. Remove from the shelves all the things you will never use. Add those you know you will need. Make sure necessary items are replenished quickly.

FLOUR AND LEAVENING.
NECESSARY: all-purpose flour, cornstarch, baking powder, baking soda. *Useful but not basically necessary:* biscuit mix, cream of tartar, pastry flour, piecrust mix, potato flour, arrowroot, active dry yeast.

CEREALS AND STARCHES.
NECESSARY: rice, noodles, macaroni, spaghetti, small pasta for soup, rolled oats, cold cereal. *Useful but not basically necessary:* cornmeal, farina, fine bread crumbs (it's cheaper to make your own), barley.

SUGAR.
NECESSARY: granulated white, dark and light brown or your choice of one, icing, molasses, corn syrup. *Useful but not basically necessary:* maple syrup or maple blend, maple sugar, fruit sugar.

BEVERAGES.
NECESSARY: coffee, instant coffee powder, tea, dry skim milk, cocoa, instant cocoa powder.
Useful but not basically necessary: coffee beans, choice tea, evaporated milk, condensed milk.

CHOCOLATE.
NECESSARY: chips, unsweetened, semi-sweet.
Useful but not basically necessary: sweet chocolate, fancy imported chocolate, Dutch cocoa.

EXTRACTS AND FLAVOURINGS.
NECESSARY: vanilla, almond, maple, lemon juice, bouillon cubes, ketchup, prepared mustard, Worcestershire sauce.
Useful but not basically necessary: rum extract, soy sauce, chili sauce, condiment sauces, hot-pepper sauce, fancy mustards.

FATS AND SHORTENING.
NECESSARY: salad oil, vegetable shortening, pure lard.
Useful but not basically necessary: olive oil, peanut oil.

VINEGAR.
NECESSARY: white vinegar, cider vinegar.
Useful but not basically necessary: malt vinegar, wine vinegar, herb vinegar.

HERBS, SPICES, AND SEASONINGS.
NECESSARY: Basic spices: ground allspice; ground cinnamon; cloves, whole and ground; ground ginger; dry mustard; grated nutmeg; paprika; pepper, black, whole and ground. Basic dried herbs: basil, bay leaves, marjoram, orégano, sage, savory, thyme. Also coarse salt, fine table salt, monosodium glutamate.
Useful but not basically necessary: Spices: whole allspice, cardamom pods, cinnamon sticks, coriander berries, mace blades, whole nutmeg, white pepper. Herbs: dried chives, powdered garlic, powdered onion, dried parsley, dried tarragon. Also seasoned salt.

DRIED FRUITS, LEGUMES, AND NUTS.
NECESSARY: currants, dates, prunes, seedless raisins; navy beans, split peas, yellow peas; coconut, walnuts.
Useful but not basically necessary: almonds, Brazil nuts, pecans; maraschino cherries, candied fruits, muscatel raisins.

MISCELLANEOUS: unflavoured gelatin, flavoured gelatin, food colouring, grated cheese, olives, pimentos, tomato sauce; a few cans of cream soup to be used as sauces or in casseroles (celery, mushroom, tomato).

Many other items would be good to have, but buy them only as they are needed. An overstocked cupboard can become a mess and requires a lot of attention. After all, there is no use cluttering up valuable space with items you rarely use. This applies even to the list above. If there are items on it you are sure you will never use, then by all means omit them. The list is only a guide to get you started. Don't plan to buy them all at once; perhaps each week you could add another staple or another spice.

SHELF LIFE

How long to keep the most-used foods on your pantry shelf

FOOD	TIME
Baking powder, baking soda, cream of tartar	8 to 12 months
Cake, biscuit, pancake, piecrust mixes:	
opened	2 to 3 months
unopened	6 to 8 months
[1] Canned foods (kept in a cool dry place)	1 year
Cereals (dry) and flours	2 to 3 months
Chocolate, cocoa, instant cocoa	1 year
Coconut, unopened can	6 to 8 months
Coconut, opened box	2 weeks
Instant coffee powder	6 to 8 months
Tea, unopened box	3 to 4 months
Tea, opened box	2 weeks
Instant tea	6 to 8 months
Potato chips	7 to 10 days
Dry bread crumbs in covered container	6 weeks
Dried fruits and dry legumes	6 to 8 months
Extracts, flavorings	8 to 12 months
Herbs, spices, seasoning salts	8 to 12 months
Macaroni, noodles, spaghetti, etc.	3 to 6 months
Milk, dry (discard it if it gets lumpy)	1 year
Nuts, in shell	1 year
Nuts, shelled	2 to 3 months
Shortening, lard, salad oil	3 to 4 months
[2] Sugar, syrups	1 year

[1] Canned baby foods should be used within 6 months because of vitamin deterioration, even in the unopened can or jar. Evaporated milk and condensed milk should be used within 3 months.

[2] Maple syrup, when opened, should be transferred to a glass bottle. It should be refrigerated if kept for longer than 10 days. Under refrigeration it will keep for 6 to 8 months.

MEASURES

The spoons, cups, saucepans we use are designed according to ancient patterns. There is no particular reason why a cup should hold an arbitrary 8 ounces (225 ml) but it does. On the other hand, recipes often call for tablespoons or cups of something that you have bought by the pound, and it seems like differential calculus to get these measures to mesh.

Another problem that exists for us Canadians is that we use U.S. cookbooks as well as French, English and other cookbooks using metric measurements. A complete comparison of all these measures would require a large book, so in the tables that follow you will find only a short summary as a guide and reference.

You will notice that there are 2 kinds of pints and quarts, imperial and U.S. While the cup is the same standard 8-ounce measure, the imperial pint and quart hold more cups than the U.S. pint and quart. This presents a problem only in recipes calling for pints and quarts. For recipes from a Canadian or Commonwealth source, use the imperial measure; for U.S. recipes use the 2-cup pint and the 4-cup quart.

EQUIVALENT MEASURES

EQUIVALENT COOKING MEASURES — IMPERIAL AND U.S.

a few grains	= less than 1/16 tsp
a pinch	= less than 1/8 tsp
1/2 tbsp	= 1 1/2 tsp
1 tbsp	= 3 tsp or 1/2 oz
1/8 cup	= 2 tbsp or 1 oz
1/4 cup	= 4 tbsp or 2 oz
1/3 cup	= 5 tbsp plus 1 tsp
1/2 cup	= 8 tbsp or 4 oz
2/3 cup	= 10 tbsp plus 2 tsp
3/4 cup	= 12 tbsp or 6 oz
1 cup	= 16 tbsp or 8 oz
2 cups (8 oz each)	= 1 pint (U.S.)
2 pints (16 oz each)	= 1 quart (U.S.) or 4 cups
1 imperial quart	= 5 cups or 40 oz
1 U.S. quart	= 4 coups or 32 oz

EQUIVALENT COOKING MEASURES —
METRIC

The metric equivalents of imperial measurements in common use are not exact. For instance, 1 pound is precisely 453.592 grams; but for the sake of convenience, 500 grams is considered to be equal to 1 pound. The approximate metric equivalents given here are those in common use.

Abbreviations and symbols	
centimetre	= cm
gram	= gr
kilogram	= kg
litre	= L
millilitre	= ml
millimetre	= mm

Volume: Liquid measures

¼ cup	=	60 ml
⅓ cup	=	80 ml
½ cup (4 oz)	=	125 ml
¾ cup (6 oz)	=	200 ml
1 cup (8 oz)	=	250 ml
4 cups	=	1 L

Volume: Dry measures

¼ cup	=	50 ml
⅓ cup	=	80 ml
½ cup	=	125 ml
¾ cup	=	190 ml
1 cup	=	250 ml

Weight

1 oz	=	30 gr
1 lb	=	500 gr
1 kg (1000 gr)	=	2.2 lb

Length

⅛ inch	=	3 mm
¼ inch	=	6 mm
½ inch	=	1.25 cm
1 inch	=	2.5 cm
2 inches	=	5 cm

Small measures, liquid and dry

¼ teaspoon	=	1 ml
½ teaspoon	=	2 ml
1 teaspoon	=	5 ml
1 tablespoon	=	15 ml
2 tablespoons	=	30 ml
3 tablespoons	=	50 ml

Note: ml means millilitre;
      1000 ml = 1 L

EQUIVALENT TEMPERATURES

Temperature
Water boils at 212°F (100°C)

Oven temperatures

Very slow oven	250° to 275°F (120° to 135°C)
Slow	300° to 325°F (150° to 165°C)
Moderate	350° to 375°F (175° to 190°C)
Hot	400° to 425°F (205° to 220°C)
Very hot	450° to 465°F (230° to 235°C)

Fahrenheit and Centigrade temperatures for sugar boiling

228° to 234°F = 109° to 112°C
Thread or very soft-ball stage; the syrup cannot be formed into a ball hard enought to pick up.

234° to 240°F = 112° to 116°C
Long-thread or soft-ball stage; the syrup can easily be formed into a soft pliable ball; it can be picked up.

240° to 248°F = 116° to 120°C
Rather firm ball that maintains shape when removed from water.

250° to 256°F = 121° to 124°C
Very firm ball that forms into hard-ball mass.

CHAPTER 4

Science
and seasoning

DURING my early training, I asked why it was necessary to learn so much about food chemistry when all I really wanted was to learn how to cook. My Paris friend and teacher Dr. de Pomiane gave me this answer: "In cooking, as in everything else, always remember that science must come first, because it is science that makes it possible to understand the mechanics. Once the mechanics are understood, creativity follows, and at that point cooking becomes an art." I have recognized the truth in Dr. de Pomiane's statement throughout my life. That's why I feel it is important to explain some of the chemistry and the basic mechanics of cooking.

It would take years to learn all about the chemical reactions that come into play every time you apply heat to food, or add salt, sugar, lemon juice, baking powder or yeast, or mix diverse elements to make a new food entity. Once you understand what happens when you add an acid or a sweet to food, or how heat changes meat fibres and egg protein, you become a better cook. Yes, the art of cooking requires theoretical knowledge as well as practical experience. One reinforces the other.

Do not expect a long lecture about these subjects. You will find bits of information all through the chapters that follow; for instance, the effect of heat on eggs is discussed in the egg chapter, and the process of emulsion — mixing oil and water — is described in the chapter on sauces. Here I will include only the basic techniques that are indispensable from the outset, and the most simple information on the effect of heat on food, and what happens when you add acid, salt and sugar.

THE MECHANICS OF COOKING

HERE'S WHERE THE MECHANICS COME IN

Before foods are cooked and often after they are cooked but before they are eaten, they are subjected to a variety of procedures — washing, scraping, peeling, cutting, chopping, grinding, mashing, whisking, stirring, folding, kneading, rolling, shaping. These are the mechanics of cooking. Without an understanding of most of these terms, cooking could remain a mystery forever, since all of them are used in cookbooks. And without some practical experience in these mechanics, cooking will be a chore. Even as simple a task as slicing a vegetable is not easy at first. You will become more skilled as you practice.

Mixing

This consists of stirring two or more ingredients by moving them around with a spoon or fork. Sometimes a spoon will mash down the ingredients, while a fork can give a lighter mixture.

Blending

This involves mixing thoroughly, but without beating, by stirring around and around until all the ingredients are well mixed, with the particles spread evenly throughout the mixture. A wooden spoon of the proper size is the best tool. First stir to mix, then move the spoon following the shape of a figure 8 to reach all areas.

This term is also used to describe the action of an electric blender, although the process is somewhat different. In an electric blender the ingredients are broken into much smaller particles at tremendously high speed.

Whisking

This consists of agitating with a light rapid motion, using an instrument that will froth such ingredients as eggs and creams by incorporating as much air as possible. Nothing can replace the French wire whisk for this operation. It is perfect to aerate a single food, like egg white or whipping cream. It is the only utensil that incorporates enough air bubbles to produce a perfect meringue and a full-bodied whipped cream. It is also the only tool that makes it possible to keep beaten egg whites perfect for 10 to 15 minutes, and whipped cream fluffy for a few hours.

Incorporating

This involves forming a light ingredient and a heavy ingredient into one body. A good illustration is the emulsifying action that takes place when you make hollandaise sauce or mayonnaise. In hollandaise, butter is slowly incorporated in the egg yolks; in mayonnaise, oil is incorporated. The nature of the mixture determines the best tool to use, but here, too, the French wire whisk is ideal. In this process, the lighter ingredient must be added a little at a time and fully incorporated before adding the next lot.

Folding

This term describes the process of combining air-filled ingredients, such as beaten egg whites or cream, with a heavier mass, such as a batter. It has to be done in such a way that none of the air is lost; the lightness or leavening action of the air-filled ingredient is what gives the mixture its character. Angel food cake is an example of such a mixture; the egg whites act as leavening. A more vigorous method such as beating would break down the air bubbles.

An orange-wood or rubber spatula or paddle is the best utensil. Let the lighter mixture slide on top of the heavier. Then, tilt the bowl and draw the paddle or spatula through the mixture in a clockwise direction from bottom to top of the bowl and round again, using as few strokes as possible. A gentle rhythmic motion as you go down and up and cut in is also very important, and the rhythm must continue without stopping until the process is complete. It is not necessary in folding to make a mixture that is as homogeneous as a mayonnaise. For instance, when folding beaten egg whites into batters or sauces, a few flecks of white may remain on top.

Beating

This means to strike, or to crush. In its original meaning we use this term for flattening meats such as pieces of veal for making scaloppini, or sometimes for pounding to tenderize, but it is also used for the kind of mixing in which ingredients are completely blended together so that each loses its individual identity to become part of a whole.

The usual utensil used is a rotary hand beater, which takes vigorous two-handed action, one hand firmly holding the beater and the other turning the handle steadily and rapidly. This can also be done with an electric mixer and in an electric blender.

Grinding

This is one of the most ancient ways to process food. For thousands of years wheat has been ground to make flour for bread. When we grind peppercorns or other spices in a small mortar with a pestle, we are following the same method. However, most grinding is done in some sort of machine — for instance, a food grinder that can process meat to make hamburger or peanuts to make peanut butter; or an electric grinder that grinds coffee beans. An electric blender can be used to grind some kinds of food.

Mashing

Generally, mashing applies to cooked foods such as potatoes or to apples for applesauce, but the term is also used for crushing a garlic clove with the flat side of a knife to release the garlic flavor more quickly in cooking.

CUTTING IS AN ART

All sorts of foods are cut up to make them smaller for cooking or eating. Various terms are used. When a chicken is "cut up", this usually means that it has been disjointed and cut into eight pieces. Vegetables are cut into chunks. Other terms describe the size or shape of the pieces produced. Meats can be sliced, fruits dices, herbs minced, but vegetables are most often cut up.

Some cutting jobs are best done with scissors; a good example is cutting chives. Marshmallows and sticky dried fruits — dates, figs, apricots — are easier to cut with scissors dipped into hot water first.

How to hold a vegetable when cutting

The holding hand must be placed on the food so that the first two fingers present a vertical guard wall to the side face of the knife. Be sure the fingertips are well tucked underneath, out of the way. The fingers then form a right angle with the cutting board so that the face of the knife leans against them in its up and down movements. Never lift the knife higher than the height of your finger guard wall.

For quick, easy work, a 10-inch (25 cm) chef's knife is best. Never use a curved-edge knife, for the straight edge must meet the cutting board on the down stroke to cut through the whole vegetable.

TO SLICE: This is a vertical, straight cutting action used on tender or fleshy vegetables that do not have hard fibres.

To slice a mushroom as shown in the illustration, cut, do not pull, the bottom of the stem. Hold the mushroom following the rule and cut straight through in ¼-inch (6 mm) slices, starting from the outer rim. When you reach the centre, turn the mushroom around and slice as before. Some other tender or fleshy vegetables commonly sliced are asparagus, cucumbers, eggplant, onions of all sorts, tomatoes and zucchini.

TO JULIENNE: Vegetables such as carrots, potatoes cut into long thin strips are called julienne. First scrape or peel. Then cut a thin strip off one side of the vegetable to make it lie flat. Place the flat side on the cutting board and cut the vegetable into very thin lengthwise slices. Cut each thin slice into narrow long strips. A spoonful or so of julienne vegetables, perfectly cooked by steaming, makes a beautiful and tasty garnish for consommé or any other clear soup.

If you cut the long thin slices crosswise, they will be very short narrow strips like matchsticks.

TO CUT INTO CHIFFONADE: Usually a chiffonade is made with leafy greens such as spinach and lettuce. Place 6 to 8 washed leaves one over the other, then cut them into long thin shreds. Blanched chiffonade vegetables make a flavorful garnish for consommé.

TO SHRED: This kind of vegetable preparation is well known because of coleslaw. The preparation is almost the same as chiffonade, except that the vegetable

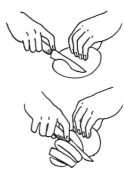

1. Two fingers, tips tucked out of harm, act as a guard to the knife.
2. From the outer rim, slice straight through in ¼-inch (6 mm) slices.

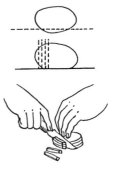

1. To make the vegetable lie flat, cut a thin strip off one side, then thinly slice the vegetable.
2. Cut each slice into strips.

used is coarse and hard, such as cabbage. To be perfect, the shreds must be very fine, so a thin-bladed sharp knife is needed.

TO CUT ON THE BIAS OR DIAGONAL: This is a method we have learned from Oriental cooking. The difference between cutting on the bias and straight slicing is the angle at which you hold your finger guard. Cut at a 45° angle to the vegetable to make the slices.

TO SLIVER: This is done by cutting into long, thin pieces on the bias. The advantage of this method is that the vegetables cook very fast because the heat can penetrate evenly.

First make a diagonal cut at one end of the vegetable. Then cut the whole vegetable parallel to the first cut, always on the bias, into long slivers as thin as possible. With a good sharp knife and a bit of experience, you will soon be able to do this very quickly.

TO DICE: Diced vegetables are cut into cubes of about ⅜ inch (9.5 mm) to make them look their best in a dish, and to help them cook quickly. Practice on a peeled cucumber, which is soft; then you will be able to dice any vegetable.

Cut the vegetable lengthwise into quarters. If it is seedy, remove the seeds. Now cut the quarter section into halves crosswise and line up 4 halves in a row. Holding them down with your hand, slice these lengthwise into julienne strips. Then place the strips in a little bundle and cut them crosswise to dice them into uniform cubes.

TO MINCE: First, gather whatever it is you wish to mince — whole nuts, mushrooms, parsley — into a small heap; then chop them with a chef's knife, using an up-and-down motion, until they are cut into coarse pieces. Heap the pieces together again. Grip the back of the knife blade near the handle with one hand and the tip with the other. Chop with short, rapid, up-and-down strokes, pushing the food back into a heap occasionally with the knife. Continue until the food is cut into very small pieces.

TO CURL VEGETABLES: Vegetables are usually curled to serve as decorations, or to be passed around as an hors d'oeuvre or appetizer. Long, straight root vegetables are the best for curling. With a vegetable peeler, slice a thin strip off one side of a peeled carrot, turnip or parsnip. Curl each strip around a finger as tightly as possible. If necessary, keep the strip curled by pinning it with toothpicks. Place the curls in a bowl of ice water. There will be vitamin loss from soaking, but these are mainly for decoration, not nutrition. Refrigerate for 4 to 5 hours. Remove the toothpicks before serving.

1. Quarter the vegetable lengthwise.

2. Cut each quarter into halves.

3. Julienne each piece.

4. Gather the strips together and cut into uniform cubes.

1. Slice a thin flat lengthwise strip from the vegetable.

2. Roll up into a tight curl and fasten with a food pick.

THE CHEMISTRY OF COOKING

THE EFFECT OF HEAT ON FOOD

By submitting food to heat we are able to change its form, color, texture and flavor. A rib roast shrinks and its contour changes. It goes from deep red to reddish brown. The soft texture of the uncooked fibres hardens and tenderizes. The flavor changes.

Some foods when heated together are completely changed and form something quite different from the original. White sauce is an example; the butter, flour and liquid, which originally had individual identies, are joined into one by heat.

How we apply heat
Heat can be applied in many ways.

Hot liquid, as in boiling, simmering, blanching, poaching, scalding.

Hot fat, as in frying in shallow fat, or in deep fat, where foods such as doughnuts are immersed in it.

Hot metal, as when a steak is panbroiled, or any food is cooked in greaseless pans.

Radiation, which is heat given off by the red hot coil of an electric stove unit, or the flame of a gas stove, or the glowing charcoals of a barbecue.

Trapped heat, which is the heat in ovens of various kinds. This, in a way, combines two basic principles — part of the baking is done by the radiated heat coming from the hot metal walls and grill of the oven, the other part by the trapped heat, the heated air. 0—🐝 When the oven door is opened, heated air escapes and the oven temperature drops. That's why oven doors should be opened as little as possible when a delicate food such as a soufflé or a cake is baking. But any food cooked by oven heat should be submitted as rarely as possible to the cold air currents that enter the moment the door is opened. For example, a roast that is constantly basted will shrink more than one that has not been disturbed. The cold air striking the hot meat accounts for the difference.

On the subject of heat adjustment, it is important to know that the heat controls on gas and electric stoves are slightly different. Gas is very easily controlled; the degree of heat is increased or decreased almost instantly by the turn of the knob. With electric units, the heat takes some time to be increased or decreased. This makes a significant difference when cooking food that requires varied amounts of heat at different stages. So, if you are cooking on an electric stove, it is better to use two burners; when a change of heat is required, simply move the cooking vessel from one burner to the other.

Microwave heat, which is a form of high-frequency radio wave similar to those used by radio. Electricity is converted into microwave energy by a magnetron tube. From the magnetron tube, microwave energy is transmitted to the oven cavity, where it is reflected, transmitted and absorbed. Microwaves are reflected by metal, just as a ball is bounced off a wall. A combination of stationary (interior walls) and rotating (turntable or stirrer fan) metal helps assure that the microwaves are well distributed within the oven cavity to produce even cooking. Microwaves pass through some materials — paper, glass, plastic — much like sunlight shining through a window. Because these substances do not absorb or reflect microwave energy, they are ideal utensils for microwave oven cooking. Microwaves are absorbed by food to a depth of about ¾ to 1½ inches (2 to 4 cm). Microwave energy excites the molecules in the food — especially water, fat and sugar molecules — and causes them to vibrate at a rate of 2.45 billion times per second. This vibration causes friction, which produces heat. The internal cooking is then done by conduction. The heat produced by friction is conducted to the centre of the food.

Foods also continue to cook by conduction during standing time, which keeps the cooked food warm for 4 to 10 minutes after it comes out of the oven — making it possible to cook three or four dishes with only one oven and to serve everything warm.

Room temperature heat is another kind that we tend to ignore. This will warm up cold food from the refrigerator, such as fruits, cheese and cooked meat. As with cooked food, it is heat that brings out the best in the food. Refrigerators should be used to store food and to keep it fresh. However, too many foods are served without being brought back to perfection by returning them to room temperature. **0➝** Melons or peaches, for example, lose most of their quality when served cold. **0➝** Any cheese served cold would be better not served at all. When refrigerator-cold, cheese has practically no smell or taste and it is hard, so that its natural texture is impossible to appreciate. Brought to room temperature, the flavour and texture return and cheese becomes a joy to eat. **0➝** Cold roast beef should be placed at room temperature for two to three hours before being served. It makes a world of difference in flavour.

This should not be misconstrued as unnecessary fussiness. The human palate has very definite and well-defined sensations; first, the sense of taste, which combines with the sense of smell; secondly, the texture of food, be it soft, hard, brittle or crisp; thirdly, the temperature, hot or cold; fourthly, the inner sense of taste, which is the real pleasure derived from food.

Understanding the play of hot and cold on food is most important, because they affect all of these sensations.

ACIDS

Acids used in cooking are lemon or lime juice, orange or grapefruit juice, vinegar and wine. Acid gives a clean taste to food, brings a feeling of freshness to the palate and saves any dish, cooked or uncooked, from monotony.

Although they are added before and after cooking, acids are classed as seasoners because they have the faculty of bringing flavour to a large surface of the palate.

There is a difference between the acid of vinegar and the acid of citrus fruits. Vinegar, whether wine, cider, malt or herb vinegar, has an aromatic flavor of its own.

0➝ Citrus fruits are essentially acid and play a role in enlarging and refreshing flavour, but if an aromatic is needed, the grated rind of the fruit must be added, because it contains the aromatic oil. Here is an example: squeeze the juice of a wedge of lemon over a piece of fried fish and it will add freshness to the flavour. Do the same, but add the grated rind of the lemon to the butter or cream sauce served with the fish. The freshness and aroma are combined, because the intense lemon flavour carried in the oil of the rind is more lasting.

A knowledge of the action of acids can be very important to people on salt-free diets, because they can give life to foods that would otherwise be dull.

How much acid to use in food, and how to use it, is a matter of taste. In order of decreasing sharpness, cooking acids can be classified as follows:

Wine, cider, malt vinegar
Lemon juice, lime juice
Orange juice, grapefruit juice
Dry red or white wine

They are interchangeable, depending on the acidity your desire. Taste and add as you please.

When a recipe calls for wine — for example, ½ cup (125 ml) of white or red wine — it can be replaced by half water and half of another chosen acid, or by ½ cup (125 ml) of apple juice accentuated with 1 tablespoon (15 ml) of a chosen acid. The second substitution will give a milder flavour than the first one. For another possible substitution, 1 cup (250 ml) of wine, red or white, can be replaced by 3 tablespoons (50 ml) of cider or wine vinegar, or the juice of 1 lemon, plus enough water to make 1 cup (250 ml). Or you can use 1 cup (250 ml) of orange juice.

If a recipe calls for 3 tablespoons (50 ml) of lemon juice, use the juice of a medium-size lemon without bothering to measure. In the same way you can assume that ½ cup (125 ml) of orange juice is the amount of juice from 1 medium-size orange.

USING ACIDS

Vegetables

All cooked vegetables respond to acid. Cooked spinach is a different dish when seasoned with wine or cider vinegar, a little grated lemon rind and a pinch of grated nutmeg. Cooked potatoes respond to a seasoning of lemon juice and grated rind mixed with minced parsley. ०—ॠ Add 1 teaspoon (5 ml) of vinegar or lemon juice to the water of boiling potatoes to make them mealy.

Fruits

When preparing any type of stewed fruit, add fresh lemon or lime juice to the syrup, usually the juice of ½ lemon or lime for each 2 cups (500 ml) syrup. ०—ॠ When you put any type of dried fruit through the food chopper, for such things as fruitcake, sprinkle the fruit with lemon or orange juice, so it won't stick to the blades of the chopper.

Add a little lemon juice to jams and jellies when they have finished cooking. It deepens the color and accentuates the flavor of the fresh fruit; most of all it helps them to jell. Good proportions are the juice of ½ lemon to each 4 cups (1 L) of fruit being cooked.

Lemon juice or cider vinegar added to the bowl of water in which sliced fruits stand before cooking act as a bleach and prevents discoloration. Fruit to be served raw may also discolor when exposed to the air after peeling or slicing. ०—ॠ Sliced apples, avocados, bananas, peaches and pears will not turn brown if they are dipped into water mixed with lemon juice, or if their cut surfaces are brushed with lemon juice.

A small amount of lemon, lime, orange or grapefruit juice added to a fruit cup accentuates the flavor of the various ingredients.

Meats

Dry red or white wine, or lemon juice, or cider or wine vinegar, help to tenderize meat and poultry and keep seafood firm and white. Use 2 to 4 tablespoons (30 to 60 ml) depending on the strength, for each 4 cups (1 L) of liquid.

०—ॠ Any protein food, such as fish, chicken liver, eggplant or ham steak, should be brushed first with lemon or lime rind. This cuts the fat used in frying and protects the natural flavor.

Sauces

Butter sauce is improved with 1 tablespoon (15 ml) of lemon or other citrus juice added to ¼ cup (60 ml) melted or soft butter. White sauce for fish or white meat is enhanced by lemon or lime juice and the grated rind of the fruit. To gravy for veal, chicken, or liver add lemon or lime juice; failing this, use red-wine vinegar.

Milk and cream

To sour 1 cup (250 ml) of fresh milk or cream, add 2 teaspoons (10 ml) of lemon juice or vinegar. Or you can stir together ½ cup (125 ml) water, ½ cup (125 ml) evaporated milk 1 tablespoon (15 ml) vinegar. Let stand for 5 minutes and you will have sour milk. Mix 1 tablespoon (15 ml) of vinegar in 1 cup (125 ml) undiluted evaporated milk and in 5 minutes you have sour cream.

When whipping well-chilled cream, first sprinkle the cream with a few drops of lemon juice. It speeds up the work and gives the final product more body. ⊙━🔑 It is just as important to add fresh lemon juice to evaporated milk or to instant dry milk when either is being whipped, because it will increase the stability of the protein foam that results when these milks are whipped.

SALT

When food chemists prepare blends of different ingredients for seasoning, they refer to salt as a "bloom" because it does not flavor, taste nor bite like a spice; it simply causes all the other ingredients to "bloom" into a perfect union. You may prepare a very good soup, but a lack of salt will give the impression that it is flat. When you add the required amount of salt to taste, you will find that every flavor in the soup will come alive.

Salt is a seasoning that is neither herb nor spice but a mineral, and one that is essential to life. It is contained naturally in most foods. Salt, like sugar and acid, increases the flow of saliva. When used in the right proportion, it opens the taste buds. These two actions stimulate the appetite. Remember, the role of salt is not to give a special taste of its own to food but to intensify a natural flavour or to bring several flavours into one blended perfection. For this reason, a bit of salt in sweet dishes helps to sharpen the sweetness. Both salt and sugar act best when a small amount of one is added to the predominant use of the other.

Just as salt in the mouth makes saliva flow, it releases juices in foods. It is for this reason that you do not add salt to most vegetables before cooking; you want the juices to remain in the food. However, salt is used deliberately to release bitter juices. It helps give aroma to foods by releasing juices.

There are several types of salt — coarse or kosher salt; rock salt, which must be used with a grinder; fine sea salt, usually found at health-food stores; plain and iodized salt. You may wonder why you should bother to look for special salt, but let me assure you that a good salty salt has a most satisfying taste and is worth taking a little trouble to find.

Many recipes read "salt to taste" and very often the inexperienced cook panics. How much salt is "to taste"? Too much may spoil the dish, and too little will leave it tasteless. This is no more mysterious an operation than adding sugar to your coffee, or pepper to your steak. Of course, the amount that is "to taste" varies with the individual. The right amount is that which gives the food a certain authority to your particular taste or makes a flavourful whole of the food.

This is the best way to salt to taste: Put a little salt in whatever food you are preparing, and taste. If required, add a little more, then taste again. After the second time the taste buds become dull and the palate doesn't respond, so you must add salt a third time, about 15 minutes before tasting.

Salt always improves a sweet dish; that is why it is added to cakes, cookies and fruit desserts. ⊙━🔑 Beware when doubling a recipe, however, not to double the salt. Use the same amount as in the original recipe. Sugar does not want to remain indebted to salt, so by the same token, a pinch of sugar added to salt dishes, such as tomato sauce or vegetables, perks up flavor and color.

A touch, a pinch, a bit of salt, if you must have accurate measurements, is about 1/16 teaspoon (0.25 ml).

General rules for the use of salt

With meats: When you have all meat and no bones, use 1 teaspoon (5 ml) of salt per pound (500 gr) of meat. Cut the quantity in proportion when there are many bones.

Use no salt with corned beef, ham, bacon and dried beef until the meats are fully cooked; then add salt to taste if necessary.

With poultry: Use about 1 teaspoon (5 ml) salt for a 3-pound broiler-fryer; 1½ teaspoons (7 ml) in the water in which you poach a chicken; ¼ teaspoon (1 ml) for 2 drumsticks or 6 wings.

With fish: Except for smoked fish, salt cod and shellfish, which are naturally salty, use ½ teaspoon (2 ml) per pound.

With macaroni, noodles, etc.: Use 1 tablespoon (15 ml) salt for 3 quarts (3 L) water in which macaroni or noodles are boiled.

With rice: Use 1 teaspoon (5 ml) salt for 1 cup (250 ml) raw rice and 2 cups (500 ml) water.

With salads: For a bowl of salad to serve 4 persons, use ½ teaspoon (2 ml) salt.

With vegetables: Only potatoes are salted while cooking; use 1 teaspoon (5 ml) salt for each 4 cups (1 L) water. Salt other vegetables after they are cooked.

With fats: When substituting lard or shortening in a recipe calling for butter, add ⅛ teaspoon (0.5 ml) salt per cup (250 ml) of fat.

SUGAR

Food texture and colour are affected in different ways, depending on the type of sweetening agent used. What all sweetening agents have in common is their appeal to our sweet taste buds.

And, like salt and acid, sugars have the faculty of drawing out flavour. On the other hand, if a chemical action is needed to hold ingredients together, as in meringue, or to give texture, as in cakes, sugars are added to produce a new combination.

Types of sugar

Granulated sugar: When a recipe does not specify a particular type of sugar, this is the type to use. It comes in two forms, granulated and fine granulated. Use ordinary granulated sugar for jams and jellies.

When granulated sugar is lumpy from moisture getting into the container, sift it before using it in a recipe.

Very fine granulated sugar: This is referred to under various names, such as berry sugar, veri-sugar, ultra-fine sugar and fruit sugar. In England it is called castor sugar. In this book it will be called fruit sugar.

Its virtues are numerous. Much finer than fine granulated sugar, it dissolves quickly in cold liquid, so it should be used in cold beverages, such as lemonade, when simple syrup is not available. It should be used in caramelizing or glazing, since it melts easily; for fruit cups, or on top of raw fruits such as grapefruit and strawberries. Whenever sugar is called for in beaten egg whites, fruit sugar will give the best results, as its fineness interferes very little with the air bubbles of the beaten eggs.

Brown sugar: In English cookbooks, dark brown sugar is referred to as Demerara and light brown sugar as moist sugar. Light brown sugar has little flavor compared to the authoritative flavor of dark sugar. Brown sugar is considered more nutritious than white sugar.

Brown sugar hardens as it loses moisture, so it should be kept in a heavy transparent plastic bag, well closed, or in a tightly covered glass jar. Brown sugar should never be kept in anything made of metal because its acid will eat the metal. When only a few lumps are present, smooth them out with a rolling pin. If a large amount has hardened, place the sugar in a heatproof pan in a 200°F (95°C) oven for few minutes to soften, then roll.

Light brown sugar is lovely to sweeten fruits, raw or cooked, because it gives syrup and fruits a rich flavour.

When substituting brown sugar for white, measure as follows: Pack the brown sugar into a measuring cup so firmly that it will hold its shape when turned out. You will then get the right amount to equal 1 cup (250 ml) of granulated sugar.

To substitute white sugar for brown sugar, measure 1 cup (250 ml) white sugar, take out 2 tablespoons (30 ml) add ¼ cup (60 ml) molasses, and let stand for 1 hour before using.

Icing sugar: This also has a variety of names. U.S. recipes refer to it as confectioners' sugar, sometimes adding one to three Xs after the name, which indicate fine, finer, finest. English recipes refer to it as icing sugar. Canadian recipes call it both icing sugar and powdered sugar. In this book it will be called icing sugar.

This is an extremely fine powdered sugar with cornstarch added, which immediately indicates why it should not be used in drinks. You can see why hot liquid is usually recommended when this sugar is used for frostings; the hot liquid absorbs the starchy flavor of the cornstarch. Despite the added cornstarch, icing sugar lumps readily. It should always be sifted before using. Like brown sugar, it absorbs a great deal of humidity, so it should be kept well covered.

Honey: In a sense, honey is more than a sweet sugar, because it consists of dextrose and fructose as well as sucrose, plus small amounts of aromatic oils and traces of acids. Nature at play! Only bees can make honey. Humans have tried, but its complicated constitution has eluded all synthesis. There are many types of honey, with different kinds of perfume.

In cooking, honey should be used with caution; it cannot replace sugar quantity for quantity. You can substitute it for half of the sugar called for in desserts and jellies. As an example: 1 cup (250 ml) sugar can be replaced by ½ cup (125 ml) honey and ½ cup (125 ml) sugar. For each 1 cup (250 ml) honey used, reduce the amount of liquid in the recipe by 3½ tablespoons (55 ml) and add ¼ teaspoon (1 ml) baking soda. Or substitute corn syrup in fudge or other candies with honey, for more flavour and smoothness.

○━ A little honey as well as sugar brings out the flavour much more than salt. A summer delight, when garden-fresh tomatoes are around, is to cut a tomato — not chilled, but at room temperature — into thick slices, spread it lightly with honey and sprinkle generously with minced chives and freshly ground pepper.

Molasses: This is called treacle in England. It is used more as a flavouring than as a sweetener. In Indian and Chinese and other Oriental cuisines, small amounts of molasses are used as a seasoning for meats, to give colour and to enhance the soy sauce.

○━ Before we leave the subject of sugar, it is important to know that most foods have some kind of hidden sugar in them — fructose in fruits, lactose in milk, maltose in grains and dextrose in grapes. Maybe reading this will cause dieters to despair, but remember that the hidden sugar is Nature's unique contribution to give each food a special appeal.

HOW SEASONINGS WORK

Now that we have learned about the use of the three basic kinds of seasonings — salts, acids and sugars — it is important to understand the role they play in the preparation of all foods.

Different tastes or seasonings do not stimulate reactions at the same speed. When I was a student, I had to go through the experience of tasting different seasonings. It was a great help to close my eyes and concentrate on the taste buds. I learned then that acid was the taste I could always taste first. This was followed by the most usual and natural, salt; then came the sweet taste. Although the sweet taste buds are at the tip of the tongue, the first part of the tongue to receive the food you are tasting, their reaction is the slowest.

Keep this in mind when adding sweetening. For instance, when you are adjusting the sweetening on fruit, put a drop of syrup on the tip of your tongue and keep it there for 10 to 12 seconds. Because the sweet taste buds are so slow to react, you must allow enough time to be sure you do not add too much sweetening.

Seasoning of any type should not be left to measuring spoons. It should be a truly personal matter. Many dishes have been saved by the addition of something special in just the right quantity! This makes all the difference. If you become familiar with ther effects of salt, acid and sugar, and learn about herbs and spices, and then if you use them, cautiously to begin with, and learn to really taste them, you will soon acquire a true wisdom about seasoning.

Although the words seasonings and condiments are often used interchangeably, there is a subtle difference. To season a food means to add a substance at some point during the cooking to improve or enhance the flavour. Of course, additional seasoning can be added to the completed dish, as one adds salt and pepper at the table. A condiment is a prepared pungent mixture, sometimes quite complex, which is served with food after it has been prepared and usually is added by individual diners at the table. Chutney and ketchup are examples.

MONOSODIUM GLUTAMATE (MSG)

This, in a sense, is a miracle seasoning, but it is a very ancient product, even if today's method of making it is different from the original Oriental seaweed recipe. The Chinese call it *mei jiung* and the Japanese call it *ajinomoto*. Many people also refer to it as "taste powder", and maybe this best describes MSG, since it neither salts nor perfumes, but accentuates the natural flavor of foods to which it is added. Although MSG cannot replace salt in food, it increases the saltiness of salt. It cannot replace sugar either, but it accentuates the natural sweetness of such vegetables as carrots and squash. It enhances the flavor of meat. On the other hand, inherent sourness in a food is slightly reduced by MSG. And it removes the bitterness from spinach and liver. It blends aromas and makes things smell better. It is the only ingredient capable of spreading taste rapidly in the mouth while sending a fully blended odour to the nose. It may be used also as a means of blending seasonings. Very little is required. Too much may be detrimental to foods and may even cause discomfort. Health and Welfare Canada does not consider it harmful, but recommends that it be used sparingly.

MY FAVORITE SEASONINGS

As a last word, I cannot resist mentioning what I consider the Three Great Seasonings. If I have nothing else, I am sure that with them I can season all I want. They are lemon or lime juice, fresh gingerroot and vanilla beans.

It is easy to obtain fresh lemons or limes, so I don't need to say more about them. As for fresh gingerroot, I always have a supply on hand in my freezer. It is an amazing seasoner with the most fragrant perfume, equally at home with acids or sweets. Vanilla beans can provide the most delicate and gentle flavor in the world for so many foods. Since the vanilla bean is a dried pod, it is easy to have it always on hand.

These three seasoners can make a unity of many flavours without ever being overpowering themselves. When a definite flavour of any one of the three is desired, use it in a larger quantity. In the chapter on herbs and spices, you will find complete descriptions of ginger and vanilla.

CHAPTER 5

An introduction to herbs and spices

ERBS were once thought to possess magical properties and were often used as symbols of supernatural powers. Their nature and efficacy were attributed directly to the gods by the alchemists; to the sun, moon and stars by the ancient astrologers. The alchemists were well acquainted with the chemistry of herbs and used them as the basis of perfumes, cosmetics, and medicines, for which they are still used today. Herbs and spices were also used by the ancients to flavour foods. The basic difference between these two families of seasonings is that herbs grow in temperate climates, while spices come from the tropics. With herbs, the leaves usually provide the seasoning; the leaves of spice plants are seldom used for this purpose.

While herbs and spices can enhance the flavour of foods, they must be used properly so that the flavour is a subtle one. Do not be heavy-handed with them, because most foods have a distinct flavour of their own that should not be overpowered or destroyed. Remember that you are trying to *enhance* the flavour of a dish.

Since the individual strength of herbs and spices varies so much, it is next to impossible to state exact quantities to be used. Seasoning and flavouring is, curiously enough, an expression of one's personality. Are you an overcautious person? Strong and domineering? Or are you a real artist who knows all about balance and proportion instinctively? The way you season food will give a very good indication of your personality.

To begin with, use only a tiny amount: ½ teaspoon (2 ml) of mild herbs and ¼ teaspoon (1 ml) or less of strong herbs or spices. Experience and your own personality will soon take over and you may add to or substract from the amount of each to suit your own taste and the particular dish.

All herbs and spices have essential oils that are the source of their characteristic aroma and flavour and constitute their main value. These oils are released either by grinding or by fine chopping. This is one reason why herbs and spices bought already ground or powdered lose their character much more quickly than whole leaves or seeds.

☛ As soon as herbs or spices lose their scent replace them. ☛ Also, keep them away from the light by using metal containers or bottles that are nearly completely covered by wrap-around labels. Otherwise they will lose their colour and flavour.

HERBS

THE BASIC THREE	Parsley, Mint, Bay leaf
Add the following two for THE BEST-KNOWN FIVE	Thyme, Sage
Add the following five for THE BEST-KNOWN 10	Dill, Basil, Savory, Marjoram, Tarragon
THE GARDEN 10	Borage, Chervil, Chives, Lemon balm, Lemon thyme, Lemon verbena, Lovage, Marigold, Nasturtium, Spearmint
THE GOURMET'S TWO	Rosemary, Saffron

Parsley *Petroselinum crispum*
This is the most familiar of all herbs, with its crinkly green leaves and fresh smell. It is sold fresh year-round and dried flakes are also available. Parsley grows indoors, so you can have it fresh all year long.

Whole sprigs are used as a decorative garnish; finely chopped parsley adds flavour, aroma and colour to many foods.

Mint *Mentha*
This large family of herbs has many members, including curlymint, applemint, orangemint, peppermint and spearmint (more about spearmint later). Mints are used to flavour sauces, vegetables, jelly, fruits and alcoholic beverages, as well as tea and candy. Mint is not available fresh year-long, but the dried flakes retain their flavour quite well. Mint is easily grown in the garden; it is a perennial and a well established bed of it will be a permanent addition. ☞ The use of mint can be traced as far back as the Greeks and Romans. The Romans used to sprinkle mint into their wine, and sometimes they made a thick green paste by mixing chopped mint with honey and used it to remove wine breath. It makes a delicious spread for toast.

Mint sauce is the perfect accompaniment to roast lamb. ☞ Chop mint leaves fine, then pour 1 to 2 tablespoons (15 to 30 ml) boiling water over them before adding the other ingredients. This releases the full flavour of the mint.

Mint lemonade

¼ cup (60 ml) boiling water

1 cup (250 ml) chopped mint leaves

Juice of 6 lemons

Grated rind of 1 lemon

Juice of 3 oranges

1 cup (250 ml) fruit sugar

Ice water, soda or ginger ale

Pour boiling water over the mint leaves. Add the lemon juice, grated lemon rind and orange juice. Stir in fruit sugar. Refrigerate in a tightly capped bottle. To make lemonade, pour enough of the liquid into a glass to make it one-fourth or one-third full; then add ice water, soda or ginger ale. Add ice. The mint syrup will keep in the refrigerate for up to 2 weeks. Makes about 4 cups.

Here are some other uses for mint. **0—** Boil a few sprigs of fresh mint with green peas or new potatoes. **0—** Add chopped fresh mint to potato salad, canned green-pea soup, seafood salad, applesauce and fruit salad. **0—** Add 1 tablespoon (15 ml) chopped fresh mint or 1 teaspoon (5 ml) dried mint to cabbage while it is boiling. Delicious! **0—** Put a few sprigs in your bottle of cider or wine vinegar. **0—** Mash mint leaves with butter and cream cheese for a light and refreshing sandwich.

Bay leaf *Laurus nobilis*
Fresh leaves are dark green, shiny and from 2 to 3 inches (5 to 7.5 cm) long. These smooth-edged leaves are sold dried; though they lose some of their colour when dried. In general, the greenest leaves are the best. They are almost indispensable in cooking.

A bay leaf is always a part of the bouquet garni, which is a combination of herbs tied together with string, or put into a cotton bag and used to flavour soups, sauces and various meat and fish dishes. The whole little bundle or bag of herbs is lifted out and discarded when the dish is cooked.

Simple bouquet garni
0— Sprinkle a pinch of thyme on a few dried celery ribs. Add 1 bay leaf, and tie in a small cotton bag. If you use fresh herbs, they can simply be tied together in a small bundle and added to the food you are cooking. If you wish to elaborate on the simple *bouquet garni,* add ½ carrot, a piece of leek or onion and a few celery leaves.

0— The Welsh use bay leaves to flavour custard by simmering a bay leaf with the milk used to make the custard.

Herb bouquet 0—
Chop ¼ cup (50 ml) fresh parsley with 2 green onions, then add 2 bay leaves crumbled in your fingers. To this add ½ teaspoon (2 ml) basil, either fresh or dried. Chop all of this together for a few seconds. It does not have to be tied in a bag. Use it to flavour soups, sauces and stews, especially beef and lamb stew, and tomato salad.

Thyme *Thymus vulgaris*
Thyme is one of the oldest herbs in use. The Romans and Egyptians found that it stimulated their appetites and helped them digest rich, fat foods. It is a sweet

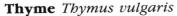

This dressing can be used for salads of canned or fresh fish and mixed vegetables.

Thyme and lemon dressing

1 lemon

¼ tsp (1 ml) dried, crumbled thyme

Pinch of sugar

3 peppercorns

½ cup (125 ml) olive oil

1 tsp (5 ml) salt

¼ tsp (1 ml) curry powder.

Grate the rind of the lemon into a small bowl. Extract the juice from the lemon and set it aside. Add the thyme and sugar to the grated rind and mix well. Crush the peppercorns in a mortar with a pestle until broken into coarse pieces. Blend these with the rest of the mixture.

Place the reserved lemon juice, olive oil, salt and curry powder in a bottle. Cap the bottle and shake the mixture well. Add the mixture containing the thyme and shake again.

This dressing will keep in a cool place for a month. If it becomes cloudy, bring it to room temperature and you will find it will clear. Shake the mixture well each time before using. Makes about ¾ cup (200 ml).

herb, with a penetrating and sharply attractive scent. Traditionally it is associated with courage, graceful elegance and energy. Because bees love it so it strongly influences the flavor of the famous Greek honey from Mount Hymettus, where the hills are covered with thyme. It is also the important ingredient of Benedictine liqueur.

Thyme is easily grown outdoors or in pots indoors. Dried and ground thyme can be found in all markets.

Because the flavour and odour of thyme are penetrating and very distinctive, you must exercise care when using it. A small pinch does have its place in flavouring all types of meats, vegetables and soups. You can combine it with parsley to flavour chicken or veal stuffing. Thyme is also perfect in cheese sauce and is a must in meat loaves. It can be combined with savory to flavour roast-beef or corned-beef hash.

Sage *Salvia officinalis*

Sage is said to ensure a long life. A woody plant, it is an easily grown garden perennial. Dried sage is available as whole leaves or ground leaves.

This is a powerful, assertive herb requiring care in its use. It is familiar to us in the traditional sage and onion stuffing for pork, duck and turkey. A pinch will also give a racy tang to braised meats, soups, croquettes and stews.

0—🔑 To make an excellent cheese spread, blend sage to taste with a mixture of half cream cheese and half grated Cheddar.

0—🔑 Another delicious spread, a sweet one to use on tea biscuits or toasted brown bread, can be made by adding ½ teaspoon (2 ml) crumbled dried sage, or minced fresh sage, to the grated rind of 1 lemon in 1 cup (250 ml) of honey.

Sage tea
0—🔑

This is inspired by the famous Moroccan mint tea.

1 tsp (5 ml) green tea leaves

½ tsp (2 ml) minced fresh sage

2 tsp (10 ml) minced fresh mint

3 tbsp (50 ml) sugar

3 cups (750 ml) cups boiling water

Lemon slices

In an earthenware teapot place the tea leaves, sage, mint and sugar. Stir until sugar is well blended. Pour in the boiling water. Stir again for a few seconds, then cover to keep warm. Allow to brew 5 to 10 minutes, then serve in small glasses or demitasse cups, with a plate of lemon slices on the side. Makes enough for 4 to 5 teacups, or 6 demitasse cups.

Dill *Anethum graveolens*

Dill, a hardy annual of the parsley family, is easy to grow. The name is said to derive from the Old Norse *dilla*, which means "to lull" and no doubt refers to its soothing properties. The herbalists used to call dill "the witches' herb" because it was not only said to cast spells but was given credit as a charm against witchcraft. Fresh dill leaves are available in late summer and early fall. Dried and ground dill and dill seeds are sold, and many flavourings include ground dill.

The flavour of dill is sharply aromatic, with a faint lemony taste. It is delicious in lentil, bean or pea soup, especially when the soup is combined with tomatoes. It is good in all egg dishes. Try it also in a white sauce you serve with boiled cauliflower. **0—🔑** You can add a few seeds when you are boiling cabbage. It is the perfect herb to use with all kinds of smoked, pickled or boiled fish. You can make dill vinegar to use with cucumbers, beets and canned fish salad; add a few sprigs of fresh dill to cider vinegar and let stand. **0—🔑** Try a few seeds in apple pie for an unusual taste.

¼ cup (50 ml) minced fresh dill

or 1 tbsp (15 ml) dillweed

or 1 tsp (5 ml) dill seeds

1 tbsp (15 ml) plain or dill-flavored cider vinegar

1 tbsp (15 ml) butter

2 tbsp (30 ml) flour

1 cup (250 ml) lamb broth

½ cup (125 ml) light cream

Salt

White pepper

Put the fresh dill or dillweed or dill seeds in a bowl. Add vinegar and stir well. Let stand until the lamb is cooked. Then make a sauce with the butter, flour, cup of broth in which the lamb was cooked and the light cream. When smooth and creamy, season to taste and stir in the dill-vinegar mixture. Simmer for 1 or 2 minutes. Makes about 1⅔ cups (410 ml).

Dill sauce for lamb

---

3 tbsp (50 ml) peanut oil

1 garlic clove, crushed

1 tsp (5 ml) minced fresh basil

1 tbsp (15 ml) butter

½ lb (250 gr) fresh mushrooms, chopped

Salt and pepper

4 large tomatoes, ripe but firm

2 tsp (10 ml) sugar

½ cup (125 ml) fine dry bread crumbs

Heat 1 tablespoon (15 ml) of the oil over low heat. Crush the garlic with the flat side of a knife and add the garlic and the basil to the hot oil, stirring until the garlic starts to brown slightly. Add the butter; when hot, add the mushrooms. Stir quickly over high heat for 2 minutes, then remove from heat. Add salt and pepper to taste.

Cut tomatoes into halves. Sprinkle each half with ¼ teaspoon (1 ml) sugar and lots of pepper, but no salt. Mix breadcrumbs with remaining 2 tablespoons (30 ml) oil and spread on the cut surfaces of the tomatoes. Bake in a 425°F (225°C) oven for 20 minutes. Pour the mushroom mixture over the tomatoes. Makes 4 servings.

Baked tomatoes with mushrooms and basil

Basil *Ocimum basilicum*

There is an aura of magic about basil. In India it is sacred to Krishna and Vishnu, deities worshipped in the Hindu religion, and is regarded as the protecting spirit of the family. Basil is an easily grown garden annual, and makes a fine pot plant as well. Crumbled dried basil leaves are available. There is both green and purple basil; the purple has a more intense flavor.

Basil is a lively scented herb with a delicate, clovelike tang. It is an ideal accompaniment to soups, sauces, sausages, liver, salads and fines herbes mixtures.

It is excellent in fish sauces, and is always found in Italian tomato dishes — even on top of canned tomatoes and tomato paste.

Try a pinch in canned tomato soup, or with your scrambled eggs. It can be a subtle addition to any recipe for cheese soufflé; add ¼ to ½ teaspoon (1 to 2 ml) minced basil to the grated cheese.

Savory *Satureia*
There is a summer savory (*S. hortensis*) and a winter savory (*S. montana*). Summer savory is an annual and the more popular of the two. Winter savory is a perennial with a slightly coarser and more pungent flavour. They are used in the same manner.

The ancient Romans loved savory sauce with their roasted wild meats making a sauce with vinegar and honey.

Savory has a warm, aromatic, rather spicy and peppery quality. It closely resembles both thyme and marjoram, and for this reason can be substituted for them successfully; however, they do not combine well. In Germany, savory is added to the water when fresh green or wax beans are cooked. It is equally good to flavor dressing for a bean salad. In Denmark, a pinch of savory is added to horseradish sauce to be served with boiled beef or tongue.

o—x Add some minced savory and grated lemon rind to the breadcrumb coating used on veal and fish, for an interesting flavor. **o—x** Split-pea soup is always delicious when flavored with a pinch or so of savory.

Herb-flavored vegetable soup **o—x**

1 tsp (5 ml) minced savory

½ tsp (2 ml) dill seeds

¼ tsp (1 ml) minced marjoram

1 19-oz (540 ml) can stewed tomatoes

1 tsp (5 ml) sugar

1 garlic clove, crushed

2 quarts (2 L) water

4 cups (1 L) chopped or diced vegetables

⅔ cup (160 ml) uncooked long-grain rice

Salt and pepper

Mix the herbs and add them to the tomatoes, along with the sugar and garlic. Mix well, cover and let stand in the refrigerator overnight. The next day, add the water and vegetables. Bring all to a boil. Reduce heat, cover and simmer over very low heat for 3 hours. Add the rice and cook for 20 minutes more. Season with salt and pepper to taste. Makes 8 to 10 cups (2 to 2.5 L).

Marjoram *Marjorana hortensis*
Marjoram is a perennial of the mint family; however, it is so tender that it does not survive our winters and we have to treat it like an annual. It is one of the sweetest and most adaptable of herbs in cooking. It smells and tastes both sweet and spicy and is moderately pungent. You may detect a suggestion of mint or cloves in the flavour.

Marjoram, even today, is sometimes scattered on Greek graves to bring happiness and good fortune to the deceased in the afterlife. For the ancient Romans it was one of the ''strewing herbs'' used to sweeten the atmosphere by being scattered on floors. They also used it as ''sweet bags'' in much the same way we use lavender today, and to perfume baths.

Use marjoram freely with veal and pork roasts, sausages and frankfurters. Use it discreetly with hamburgers, mushrooms, meat soups and omelets. It is excellent combined with basil in a spaghetti sauce. Marjoram can also be used to replace oregano, although marjoram has a more delicate taste.

This makes a perfect summer luncheon served with toast spread with cream cheese.

Tomato salad with marjoram

2 or 3 ripe, firm tomatoes

Salt and pepper

Sugar

1 green onion, minced, or 1 tbsp (15 ml) minced chives

1 tbsp (15 ml) minced fresh or dried marjoram

2 or 3 tbsp (30 to 50 ml) olive oil

Lettuce

1 small cucumber, peeled

Wash unpeeled tomatoes and cut into slices ½ inch (1.25 cm) thick. Place these in a shallow dish and sprinkle with salt and freshly ground pepper to taste, along with a few pinches of sugar. Do not mix. In a bowl, mash together the onion or chives and the marjoram. Stir in the olive oil. When well mixed, pour a spoonful at a time over the tomatoes. Again, do not mix. Cover and refrigerate 2 to 3 hours.

To serve, shred some lettuce and grate the cucumber. Make a circle of grated cucumber around the tomatoes on a serving platter, and a circle of shredded lettuce around the cucumber.

Tarragon *Artemisia dracunculus*

Tarragon described by the ancient herbalists as "highly cordial and friend to head, heart and liver." It is an herb of character with a hidden strength and must be used with caution. Its distinctive flavour is a little bit like a combination of licorice and anise, with a sweet and aromatic scent. Dried tarragon is available wherever herbs are sold. It is a perennial, but won't survive a very cold winter.

Much used in French cooking, it is the herb used to flavor béarnaise sauce, sister to hollandaise. It is the English, however, who have given us tarragon vinegar, which is so good served with poached salmon. This is very easy to make when you have fresh tarragon. Add a sprig or two to a pint of good-quality cider or white-wine vinegar and let it stand. As it ages it gets better and better. Tarragon vinegar can be mixed with dry mustard or added to tartar sauce.

Tarragon butter

Make tarragon butter for your grilled steak or fish fillets by mashing ½ cup (125 ml) butter with 1 teaspoon (5 ml) crushed dried tarragon leaves or some chopped fresh tarragon leaves. Refrigerate for 30 to 40 minutes. Shape into little balls, roll each one in minced chives or parsley, and place on a sheet of foil. Cover and refrigerate. These will keep refrigerated for 2 weeks. To use, simply place on top of hot grilled steak or fish when it is served. The heat of the food will slowly melt the butter balls.

Normandy tarragon liqueur

This liqueur's flavour closely resembles that of Benedictine. It is special for me because of my maternal grandmother, whose mother brought the recipe from Normandy. Fresh tarragon is a must. The recipe calls for orange-flower water, which you can find at food specialty shops and some drugstores.

½ to ¾ cup (125 to 190 ml) washed tarragon leaves

32 oz (110 ml) brandy

1½ cups (375 ml) sugar

¼ cup (60 ml) water

2 or 3 oz (55 to 85 ml) orange-flower water

Wash fresh tarragon under running water and pull the leaves from the stems until you have the required amount. Pour the brandy over the tarragon. Cover tightly and place in a dark cupboard for 5 or 6 days.

Make a syrup by simmering together over low heat the sugar and water. When the sugar is completely dissolved, bring to a boil and boil for 1 minute. Cool a little, then add to the brandy mixture. Let stand for 1 hour.

Place a double layer of cheesecloth over a strainer set over a bowl and slowly pour in the mixture. When all the liquid has passed through the cheesecloth, lift off the cloth. Add the orange-flower water. Bottle the liquid and cork it. Let it ripen for a week before serving. Makes about 5 cups (1.25 L).

THE GARDEN 10

Why not grow herbs of your own? All you need is a sunny window box, a few pots or bit of backyard where you can place tubs or boxes or dig a special bed. For that matter, it is not necessary to grow them in a special herb garden. If you have a garden, intermingle them with the flowers or vegetables. All of them are decorative and well worth growing for their appearance as well as taste. The following herbs are referred to as "the garden 10" since most of them have to be grown if you want them fresh. A few of them can be found in dried form.

Borage *Borago officinalis*
Mild and refreshing borage was one of the four cardinal flowers of the ancient herbalists. Whenever borage grows among flowers, bees seem to be around in great profusion. Borage is an easily grown garden annual.

In Victorian times, borage's sky-blue, five-point flowers were candied and used as a delicate decoration on top of compotes or cakes. Borage is the distinct secret flavour of the world-famous Pimm's No. 1 drink mix, which is sometimes served with a borage leaf floating in it.

Young borage leaves chopped up are a pleasant addition to a salad because of the flavor of fresh cucumber they give.

Sugared borage flowers
To have a supply of borage flowers all winter to garnish birthday cakes, decorate Easter eggs or top fruit salads, preserve them in sugar. They are not only lovely to look at but are quite tasty.

To preserve them, pick the blue flowers when in fresh full bloom, each one with a bit of stem. Spread them on a clean towel and shake each gently to be sure it is free of garden pests. Place each flower on a fine mesh cake rack or a piece of screening, passing the stem through so that each sits on top of the screen. With a small camel's-hair paint brush, coat each flower carefully with egg whites that have been beaten just enough to lose their slippery texture. Then sprinkle gently with fine fruit sugar through a shaker or a fine sieve. Let them dry in a cool place for 48 hours. After this, examine them; if any part of the flower is uncovered, repeat the process. They will also keep longer when treated twice. When the flowers are thoroughly dried, set them, one next to the other, on cotton wadding in a little box. Cover the box with transparent plastic wrap and over this place the lid of the box. In a cool place, these will keep for 4 to 6 months.

Chervil *Anthriscus cerefolium*
Chervil, a small annual herb with delicate feathery leaves, slightly resembles parsley in appearance, although its flavour is not the same. It has a mild pleasant taste of anise. Dried chervil can be found in some stores.

    0–⚡ Cream soups and creamy sauces flavored with fresh chervil are a gourmet's treat. The French relish it as flavour in an omelet, and in the summer they use it as part of a *bouquet garni*. 0–⚡ Chopped fine and mixed with a tiny bit of grated lemon rind, chervil gives a subtle, pleasant flavor to fried fish.

Chervil butter 0–⚡
Chervil is delicious with barbecued chicken or trout. Cream a few tablespoons of unsalted butter, then add fine-grated lemon rind and enough chopped chervil to make a green butter. When cooled, shape the butter into little balls, then wrap them in foil and keep refrigerated. When barbecued chicken or trout is ready to serve, simply pop a ball of chervil butter on top of each serving.

Chives *Allium schoenoprasum*
Chives take a long time to grow, but you can buy a small pot when spring is around the corner and plant the bulblets in your garden. They will grow all summer. If you wip off the tops, new shoots will appear. Chives may be used delicately or lavishly, depending on taste.

    Chives are often called the most lady-like member of the onion family, since they have such a gracious way of mixing with other herbs. They are the crowning glory of an omelet or scrambled eggs, and they equally enhance cucumbers, tossed green salad, fresh seafood salad, vichyssoise and jellied or hot consommé, especially consommé madrilène. They are perfect with poached white fish, too.

Fines herbes with chives 0–⚡
This herb mixture can be used with countless dishes. It can be made with fresh herbs or a mixture of fresh and dry herbs. Start with an equal amount of chives and parsley chopped fine, then add any of the following, either dried or fresh:

> ¼ teaspoon (2 ml) minced chervil and ¼ teaspoon (1 ml) minced tarragon

> ½ teaspoon (2 ml) minced basil and ¼ teaspoon (1 ml) minced thyme

> 2 tablespoons (30 ml) grated lemon rind

Lemon balm *Melissa officinalis*
Lemon balm is both refreshing and soothing. It has the fragrance of lemon without the sharpness. It is a perennial and will grow in any temperate climate.

    In the 1600's it was the "in" thing to have a glass of Canary wine (sherry) with a few leaves of lemon balm floating in it because it was said to renew youth, strengthen the brain, relieve languishing nature and prevent baldness. It is not the miracle herb it was thought to be, but it does add a fresh flavour, a flavour somewhere between lemon and mint, that can perk up practically any drink. 0–⚡

Lemon balm is most interesting with gin and tonic. **0—🗝** Try adding a few crushed leaves to carrots or small new potatoes.

0—🗝 Add some finely chopped leaves to your next fruit salad, or stir some into the sugar of the next raspberry pie you make.

Lemon balm iced tea

0—🗝

12 leaves of lemon balm

2 tsp (10 ml) sugar

Juice of ½ a lemon

1 whole clove

4 tbsp (60 ml) green tea or English breakfast tea

4 to 5 cups (1 to 1.25 L) boiling water

Crush the lemon balm leaves with the sugar, lemon juice and clove to make a thoroughly blended green paste. Add the tea leaves and pour the boiling water on top. Stir, cool, cover and refrigerate. To serve, strain the mixture and serve it with a bowl of ice, a small dish of lemon balm leaves and a jar of honey. Each guest can flavor and sweeten to taste. Makes enough for 6 teacups.

Lemon thyme
Thymus serpyllum, var, citriodora
A plant related to thyme, the stems and leaves of lemon thyme contain an aromatic volatile oil. The lemon flavour is very strong, but extremely pleasant. This easily grown perennial is a low, creeping plant especially suited to rock gardens. Lemon thyme is one of the best fresh herbs to flavour any type of salad. The uses of thyme apply to lemon thyme.

Lemon verbena *Lippia citriodora*
Lemon verbena is a fragrant herb with long, delicate, yellow-green leaves. When the leaves are lightly rubbed with the fingertips, they can perfume the whole hand.

The Spanish conquerors of South America first brought lemon verbena to Europe, touting it as an exciting find to make a tea to prevent digestive ailments. It remains a favorite tea all over Europe **0—🗝** Measure 1 teaspoon (5 ml) fresh or dried leaves per cup and pour boiling water on top. Let the leaves steep for 5 minutes, then serve with honey and very thin slices of lemon.

0—🗝 Try lemon verbena leaves chopped and sprinkled over a spring green salad or a tomato salad. **0—🗝** It is excellent to flavour a white sauce being served over fish. To make this, add to 2 cups (500 ml) medium white sauce the juice of ½ lemon and 5 to 6 chopped verbena leaves.

Lovage *Levistecum officinale*
Lovage is a perennial plant with ribbed stalks resembling celery. An aromatic scent pervades the plant. The flowers grow in yellow umbels. **0—🗝** When the plants dry in the autumn, the seeds can be gathered to be used during the winter to give a celery flavour to stews and soups. **0—🗝** The young leaves are very tasty when chopped and added to lettuce.

Plant lovage seeds along a fence; they will start to grow very early in the spring and last well into autumn. The plants will grow to 5 or 6 feet, and will live for years.

This potpourri can be used to perfume a room, the linen closet or a clothes cupboard. If a jar with a perforated top is placed on the fireplace shelf, the heat of the fire will cause the potpourri to fill the room with its fragrance. Use thoroughly dried leaves and blend them with a pestle in a mortar, or use a wooden spoon in a bowl.

Herb potpourri with verbena

2 cups (500 ml) lemon verbena leaves

1 cup (250 ml) thyme leaves

1 cup (250 ml) marjoram leaves

1 cup (250 ml) sage leaves

2 cups (500 ml) lavender flowers

2 cups (500 ml) green or purple basil

2 tbsp (30 ml) allspice berries

20 whole cloves

2 tbsp (30 ml) dried lemon rind*

2 tbsp (30 ml) powdered orrisroot.**

Thoroughly mix the ingredients and place them in a small jar. Make a few holes in the cover and place it wherever you please. If you own any of those beautiful English potpourri jars of perforated porcelain, by all means use them.

* To dry the lemon rind, simply grate into coarse shreds, spread on waxed paper and leave in a warm dark place for 2 to 3 days.
** Orrisroot can be purchased at some drugstores and herb stores.

In Europe a very pleasant cordial is made with the fresh seeds gathered before the lovage plants dry.

Lovage cordial

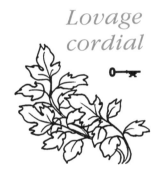

½ cup (125 ml) fresh lovage seeds

3 to 4 cups (750 ml to 1 L) brandy

1 cup (250 ml) sugar

¼ cup (60 ml) water

Steep the seeds in the brandy for a week. Then make a syrup with the sugar and water and boil it for 10 minutes. Add this to the brandy and lovage seeds. Let stand for a month. Then strain to remove the seeds, and the cordial is ready. Makes about 4 cups (1 L).

Marigold *Calendula officinalis*
Marigolds are a very old potherb of the past. For thousands of years marigold petals were used for colouring instead of saffron; they are still used for this in Mexico and Italy. In the old days they were often referred to as "herb of the sun" or "marsh gold" because of their bright golden colour.

Marigold is a hardy annual, easy to grow, and will bloom all season until frost. The flavour of marigold is at its best when it is gathered in fine weather, early in the morning, as soon as the dew has dried.

The flavour of marigold is mild, pleasant and slightly peppery. The dried petals improve in dried pea and bean soups, stews, chowders, roast pork or veal, fried liver, rice and noodles. If you like to bake bread, add 1 tablespoon (15 ml) dried petals to your next batch when you add the flour. It will make the bread a beautiful pale-yellow color and will add immeasurably to the flavour. You can also use marigold in a poundcake, by adding 1 teaspoon (5 ml) dried or fresh leaves.

Marigold in a salad 0—⚷

Brown 1 cup (250 ml) diced bread cubes lightly in butter; when these are done, place them on a plate and sprinkle 1 tablespoon (15 ml) marigold petals, fresh or dried, on top. Cover with waxed paper and let stand at room temperature for a few hours. Make a green salad with French dressing and pour the marigold croutons on top. Toss the salad again at the table when ready to serve.

Nasturtium

Tropaeolum majus or minus

The beautiful nasturtium, with its many gorgeous colours, originated in Peru. There are dwarf nasturtiums and climbers; the brilliance of the flowers makes them attractive plants in a border or window box. Nasturtium, an annual, is easy to grow in sunny locations. The flowers have a light peppery flavour somewhat like cress and are as delightful to the taste as they are to the sight. The name is derived from Latin words meaning "to twist the nose," no doubt a reference to its peppery quality.

Nasturtium is rarely used in cooking, but its flowers, leaves and seeds can be used.

0—⚷ In France, a summer salad often has the leaves and flowers of nasturtiums added to it; they are chopped fine and used as parsley would be. After the salad has been tossed, a few whole flowers are used to decorate it.

0—⚷ In Italy, the flowers are often dipped into either crêpe or fritter batter, then fried in deep fat. When sprinkled with sugar, they are crunchy and full of flavour as well as being colourful.

0—⚷ To give a new flavour to cottage cheese, add a few chopped nasturtium leaves. 0—⚷ Mix some chopped leaves and flowers with creamed butter, salt lightly, and spread on brown bread to make dainty tea sandwiches. 0—⚷ To make a relish similar to capers, pickle the seeds by pouring hot vinegar on top of them. Add 1 teaspoon (5 ml) sugar to each cup (250 ml) vinegar. Then cover and let the seeds ripen for 1 month before using.

0—⚷ Nasturtium flavouring for fresh green-bean salad

Cook green beans, keeping them a bit firm. Rinse under cold water as soon as they are cooked and drain thoroughly. Place in a salad bowl and add 2 green onions chopped fine and 6 to 8 nasturtium flowers, also chopped. Toss with French dressing and serve.

Spearmint

Mentha spicata, var, viridis

Spearmint is an easy perennial to grow. Its pleasant, mild flavor has long been glorified in the famous mint julep of the Old South.

The ancient Greeks and Romans used it to scent their baths. In combination with aniseed and cuminseed, they used it to flavour their foods, especially lamb. The herbalists prescribed smelling spearmint as "comfortable for the head and the memory." Since the 14th century, spearmint has been used to flavour tooth powder and toothpaste.

It is excellent in fruit salads, with cream cheese, in lentil soup and fresh green peas, and added to the stuffing for broiled chicken. In any recipe that calls for mint, spearmint can be substituted.

Applesauce with spearmint or lemon verbena 0—⚷

Wash 20 to 30 apples; do not peel them, but cut into coarse pieces. It is not necessary to remove pits or cores. Place the pieces in a large saucepan with enough cold water to reach to about the middle of the apples. Add a generous handful of either spearmint or lemon verbena and bury this right in the middle. Cover and cook over medium heat, stirring once or twice, until the apples are mushy.

Put 2 to 3 cups (500 to 750 ml) sugar in a large bowl. Pour the apples into a food mill or strainer and stir over the bowl of sugar until all the apples have been strained. Stir with the sugar until the sugar is completely dissolved. Taste; add more sugar for more sweetness, but remember that the applesauce will be sweeter and thicker when cold. In the bottom of plastic or glass containers, place a few fresh leaves of spearmint or lemon verbena, pour in the sauce and close. Cool and serve or freeze. Makes 3 to 4 quarts (3 to 4 L).

THE GOURMET'S TWO

Saffron *Crocus sativus*

Saffron is made from the dried stigmas of the flowers of the saffron crocus. Its cultivation in the East goes back to antiquity. Because an enormous number of stigmas is needed to produce 1 pound (500 gr) of the spice (some estimates say 60,000, others go as high as 200,000),

the cost is always high. However, a few stigmas or a pinch of ground saffron is enough to flavour and colour a dish. Its mildly aromatic flavour has a slight aftertaste of iodine. It gives a beautiful light-orange colour when mixed in food. Saffron is available as dried stigmas, looking like dark red pieces of thread, and as ground spice. Usually it is best to soak the stigmas in some of the liquid used in the recipe to be sure the colour is well mixed with the other ingredients.

Saffron is an acquired taste; some people like it and others do not. Try a pinch and find out for yourself. ⚬━┱ Add saffron to chicken consommé, or to rice while it is boiling.

Saffron is the essential flavouring ingredient in the famous French *bouillabaisse* and the Spanish *paella,* which indicates that in almost any type of fish cookery, saffron has a secure place. It is also used in breads, such an English saffron buns.

1 cup (250 ml) long-grained rice

⅛ tsp (0.5 ml) ground saffron

4½ cups (1.125 L) chicken stock

Salt

3 tbsp (50 ml) butter

1 small onion, minced

1 tsp (5 ml) curry powder

3 tbsp (50 ml) flour

1½ cups (375 ml) milk

6 hard-cooked eggs, quartered

Minced fresh parsley

Juice of 1 lime

Simmer the rice with the saffron in 3 cups (750 ml) of chicken stock. Salt may not be needed if there is salt in the stock, but taste a kernel of rice after 10 minutes and add salt if necessary. When the rice is cooked and all the stock is absorbed (about 20 minutes), stir in 1 tablespoon (15 ml) of butter with a fork.

Fry the onion in the remaining 2 tablespoons (30 ml) of butter. Add curry powder. Cook until curry powder is completely dissolved in the butter and beginning to give off its distinctive odour. Add flour and stir until well mixed. Add milk and remaining chicken stock. Cook until smooth and creamy. Season to taste. Add the eggs.

Mound rice in the centre of a warm platter, then pour the egg sauce around it. Sprinkle the sauce with parsley. Pour lime juice over the rice. Makes 6 servings.

Curried eggs with saffron rice

⚬━┱

Rosemay *Rosmarinus officinalis*
Rosemary, the herb of friendship and remembrance, has appeared at weddings and funerals for centuries. It used to be said that rosemary will grow only in the garden of the righteous. It is very difficult to grow outside of hot or mild areas. Usually, small pots can be found in nurseries in the spring. Dried leaves are available in markets, but it is very easy to dry your own. Rosemary is strongly individualistic, with a spicy, pungent, piney flavour.

O— Use a few sprigs to flavour roast chicken. **O—** To flavour roast veal, mix a few sprigs with garlic and lemon juice. **O—** A pinch of rosemary crushed almost to a powder can be added to ½ cup (125 ml) prepared horseradish. **O—** Rosemary is an absolute must with roast lamb.

In a sense rosemary may be called the Italian herb, since it grows wild all over Italy and is used a great deal there. The second favorite herb in Italy is basil. Together, these make a happy flavouring combination with pork or lamb.

OTHER IMPORTANT HERBAL SEASONINGS

All the herbs listed so far — except saffron — are the sort we call leaf herbs, although more than the leaves are used. We use seeds of dill and nasturtium and flowers of borage and marigold. We use chiefly the seeds of other plants and some we value for the bulb, like garlic, or the root, like horseradish, or a tiny part of the flower, like saffron. Here are some bits of information about a few of these other herbs.

Anise *Pimpinella anisum*
Aniseed is the dried ripe fruit of an easy-to-grow garden annual. It is native of Egypt and has been planted in the gardens of Central Europe since the Middle Ages.

In older days anise was reputed to avert the Evil Eye. Sprigs of anise, hung by one's pillow, were supposed to keep away bad dreams. Since it does help the digestion, it is possible that those who hung it by their pillows also chewed a few seeds, thus settling their stomachs and avoiding bad dreams.

Anise is highly aromatic and has its own distinctive, sweetish scent and flavour. Aniseeds are greenish gray, oval and tapered to a point. Whole seeds are sold. Anisette, the liqueur flavoured with it, is known around the world.

This herb can be used in recipes for sweet puddings, pancakes, breads, buns and cakes, but its flavour is penetrating and powerful, so use discretion. **O—** If you are interested in tisane, or herb tea, aniseed makes one of the tastiest. Just pour 1 cup (250 ml) boiling water over ½ teaspoon (2 ml) aniseeds. Let stand for 5 minutes.

Capers *Capparis spinosa*

Capers are the flower buds of a shrub extensively grown in France, Spain and Italy. French capers are very small compared to the Spanish and Italian types, and their flavour is a little different. The buds are a dark, greenish brown, sometimes mottled with bright green or pale gray.

Capers are often sold pickled in vinegar. ⚷ The vinegar, which is full of flavour, can be used in sauces or on salads. Capers are used in caper sauce for boiled meat, especially lamb, and as part of Italian antipasto. Capers are also available packed in salt; they must be rinsed before being added to recipes. Capers' saltiness and piquant quality make them a fine flavour accent for any non-sweet salad or vegetable dish and they are particularly good with tomatoes and in potato salad.

Caraway *Carum carvi*

Caraway seeds are the dried ripe fruits of a biennial garden plant similar to other umbelliferous plants such as anise, fennel, cumin and dill. If you lack seeds of one, you can always replace them with seeds of one of the others. Although there are differences in the flavours, substituting one for another does not spoil the finished dish.

Caraway seeds are dark brown, slightly curved and tapered. Their flavor is warm and aromatic, with a slight undertone of eucalyptus and mint. It is an old seed, first used by the Arabs and then by the Greeks. Whole seed are sold. It gives the popular German liqueur Kümmel its distinctive flavour.

We often see caraway seeds on top of certain dark breads and in sugar biscuits and poundcakes, but they have many more uses. For instance, caraway seeds are a natural as a flavoring for many vegetables. ⚷ Sprinkle a generous pinch on sauerkraut while it cooks, and stir it into the butter you use over boiled cabbage. ⚷ Spiced or buttered beets, or beets cooked any way, are improved with the addition of a pinch of caraway.

Sprinkle it over french fries when they are served with fish. Try it with boiled new potatoes.

You can use caraway with pork, liver, kidneys, goose and duck. Toss a pinch into soups and stews. ⚷ For a quick appetizer, cut cubes of Cheddar cheese and dip them into a little bowl of caraway seeds. ⚷ Add a few caraway seeds to spice or ginger cakes.

Celery seed *Apium graveolens*

The celery seeds used as flavouring are not the product of the cultivated celery plant, but come from a wild form with a more pronounced flavour. Most of them are imported, and the best come from France. They are sold as ground seeds or packed in salt. They have a distinctive celerylike flavour, both warm and bitter, and are strongly aromatic.

They give a lift to any food. ⚷ Tomatoes, broiled, stewed, in salads or soups, are always improved by the addition of a few celery seeds. ⚷ Potato salad as well as tomato aspic, coleslaw and tossed green salad all take on a new appeal when flavored with celery seeds. Try a pinch in meat loaves, stews and pot roasts. ⚷ Mix them with sandwich fillings of ham, cheese, egg or tuna. They are also a treat sprinkled over the ketchup or mustard spread on a frankfurter. Scrambled eggs and omelets are improved by celery seeds. ⚷ Add a pinch of the seeds to the water used to poach fish and shellfish.

Everybody knows the value of celery seeds in home-made pickles, but do you know that they go with fruits? ⚷ Mix a few with a fruit salad dressing for a new taste.

Cumin *Cuminum cyminum*

Cuminseeds are the dried ripe fruit of an annual plant much like fennel. The seeds are small, light brown and about the size of caraway seeds. They also resemble caraway seeds in flavor, but with a harsher taste and a more bitter undertone. Cumin is an important ingredient in curry powder. The Bible says these

seeds, ground with bread and wine, were taken for their stimulating and digestive qualities. Whole seeds and ground seeds are available.

0—⚷ Crush cuminseeds and sprinkle them over vegetable salads or add to dressings. **0—⚷** Toss the seeds in a little butter over medium heat, then roll bits of cheese in the butter and serve as appetizers.

You will find Dutch, Scandinavian and Swiss cheeses with cuminseed in them.

Cumin combines nicely with fennel, juniper berries and orange rind. This seed, because of its strength, warmth and aroma, is always successful when added to rich foods.

Fennel *Foeniculum vulgare*

Fennel is a yellow-flowered perennial plant closely related to dill. The feathery leaves, generally available in summer months, can be used when fresh leaves are not available. Fennel has a lovely, distinctive, penetrating aroma. Its fragrance is nearer to anise than dill, with an aftertaste of celery.

Fennel seeds are often thought of as the "fish flavour," since dried seeds or fresh leaves are good with any type of fish, either cooked with it or sprinkled on top like parsley. The slight acidity of the fennel sets off the flavour of the fish in much the same way lemon juice does. Fennel and lemon juice or lemon rind make an excellent combination.

0—⚷ Sprinkle fresh fennel leaves on salad, or mix them with cream cheese.
0—⚷ Use fennel seeds with split-pea or fresh green-pea soup and with tomato soup and borscht. Try them in lamb stew and sprinkled on roast lamb.

0—⚷ Sprinkle a few seeds on top of the crust of an apple pie before baking. Add to sweet buns and quick breads, and throw in a teaspoonful when making your next fruitcake.

Garlic *Allium sativum*

Like onions, leeks, shallots and chives, garlic is an herb that belongs to the lily family. It is so ancient that its origins have become obscured, but many believe that it came originally from southwest Siberia.

The part we use is a bulb, sometimes called a head. The bulb is made up of many little sections called cloves. Each clove has a separate skin or peel that is usually removed before using. When only a faint flavour is required, a garlic clove can be pushed through a garlic press and only the pulp used. Garlic is strong, racy and has a strong odour. Because of its high sulphur content, garlic is an excellent aid to digestion. As for garlic breath, you can take care of that by chewing a few cardamom or coriander seeds.

Garlic can be used to give background character to virtually all kinds of savory dishes. It can be combined with other flavourings, and used sparingly or lavishly as one chooses. When lightly fried in oil or butter, it loses quite a bit of its potency.

Garlic can also be bought as garlic salt or garlic powder. These can be used to season foods to be cooked, and the salt can be sprinkled on food to be served raw. Liquid extract of garlic is also available in a variety of packaging. However, none of these is as strong as fresh garlic.
0—⚷ To keep garlic at its best, store it in the refrigerator. It will not release its odour until peeled and cut.

Horseradish *Amoracia lapathifolia*

Horseradish is a long thick root with a peppery, pungent taste. It both stimulates the appetite and aids digestion. Its main role is as a condiment, either freshly grated or commercially prepared.

Fresh roots, usually sold in the late autumn or early winter, have to be peeled and grated. That is easier said than done; the person who grates the root almost needs a gas mask, and will finish the job with streaming eyes. After that it is suprising how mild and almost sweet the grated shreds are. **0—⚞** Fresh horseradish is delicious added to a cream sauce to be served with boiled beef or tongue, or blended with whipped cream to be served with roast beef.

Horseradish is also sold in a powdered form that can be mixed with water or mustard to serve as a condiment; it can be added as is to recipes. Commercial preparations are usually mixed with vinegar and hardly resemble the delicious flavor of the fresh root.

Mustard *Brassica*
This plant grows in temperate as well as tropical areas, so it is an herb as well as a spice. The leaves are used as a vegetable. The seeds are used whole in pickling and are ground to make the various forms of the familiar condiment. It is available ground, and is usually called dry mustard. The flavor must be developed by adding the crushed seeds or the dry mustard to a liquid — water, vinegar, a marinating mixture, a stew.

There are many types of prepared mustards on the market; each type is different and produces different results.

MILD YELLOW MUSTARD is a mixture of dry mustard, ground turmeric, vinegars, glucose and salt. It is the all-purpose mustard.

HORSERADISH MUSTARD is a mixture of the familiar yellow mustard, above, with freshly grated horseradish. It has a little more snap.

ENGLISH MUSTARD is a mixture of dry mustard and water. A little salt can be added if you wish. Use when a sharp pungent mustard is required. You can prepare this kind yourself. Allow at least 20 minutes for the flavour to develop.

FRENCH MUSTARD is often referred to as Dijon mustard. This contains dry mustard, sugar, herbs, flour, spices and white wine. It has a pungent but very smooth flavour. It is available in both mild and strong forms.

DUTCH MUSTARD contains dry mustard, sugar, vinegar, herbs and spices. It is pleasantly sharp and especially effective as an ingredient in cooking.

GERMAN MUSTARD is made from ingredients very like those of Dutch mustard, but the flavour differs somewhat. It is good with cold cuts and spicy dishes.

BAHAMIAN MUSTARD is not as readily available as the others. It contains dry mustard, wine vinegar, sugar, herbs, flour and many spices. It is very hot but most pleasant, especially with roasted meat and game.

Juniper berries *Juniperus*
Juniper berries are the fruits of the juniper evergreen, which grows wild in many parts of North America. They are strongly aromatic and clearly astringent.

Gin owes most of its perfume to juniper berries. In Sweden, they are used to make a very pleasant beer. In France, especially in the North, they are crushed and soaked in distilled water to make a refreshing drink.

Juniper is the perfect flavour to add to veal and lamb kidneys and to all types of wild birds. **0—⚞** The berries are excellent when mixed with an equal quantity of coriander, both crushed, to flavor beef or lamb stew. **0—⚞** When roasting duck, quail or venison, add to the gravy 8 to 10 crushed juniper berries soaked in ¼ cup (60 ml) of gin for 12 to 24 hours.

Poppy seeds *Papaver somniferum*
These tiny slate-colored seeds, which are readily available at herb counters or specialty shops, give a delectable nutty flavour to many foods. In case you are wondering about their narcotic effect, rest assured that commercial poppy seeds have positively no narcotic properties.

Poppy seeds are usually thought of in or on top of cakes, cookies and breads, and the Central Europeans have given the world the pleasure of poppy-seed strudel, but there are many other uses. **0—⚷** Add a tablespoonful (15 ml) to pie pastry when adding the flour. **0—⚷** For a quick tart or cake filling, make a paste-like mixture of poppy seeds, honey and a little lemon juice. **0—⚷** Toss a spoonful of poppy seeds into your next bread pudding.

0—⚷ Shower poppy seeds over buttered hot noodles and discover that they are not only colourful but crunchy as well. Do the same over carrots, potatoes, and turnips. **0—⚷** Mix poppy seeds to taste with cream cheese and a little sour cream for a dip to serve with potato chips.

There are several other herbs not mentioned here. Every country has some special favourites and experimenting with exotic cuisines will introduce you to new ones. You can learn more about herbs in many reference books.

SPICES

Spices stimulated some of the most dramatic chapters of human history. An important ingredient used in the Middle Ages, spices did not simply enhance the taste of food. In an area without refrigeration or quick transportation, they were needed just to make food edible. In those days, Venice held a monopoly on European sales through its control of the Mediterranean and its trading contacts with the East. The Portuguese, then the Dutch, the Spanish, the French and the English set out to break in on a trade with fabulous possibilities. In doing so, they sparked some of the greatest discoveries and some of the worst international rivalries man has known.

True spices come from tropical plants. They are the seeds of the fruits, the fleshy covering of the fruits, the unopened flower buds, the roots, barks or berries. Spices can be sweet, such as nutmeg and cinnamon, or peppery, such as black pepper, ginger and cloves. In cooking with spices, the nose plays almost as important a role as the taste buds in determining the exact amount required. For this reason it is not necessary to follow exactly the dictates of a recipe when spices are involved. Your personal taste should decide whether you prefer cinnamon to nutmeg, or feel happier with only ¼ teaspoon (1 ml) spice rather than 1 teaspoon (5 ml). Changes such as these do not affect the texture of the food nor the finished recipe. Spices, like herbs, are the food's perfume, and should be used to please one's own taste.

Grinding spices is a gourmet's delight that anyone can share, because whole spices, ground when needed, are more flavourful than already ground spices in containers. The latter have sometimes been standing for months waiting to be used. Our grandmothers used their own nutmeg graters, as well as their own mortars and pestles. If they did not possess a mortar, they crushed spices against the bottom of a flat iron by using a hammer. No spices in the old days came all ground up in little boxes. The role played by spices — to insinuate their flavours into other ingredients, which in turn helps the flavours of these other ingredients to merge with each other — is best played by pungent fresh spices.

Allspice

Allspice is the fruit of a tropical tree, Pimenta dioica, of the myrtle family. The berry is picked green and sun-dried. The flavour is a mixture of cloves, cinnamon and nutmeg, with the clove flavour predominant. Allspice can be purchased ground or whole. ⊶ The berries are easy to crush in a mortar and are at their best when used in dishes prepared by long slow cooking or in marinating mixtures. Tie the berries, whole or crushed, in a square of cheesecloth so they can easily be retrieved before serving.

Allspice combines well with lemon, orange rind and lime rind, as well as with lime juice. ⊶ No pumpkin pie should be without allspice. Mixed with lemon rind and a small blade of mace, it is also a delicious addition to blueberry pie.

Cardamom

Cardamoms are the dried ripe fruits of a large perennial herb, *Eletteria cardomomum.* Native to India, the spice is used extensively there. Perhaps its most important and primary use is in the making of curry powder. It is, after saffron, the most expensive spice, because every delicate seed pod has to be snipped off the plant by hand, and the yield is relatively low. An acre usually yields about 250 pounds (113 kg).

The cardamom fruit or pod is a small, bleached, white capsule that contains 10 to 12 little black seeds the size of small grape pips. Usually the seeds alone are used, but the pod will dissolve if it is cooked in liquid mixtures such as stews for any length of time. The taste is clean, flowery and sweet.

While the Indians use cardamom for curry, the Scandinavians use it in their sweet breads and pastries, including the well-known Danish pastry. Swedish and Finnish cooks also use cardamom to flavor the meat for their famous cold table, their meatballs and the stuffing for their cabbage rolls, which are served with a milk gravy also flavoured with cardamom. It is an Arabic custom to serve a tiny silver bowl of cardamom seeds to add to the taste of sweet black coffee.

⊶ Combined with cloves and cinnamon, cardamom makes a perfect seasoning for fried rice. ⊶ Try a few crushed seeds in mashed sweet potatoes. ⊶ The perfumed spiciness of cardamom, sometimes combined with almonds or lemon rind, is delicious in a poundcake. ⊶ Try it, sometimes combined with coriander seeds, to flavour apple or pear pies. It is also very good in gingerbread and in spicy pickles.

Because cardamom seeds have a warm flavour and scent, they are used as a pleasant way to sweeten the breath. Or chew a few seeds to relieve mild indigestion.

Cardamom can be bought ground or in pods. The pods are best because the easily detached capsule keeps the essential oil in the seeds from evaporating. The seeds are very easy to grind or to crush in a mortar.

Cinnamon

Cinnamon is the bark of a handsome evergreen, *Cinnamomum,* which somewhat resembles a birch tree because of its loose bark. The bark is peeled from the trees, rolled into quills, and dried. Ground spice is available, and it is easier to use for some preparations.

Cassia is a variety of cinnamon. Actually, it is cassia that we usually have on our shelves, stronger in both colour and flavor than cinnamon itself. This all-time favourite spice can be used in cookery from soup to nuts and lends itself very well to experimentation.

○━━ When cooking anything that contains chocolate — whether cake, pie or sauce — add a pinch or more of ground cinnamon. You may not always detect its flavour, but it does its bit to improve and intrigue.

○━━ Put a small cinnamon stick in the winter compote of dried or fresh fruits. ○━━ Simmer a cinnamon stick and a blade of mace in the milk used for plain custards or rice puddings. ○━━ Roll a cube of sugar in cinnamon, then in grated orange rind, and place it in the middle of a plain muffin before baking. ○━━ Peel and slice an orange and sprinkle it with a mixture of cinnamon and sugar, or maple syrup and cinnamon.

Cinnamon is delicious in applesauce, but use only a little. It is good combined with grated lemon rind too. A cinnamon stick in a bread sauce is a real taste thrill. ○━━ If you enjoy a glass of hot milk before going to bed, sweeten it lightly with honey and add a sprinkle of cinnamon on top.

Cloves

Cloves are the dried unopened flower buds of a large evergreen tree, *Eugenia caryophyllata.* They are small, dark brown and look something like a small nail. (Their name comes from the Latin word for nail). When the bud of the clove has separated from the little stem, they are sometimes confused with the allspice berry. This is the difference: the clove has tiny overlapping dried petals, whereas the allspice berry has a single wrinkled skin. Ground cloves are available, but the ground spice does not keep its flavour long.

Because they have a high proportion of essential oil, cloves are very aromatic, warming and astringent. The flavour is penetrating and powerful, so use them with discretion. when you want a subtle flavor, take a few of the round buds from the top of their naillike bases and crush the buds in a mortar with a pestle or with a wooden mallet.

Studding a ham with cloves is the most common use for this spice, but here are some other uses. ○━━ Sprinkle a dash of cloves into cold cranberry juice or iced tea. This spice is always good with boiled onions and on baked apples. ○━━ Next time you make apple jelly, place a clove in the glass before pouring in the jelly. Beets, sweet potatoes and squash are enhanced by a pinch or so of cloves. Add a clove or two to a jar of any type of commercial pickles. Combine one or two cloves with a small piece of cinnamon bark in baked rice pudding.

Coriander

Coriander seeds are the dried aromatic fruits of a small annual herb, *Coriandrum sativum.* The Hindus credit it with being one of the most ancient of spices. The seeds are round and pale brown and can be bought whole or ground. Whole seeds are easily crushed and retain their flavor much longer. The seeds have the unique quality of increasing their aroma with age, which is another reason for buying them whole.

Although coriander has a faint licorice taste, the general impression it leaves is pleasantly flowery, with a faint hint of orange.

Coriander is one of the flavoring agents in gin. It is also used a great deal in the East as one of the main ingredients in curry. The fresh coriander leaves called *cilantro* or Chinese parsley are used extensively by Indians and Italians, by many Central Europeans and by Mexicans. The plant grows very well in most gardens, but people do not like growing it because of its unpleasant odor. However, the lacy leaves of fresh coriander chopped over fruits are very tasty.

Experiment with a little coriander in soups, stews and sauces and with duck and game. It is particularly good to flavor goose or pork dressing. It is also delicious in apple pie. ○━━ Combine it with grated lemon or orange rind to flavor custards, fruit salads or any type of creamy dessert.

Ginger

Ginger is native to China and to this day remains one of the most important seasonings in Chinese cuisine. The root of the ginger plant, *Zingiber officinale,* is what is used. It is peeled and dried to make a spice that is aromatic, hot and biting, with a full and pungent flavour. Because it is both heartening and warming, it has long been used as a stimulant as well as an aid to digestion. It is available fresh, dried, preserved, crystallized and ground to a powder.

To know the full, delicate, pungent flavour of ginger, it must be tasted fresh. So little is needed to flavour a whole dish, and what a pleasure it is to enjoy its aromatic taste and crips texture!

To use the fresh root (or rhizome, to be exact), simply peel it, taking off the thinnest possible layer of peel, and grate, slice or chop it fine, whichever suits your recipe.

There are several ways to keep fresh gingerroot for long periods. **0—⚿** One method is to place it in a plastic container and freeze it. It can be kept frozen, in perfect condition, for as long as two years. To use, simply cut off a piece, then peel, grate or slice it without even thawing it out. **0—⚿** Another method is to peel the root and place it in a glass jar, cover with sherry and keep refrigerated. The ginger-flavoured sherry can be used as an extract to flavour sauces, custards, stews, etc. Gingerroot will keep its potency and flavour for 10 to 12 months if preserved with sherry.

To preserve fresh gingerroot to use either as a dessert or in a dessert, make a thick syrup with 1 cup (250 ml) sugar and ¼ cup (60 ml) water; add ½ to 1 cup (125 to 250 ml) peeled gingerroot, cover and simmer over low heat for 40 minutes. Pour into a clean glass jar. Keep refrigerated, or in a cool place. It will keep for 12 to 14 months.

Fresh gingerroot, wrapped in foil and refrigerated, will keep for a few days. If you do not plan to use it quickly, it is better to freeze it, or preserve with sherry.

0—⚿ When a gingerbread recipe calls for 1 or 2 teaspoons (5 to 10 ml) of ground ginger, grate 1 teaspoon (5 ml) of fresh gingerroot to replace it. What a difference! It can be used with all Chinese food and is particularly good with any bland or delicate food, such as fruit salad. Try it first by adding ½ teaspoon (2 ml) or so of grated fresh gingerroot to a can of fruit salad or sliced peaches. Cover and let stand for a few hours.

A pinch or two of grated fresh gingerroot or the dry ground spice will give body and warmth to meat or other food. **0—⚿** It is excellent with oxtail soup, creamed or buttered carrots, and white sauce for cod or salmon. For a sweet white sauce to be used on a pudding, flavour with the ginger syrup, above, to taste. **0—⚿** Grated fresh gingerroot or ground ginger mixed with a few tablespoons of sugar is delicious; this is a rare treat sprinkled over cantaloupes and other melons. **0—⚿** A quick and simple dessert sauce can be made by beating together ½ cup (125 ml) maple or corn syrup, 1 tablespoon (15 ml) butter and 1 teaspoon (5 ml) grated fresh gingerroot.

Remember, ground ginger loses its flavour and pungency easily when exposed to air, so be sure to keep ginger jars closed thightly.

Mace

Mace is the bright scarlet aril that covers the hard brown kernel within which the nutmeg seed is found. When ripe, the nutmeg fruit splits open to reveal one of nature's most beautiful combinations of colours as well as one of its most fascinating patterns. The first layer of fresh nutmeg is a vivid green, the next a bright orange; the third layer is the brilliant scarlet aril that protects the nutmeg kernel. It is this covering that is dried to become mace. It tastes something like nutmeg, but mace is more delicate. Mace and nutmeg can often be substituted for one another in recipes; however, it is not always successful. Mace is best used with fish, meat, cheese, soups and vegetables. It is good in a dessert or with fruit.

The best way to obtain a delicate mace flavor is to use what are referred to as "blades of mace," although the spice can be used ground. The "blades" are the fibres of the scarlet aril, which changes to a pinkish beige colour when dried.

Nutmeg

Nutmeg is the dried seed from the fruit of a sturdy evergreen tree, *Myristica fragrans*, with leaves resembling the rhododendron. The spice has a straight, sweet, aromatic quality and differs from other spices in that it is both sweet and bitter at the same time.

Nutmeg blends well; it adds richness and warmth to bland foods such as custard, milk pudding, eggnog, pears and tapioca. **0━►** To a French chef, nutmeg is a must with fresh spinach. **0━►** For a pleasant surprise, try it in mashed potatoes and scrambled eggs, but use it with discretion.

Nutmeg is available already ground but, more than any other spice, it should be freshly grated just before using; it makes a great difference in the flavour. Use a nutmeg grater for best results. You will find that a small jar of whole nutmegs goes much further than a box of ground nutmeg. On the average, one nutmeg will give you 1 large tablespoon (15 ml) of grated spice.

Pepper

Pepper, the berry of a beautiful vine of the tropics, *Piper nigrum*, is perhaps the most important spice of all. It has more than 5,000 years of history behind it, — and peppery history it has been. This spice is in no way related to *Capsicum* peppers, despite the similarity of the names.

0━► One important thing to remember about pepper is that much of the biting quality it possesses is lost during cooking, so add it after cooking.

Pepper stimulates the gastric juices and the digestive processes. It does not make food as "hot" as most people believe; cayenne pepper and other forms of *Capsicum* peppers are much hotter. Pepper enhances the flavour of food, bringing out and strengthening the inherent flavour of any food to which it is added. It never camouflages natural flavour. It will not mask a bad dish, but it will bring out the best in a good one.

Both black and white pepper come from the same seed. When first harvested, pepper seeds are red, odourless and tasteless. When dried in the sun, they become black and spicy. White pepper emerges after the black coating is taken off by abrasion. White pepper is far less aromatic and therefore less effective than the black.

To achieve the best results with pepper, buy it as peppercorns, which you grind in a pepper mill as needed. A good pepper mill is a truly useful utensil. You can have a more flavourful spice this way, and you can also adjust the grind from coarse to very fine to suit your recipe. Ground pepper loses much of its quality in a short time.

There is often a question about the difference in cost between ground pepper and peppercorns. There are many types of peppers, and they are grown in different parts of the world, including Java, Johore and Penang in Malaya, Trang in Thailand, Saigon in Vietnam, Singapore, which produces a superb smoked pepper, and Malabar in India, where Tellicherry pepper comes from. These areas sometimes have two or three different types each. The price varies according to the quality of the berries. When you buy peppercorns, they are of one kind only and of uniform size. Naturally, they are more expensive than ground pepper, which can be made from a mixture of various kinds and sizes, perhaps even mixed with less flavourful seeds of similar spices. In this case, the more expensive product is definitely superior. Once you have become acquainted with fresh-ground pepper of a kind you like, you will never want to go back to commercial ground pepper.

CAPSICUM PEPPERS

Capsicum peppers are the fruits of a large plant genus or group of plants, generally the product of subtropical and tropical countries, but some species grow in temperate zones. The genus includes chili peppers, cayenne peppers, paprika peppers, pimientos, bell peppers and others. Each has qualities of its own, as well as characteristics shared with the others.

Sweet bell peppers are a familiar garden plant whose fruits are used as vegetables, usually when they are still mature and green in colour. Fully ripe peppers are red. They are delicious at either stage.

Chili peppers

These are peppers of a small pungent species, usually eaten dried. They are red or green, sometimes yellowish, with a shiny lacquered surface. As they are bitingly hot, so use them with caution. ⚬⟶ Chili peppers' hotness increases with prolonged cooking, as in spaghetti sauce. They are also used in curry and other mixes to give pungency.

Cayenne peppers

These are the ripe fruits of another *Capsicum* species. The long twisted pods are dried, and usually sold as ground spice. Salt and other spices are often added to commercial varieties of ground cayenne pepper to vary the taste and the pungency.

Cayenne pepper is biting and pungent, with a most pronounced flavour. Always use it sparingly.

Tabasco peppers

These are very slender small peppers that grow in Central America and in the southern United States. This pepper is used most familiarly in a fiery-hot liquid sauce.

Pimientos

These are the shiny red fruits of another *Capsicum* species. Sweet and mild, they leave an acid aftertaste. They are used a great deal in Spanish and Mexican cooking. We usually get them peeled and canned. Because of their mildness, they are used as a vegetable or garnish rather than as a spice.

Paprika

This spice is made by grinding the dried stemless pods of a mild *Capsicum* pepper. Because of its use in Hungarian cuisine, it has earned a universal reputation.

There are marked differences in paprika. The everyday type that is found, bearing no identification, on the shelves of markets everywhere is fine to sprinkle here and there for color and a pleasant garnish. But more attentive care should be exercised in choosing a paprika to be used for cooking.

Hungarian paprika, with its distinctive warm flavor and beautiful deep-red color, comes in a range of tastes, from very mild to very pungent. Spanish paprika is harsher. They can be combined with great success. ⚬⟶ Use a mixture of both on meats. First brush the meat with oil to help release flavor. ⚬⟶ Add Hungarian paprika to the flour used to coat fish before frying. ⚬⟶ Sprinkle both kinds on hashed brown potatoes to help them brown faster and taste better.

Sesame

Sesame seeds, called benne seeds in some parts of the world, are the dried fruits of a beautiful tropical herb, *Sesamum indicum*. The herb is the basis of the famous Middle East sweet *halva*.

Oil of sesame is considered one of the healthiest herb oils in the world. Many Chinese dishes are prepared with a dark, heavy sesame oil, in contrast with Indian curries, which are prepared with a pale, light sesame oil. Sesame oil, which has been used from the very beginning of man's culinary efforts, is highly valued

by diet-conscious people who recognize it as one of the best kinds of polyunsaturated fat.

The cream-coloured little sesame seeds have a warm, nutty flavor that resembles the flavor of toasted almonds. When toasted to a golden brown, either in butter or spread on a baking sheet in a 300°F (180°C) oven, the flavour is accentuated. The seeds can be used as a substitute for nuts.

⊶ A generous sprinkling over chicken, fish, noodles or vegetable casseroles can take the place of buttered crumbs to give a dish a crunchy topping. **⊶** Add toasted sesame seeds to rice dishes or sprinkle them on baked potatoes. **⊶** Plain or toasted sesame seeds make an interesting garnish for hot cream soup and a pleasant addition to salads. Cakes, cookies, biscuits and crackers are improved with a sprinkling of sesame seeds. They also make a delicious and very healthy candy. Simply use the seeds to replace the nuts in any nut brittle candy recipe.

Turmeric

Turmeric belongs to the ginger family. The rootstalk of the plant, *Curcuma longa,* is the part used; it is dried and ground to a powder. Turmeric was used as a yellow dye centuries before Christ, and in the East it is still used that way.

Most people know turmeric only as an ingredient used to colour mustard pickles or prepared mustard, but it is a spice of great character and has many more uses. An aromatic spice with warm, musky overtones, turmeric is one of the basic ingredients of curry powder and gives it its familiar colour. Light-coloured Madras turmeric, usually sold in small airtight cans, is the best. There is a great variation in colour, depending on where it originates. Colour alone is not a reliable guide to quality.

⊶ If you have a good Madras turmeric, combine it with ginger and cardamom in the quantity you prefer for a quickly mixed curry powder. Often a pinch or two of turmeric is added to a dish merely to give colour. **⊶** Before roasting or barbecuing chicken pieces, roll them in turmeric mixed with a little flour for a beautiful gold colour as well as added flavour.

⊶ Turmeric can replace saffron in a recipe for the colour, but the flavor will differ, of course.

Vanilla

This familiar flavouring is native to Mexico, where it begins life as a beautiful orchid, *Vanilla planifolia*. Its exquisitely fragrant blossom lasts for only a day and then gives way to a cluster of long green pods, which are the vanilla beans. The 16th-century Spanish explorer Hernando Cortés brought it to Europe from Mexico, where it was used as a flavouring for chocolate. Soon all of Europe was drinking hot chocolate flavoured with vanilla.

Vanilla has remained one of the most popular flavourings in the world. Most people use it in the form of extract, but you must learn to use the beans. This also is the best way to combine quality with economy.

Because vanilla trees must be pollinated by hand, harvested by experts and cured by a demanding process requiring many months, the perfect vanilla bean is expensive. It is a long, thin, shriveled brown bean, soft and pliable and usually between 6 and 10 inches (15 to 25 cm) long. The best and the most flavour are trapped in the pod, so the cost becomes relative when we learn how to use it and get the most out of it. One fact is certain: The flavour can never be imitated.

USES OF THE WHOLE BEAN

For rice or other puddings, custards and even packaged puddings, add the whole bean to the milk and simmer. Place the bean in the syrup you make to poach fruit. Bury it in a bread pudding. And no matter how you use it, when you are through with it, rinse it off under running cold water and place it on waxed paper to dry. It can be used over and over again.

You can keep vanilla beans buried in a jar of fine fruit sugar. After a week, the entire jar of sugar becomes flavoured with vanilla. European cooks long ago learned how good vanilla sugar is when sprinkled on fruits or on top of cookies, or used instead of the bean itself for everyday dessert, or in making a cake. As you use the sugar, keep replacing it, but keep the jar tightly closed. The beans buried in sugar will keep soft for a long time.

After many uses, when the bean really dries out, grate it for flavouring such foods as fruits, custards and cakes.

USES OF THE SPLIT BEAN

For a special dish, or when additional flavour is required, or when you want the flavour to work faster, cut a 1- to 4-inch (2.5 to 10 cm) piece of the bean and split it open. Scrape the split pod with a knife to get out the seeds, then add them to the food. Do not discard the split pod; simply bury it once more in sugar.

In places such as the West Indies and Martinique, it is the custom to keep 2 or 3 pods of vanilla in a tall, narrow bottle filled with rum or brandy. With time this becomes a perfect extract. It is more economical for us, though, to buy and use the commercial extract.

Curry powder

Curry powder is a mixture of spices pounded together and used as a seasoning. There are many brands on the market; try several to discover which you prefer. In India, where curry is like salt and pepper to us, each woman grinds or pounds on stone her own favourite mixture, often from seeds she gathers herself.

Curry powder

Here is a recipe for mild curry powder. You can adjust the ingredients to suit your own taste.

3 tbsp (50 ml) black peppercorns

4 tbsp (60 ml) coriander seeds

2 tbsp (30 ml) caraway seeds

1 tbsp (15 ml) cumin seeds

1 tbsp (15 ml) whole cloves

2 tbsp (30 ml) cardamom seeds

1 tbsp (15 ml) cinnamon

¼ tsp (1 ml) ground hot chili pepper

Use an electric blender, or mix and grind as needed in a mortar with a pestle. Be careful if you are using the mortar. These spices release volative oils and dusts that can be very irrating to eyes and mucous membranes. When the curry powder is mixed, store in a tightly covered jar and keep in a dark place.

In India, women sprinkle a pinch or two on top of most foods. It is a pleasant change on boiled potatoes and cabbage. For a curried dish, you might add some grated fresh gingerroot, some ground turmeric and some crushed garlic in amounts to suit your taste.

CHAPTER 6

Marinades and stocks

MARINADES

A MARINADE is a liquid that seasons and sometimes tenderizes the foods soaked in it. It was originally used by sailors to preserve fish. The word comes from the French and means to pickle in brine. Before marinades were used as preservatives, salt alone was used.

A marinade also can be used to flavour bland food and to give a zesty new flavour to leftovers. With certain foods it can be used to bring out specific flavours. It is a great asset in barbecuing for sharpening flavours and for supplying fat (through oil penetration) to meats lacking in natural oils. Certain meats — spareribs, shoulder pork, lamb chops, short ribs — can be tenderized by the acid penetration of the marinade, thus shortening the cooking time. Marinade can also be used as a flavourful basting sauce, applied with a brush or spoon.

Basically, a marinade is a combination of oil and wine with vinegar, lemon juice or consommé, and spices and herbs, and often garlic and/or onions. This is how it works: The acid breaks down the fibres and the oil enters, with it the flavours of the seasonings.

Marinades can be made with olive oil or salad oil. You can use any of the different types of vinegar, or any white or red wine. You can use any of dozens of different herbs and spices, fresh or dried, to season a marinade to your personal taste.

Meat, fish, poultry, vegetables and fruit can be marinated, although where fruits are concerned, the word ''macerate'' is more accurate.

When meat is being marinated, it does not have to be covered with the marinade, so long as it is turned frequently while it is marinating. It is usually better to cover other foods with the marinade. When working with meat, place it in a glass, enamelware or ceramic container and pour on the marinade; turn the meat frequently. Most foods require only two to six hours at room temperature, but large or tough cuts of meat should be kept in the refrigerator for a few days and covered tightly to prevent their strong seasoning odours from reaching other foods.

After being used, a marinade will keep, well covered and refrigerated, for two to three weeks; so when you drain the food from the marinade, strain the liquid and store it to use again.

Sometimes a marinade is used in the cooking process that follows its use. For example, a piece of marinated meat may be drained, wiped dry, browned on all sides, then pot-roasted with the strained marinade used as part of the cooking liquid.

The recipes that follow are all for uncooked marinades; the ingredients are mixed cold or at room temperature and poured over the food without any further preparation. Marinades can also be cooked, like a court bouillon, before being poured over the food.

If you have a very large amount of food to marinate, you may want to double or triple the amounts of the ingredients.

Marinade for fish

6 tbsp (90 ml) salad oil

3 tbsp (50 ml) vinegar

3 to 6 parsley sprigs, chopped

⅛ tsp (0.5 ml) ground thyme

1 tsp (5 ml) salt

½ tsp (2 ml) crushed peppercorns

Juice and rind of 1 lemon

Few green onions, chopped

Combine the ingredients and place in a shallow dish. Add fish fillets, fish steaks or whole fish. Marinate in the refrigerator for 2 to 10 hours. Drain and cook. Makes about ¾ cup (200 ml).

Wine marinade for meat

½ cup (125 ml) salad oil

½ cup (125 ml) dry red wine or dry vermouth

½ tsp (2 ml) dry mustard

1 bay leaf

1 tsp (5 ml) crushed peppercorns

Mix the ingredients and place in a dish just large enough to hold the meat. In this way only a small amount of liquid can cover a large piece of meat. Marinate in the refrigerator for 2 to 10 hours. Drain. Makes 1 cup (250 ml).

Oriental marinade

¼ cup (60 ml) soy sauce

¼ cup (60 ml) sweet vermouth, sake, or consommé

1 tsp (5 ml) cider vinegar

1 garlic clove, crushed

½ tsp (2 ml) grated fresh gingerroot or ground ginger

1 tsp (5 ml) MSG (monosodium glutamate)

Mix and use as above. Makes ½ cup (125 ml).

Marinade for chicken

This is an example of a "dry" marinade. It has very little liquid and it is brushed on the chicken rather than poured over it.

1 or 2 garlic cloves, crushed

½ tsp (2 ml) curry powder, or 1 tsp (5 ml) crushed cuminseeds

½ tsp (2 ml) dried tarragon or basil

1 tsp (5 ml) salt

1 tbsp (15 ml) salad oil

Juice of 1 lime or 1 lemon, or 2 tbsp (30 ml) brandy

½ tsp (2 ml) crushed peppercorns

Mix. Brush chicken with the mixture. Cover the chicken and refrigerate overnight.

½ cup (125 ml) orange juice

¼ cup (60 ml) sweet vermouth, red wine or lime juice

1 thick onion slice

10 juniper berries, crushed

Handful of parsley

½ tsp (2 ml) aniseeds

Mix. Pour over duck or game. Cover, and refrigerate for 2 to 6 hours. Makes ¾ cup (200 ml).

Marinade for duck and game

¼ cup (60 ml) wine or cider vinegar

⅔ cup (160 ml) salad oil

¼ tsp (1 ml) prepared mustard (English or Dijon mustard is best)

¼ tsp (1 ml) sugar

½ tsp (2 ml) dried herb

½ tsp (2 ml) salt
¼ tsp (1 ml) pepper

Place mixture in a bottle, shake hard, and pour over cooked vegetables. Refrigerate for 3 to 4 hours before serving. Makes about 1 cup (250 ml).

Marinade for vegetables

Any of the preceding marinades can be varied by adding other ingredients or substituting different ingredients. For example, you could add any of the following:

1 garlic clove, crushed

¼ tsp (1 ml) celery seeds

1 tsp (5 ml) toasted sesame seeds

1 fresh tomato peeled and diced

1 tbsp (15 ml) capers

2 hard-cooked eggs, chopped

Or you could replace the vinegar with an equal amount of fresh lemon juice.

Variations on the basic marinades

½ cup (125 ml) orange juice or any other fruit juice

Grated rind and juice of ½ lemon

¼ cup (60 ml) maple or corn syrup

1 vanilla bean, or 5 or 6 coriander seeds, crushed or ¼ tsp (1 ml) aniseeds

¼ cup (60 ml) brandy or liqueur (optional)

Mix the ingredients well and pour over fresh fruits that have been peeled and sliced, diced or quartered. Gently mix all together thoroughly. Cover and refrigerate for 4 to 6 hours. Makes 1 cup (250 ml).

Marinade for fruits

STOCKS FOR SOUPS AND SAUCES

A stock is a liquid made by cooking various foods in water for a long enough time to extract the flavour and nutrients from the solid particle. The liquid becomes flavourful and nutritious, and the solid particles that remain are discarded. Stocks must be seasoned and flavoured very cautiously because they will be concentrated when they are finished and probably reduced even further when used as ingredients in other preparations.

Stocks made with calf's feet or other veal bones, and well reduced, can be clarified to make aspic jelly. When additional seasoning is added, a clarified stock can be served alone as a clear soup, but it is more likely to be used as an ingredient in a soup. Stock can be used in recipes instead of other liquids to give added nutritional value to the dish. Good stock is the secret of a delicious sauce.

Stock can be an extremely economical ingredient, since it is usually made from foods often thrown away and thus wasted. Whenever your butcher removes any bones from meat you purchase, make sure you have him include them in your parcel. These, as well as bones left over from cooked meats and poultry, can be used in the making of stock. You can also use vegetables, cooked cereals such as rice, pasta, herbs and bits of meat.

Bones used in the making of a stock should be cracked, if possible, to release the minerals, especially calcium, and vitamins in the marrow. These add to the nutritional value.

Stock can be made in a pressure cooker. Fill the cooker three — quarters full with bits and pieces of vegetables, meat and bones. Then add liquid to about the halfway mark. Toss in a bay leaf, a few peppercorns and a pinch of salt. Cover and cook for 20 minutes, then let the pressure reduce. Once the pan is cooled, remove the cover and strain the contents. This makes a very tasty stock that turns into a thick, clear jelly when refrigerated.

A good measure for stock is 2 cups (500 ml) of water and 2 cups (500 ml) of soup greens for each pound of bones.

Basic meat-bone

2 lb (1 kg) bones

4 cups (1 L) cold water

1 to 2 cups (250 to 500 ml) cooked or uncooked vegetables

1 small onion, sliced

2 slices of parsnip (optional)

Few parsley sprigs

10 peppercorns

1 tsp (5 ml) coarse salt

1 tsp (5 ml) dry mustard

1 bay leaf

Cut any bits of meat away from the bones and place in a heated large and heavy saucepan. Sear over high heat until browned here and there; this gives flavour to the stock. Remove the pan from the source of heat and add the cracked bones, cold water, vegetables (preferably mild types such as celery and carrots), the onion, parsnip, parsley, peppercorns, salt, mustard and bay leaf.

Bring to a fast rolling boil. Cover very tightly and simmer over low heat for 2 hours. When finished, pass through a fine sieve. For a very clear stock, line the sieve with 2 layers of cheesecloth. Store the strained stock in a covered glass jar in the refrigerator. Before using, remove any fat that has accumulated on top. This stock will keep refrigeraated for 8 to 10 days. Makes about 3 cups (750 ml).

A fish stock is very useful if you are making a fish sauce, soup, chowder or bisque; it can also replace clam juice in a recipe. Fish stock is a nice change when served as a soup, garnished with very fine noodles or tiny croutons. You can usually get the chief ingredients — fish heads and tails — from your fish store for free. The more you use, the stronger the stock will be.

Fish stock

2 to 3 lb (1 to 1.5 kg) fish trimmings (heads, tails, etc.)

1 bay leaf

1 small carrot, chopped

1 celery rib

½ tsp (2 ml) salt

¼ tsp (1 ml) pepper

4 cups (1 L) cold water

¼ cup (60 ml) dry white wine (optional)

Place everything except the wine in a large saucepan. Bring to a fast rolling boil. Cover tightly and simmer for 30 to 40 minutes, or until the flesh drops from the bones. Strain as for meat stock.

If you use the wine, pour the strained fish stock back into a clean saucepan, add the wine, and bring to a boil. Remove from heat and cool. Refrigerate, covered, until ready to serve. It will keep for 6 to 8 days. Makes about 3 cups (750 ml).

A vegetable broth can be an extremely tasty meatless stock, chock full of vitamins. Use it to add to soups and sauces, and for cooking meats, such as pot roast, when a liquid is required. It is another economical stock, because it is made with foods that are usually thrown away.

Vegetable broth

1½ cups (375 ml) chopped celery tops

½ cup (125 ml) chopped parsley stems and leaves

1¼ cups (315 ml) chopped spinach leaves

¼ cup (50 ml) chopped green onions or leek tops

1 cup (250 ml) chopped carrot tops

2 cups (500 ml) shredded outer leaves of salad greens

1 tsp (5 ml) salt

1 pinch of dried thyme

6 peppercorns

5 cups (1.25 L) water

Place all the ingredients in a saucepan and bring slowly to a simmer. Continue to simmer for 25 minutes. Strain as for meat stock. Makes 4 cups (1 L).

For a simple, nutritious soup, serve vegetable broth with a poached egg in it or garnished with chopped watercress.

Clarifying stock for aspics

Put 4 cups (1 L) strained stock, with all fat removed, in a large saucepan and add 2 egg whites, well beaten but not stiff. Stir the egg whites into the stock and very slowly bring the mixture to a boil, stirring continuously. When it reaches the boiling point, lower the heat to keep the stock at a steady simmer and let it simmer, without stirring, for 30 minutes. Then strain through a clothlined sieve. All particles will cling to the egg whites and the liquid will be perfectly clear and sparkling.

Stock for aspic can be flavored with wine or other seasonings, but it is important to do this before clarifying, because the addition of even salt might cloud the aspic.

A stock made with veal bones or calf's feet may jell completely without gelatin. To be sure, test it by placing a few spoonfuls in a saucer and chilling it. The sample should be firm in about 20 minutes. If it does not jell, add unflavoured gelatin; measure 1 envelope gelatin for 2 cups (500 ml) liquid. Use half that amount if the stock is half jelled. Soften the gelatin in 3 tablespoons (50 ml) cold water, then stir it into the hot stock until completely dissolved.

CHAPTER 7

Sauces and salad dressings

THERE is almost no limit to the number of ingredients, both cooked and uncooked, that can be mixed together to create delicious sauces. Once you have mastered the best-known classic sauces, some methods of preparing them and the basic ingredients, you will be able to use your imagination to develop other variations.

The perfect sauce enhances both the appearance and the flavour of the food with which it is served. But sauces perform other important functions as well. They often are used to bolster the flavour of an insipid or uninteresting dish, and to bind several different kinds of food together into a unified whole, as white sauce does in making croquettes. Sauces made with aspic, such as jellied mayonnaise, keep foods from drying out while on the buffet table. Other sauces, such as mayonnaise and vinaigrette, offer a contrast in flavour and texture to the salads or vegetables they dress. A sauce should make a real contribution to the dish for which it is designed, and should possess its own well-defined flavour as well.

There is no need to become a slave to sauce recipes. Both seasoning and flavouring are largely a matter of taste. Herbs, extracts, spices and salt do not change a basic recipe, so you can use more or less than is called for. When you begin, add only a part of the flavouring and seasoning ingredients, then taste. You can add a little more of this or that according to your personal taste.

To determine the amount of sauce you require, use this as a general guide: 7 tablespoons (110 ml) is the equivalent of 1 portion. If the sauce happens to be particularly rich, you can reduce each portion to 3 tablespoons (50 ml). However, there are occasions when you will want no more than 1 tablespoon (15 ml) per portion of a particular sauce.

HOW TO THICKEN A SAUCE

While it is possible to pour a little liqueur or cream over some food and consider it a sauce, a true sauce is thick enough to have body and to adhere to the food it is served with. There are various ways to achieve this thickening.

Reducing a sauce
This is done to give a sauce a more concentrated flavour, as well as to thicken it. Boil the sauce, uncovered, over low heat, stirring frequently, until the desired quantity is obtained. It can be reduced only a little or by half or more. Sauces to be reduced must be seasoned cautiously because the seasoning will also be concentrated. Reducing often results in adequate thickening.

Roux
This is a mixture of flour and fat that is mixed and cooked at the very start of a recipe before any liquid is added. This cooking eliminates the raw flour taste and allows the flour particles to absorb

the liquid added later. If the *roux* is cooked until just smooth and bubbling, you will get a pale sauce. Browning the mixture over medium heat, stirring constantly, will produce a darker ivory-coloured sauce. An even darker brown and richer-looking sauce can be produced by browning the *roux* even more. Only after you have browned the *roux* to the desired colour do you add cold liquid to finish the sauce. Remember, flour and fat must be cooked together first before any liquid is added. As a general rule, 1 tablespoon (15 ml) fat and 2 teaspoons (10 ml) flour for each ½ cup (125 ml) liquid, but these proportions can vary according to the recipe.

Beurre manié

This is a mixture of flour and butter added at the end of the sauce-making instead of at the beginning. Blend together an equal amount of soft butter and flour to make a soft ball. Add the mixture quickly to hot stock or gravy, but do not boil. Beat with a wire whisk until smooth and creamy.

Another method is to mix 1 part butter and 2 parts flour to produce a drier, more crumbly mix. You can store it in the refrigerator indefinitely. Add this to a simmering sauce a little at a time and whisk until smooth after each addition. Repeat until the desired thickness has been obtained.

Flour or other starch with cold liquid

The liquid can be cold water, milk or consommé, and the starch can be wheat flour, arrowroot, potato flour, cornstarch or fine tapioca. Each kind gives a slightly different texture to be finished sauce. Whichever liquid you use, add the starch, stir to a smooth cream or thin paste, then add to boiling stock or gravy. Beat with a wire whisk. Remember, the liquid must be cold when you mix it with the starch. To obtain a smooth, creamy texture free from any starchy flavor, boil the mixture for 3 to 4 minutes as you beat it with the whisk.

The usual proportion of flour to liquid for a flour-thickened sauce is 2 teaspoons (10 ml) flour to ½ cup (125 ml) liquid. Some recipes call for different amounts. To substitute another starch for the 2 teaspoons (10 ml) wheat flour, use any of the following: 1 teaspoon (5 ml) cornstarch, 1⅔ (6.6 ml) teaspoons rice flour, ⅔ (1.6 ml) teaspoon potato flour or arrowroot.

Egg yolks

Some classic sauces are thickened with egg yolk alone. Examples are hollandaise, béarnaise and the best-known cold sauce, mayonnaise. In other sauces, like Mornay, where egg yolks are used the amount of flour is reduced. *Any mixture enriched or thickened with egg yolks must never be allowed to boil, because this could cause the sauce to curdle. Low heat is essential.* If the sauce is too hot, the egg may cook into little hard lumps before it can expand and mix with the other ingredients. Remember, it takes only seconds to cook an egg once it is out of its shell.

Butter and cream

Butter plays its part in thickening emulsified sauces such as hollandaise, but it is used by itself to thicken some special sauces such as the white butter sauce served with fish in France. Butter and cream cooked over very low heat will thicken a sauce. Cream with other ingredients will also thicken, as you will see in the recipe for *sauce poulette* that follows. Whipped cream and sour cream also are used, for example in *velouté Chantilly* described later on, but both these creams are used in dessert sauces. You will find an example in the section on dessert sauces.

Cheese and bread crumbs

Grated cheese is used to thicken cheese sauces and to help thicken sauces like Mornay. Bread crumbs thicken *sauce polonaise,* so often served with cauliflower. They are also the thickener as well as chief ingredient in the bread sauce the English serve with roast chicken; recipe for this follows.

Purées

The best-known purée for a sauce is onion, which makes *sauce soubise,* but other purées of vegetables, nuts or fruits can be used to thicken sauces. Use your imagination.

FINISHING A SAUCE

The French chef's method of finishing a sauce is to remove it from the source of heat when ready to serve, and only then to add butter and stir until it is melted. The heat of the sauce melts the butter; it is not necessary to return it to heat for this. Called "buttering a sauce," it gives both gloss and richness. If you want a sauce that is light and fluffy, omit the butter and in its place stir in 3 tablespoons (50 ml) of whipped cream.

BASIC SAUCES

There are three basic hot sauces you should know — white sauce, or *sauce béchamel; sauce velouté;* and brown sauce. Once you have learned to make these, you will be able to experiment with hundreds of variations.

Sauce béchamel

The basic ingredients of *béchamel* are fat, flour and liquid. The classic béchamel is made with butter, flour and veal stock, but for a béchamel-type sauce, other possibilities exist...

The fat can be butter, oil, drippings or melted meat fat (removed uncooked from meat and melted). You can also mix different types of fat; for instance half oil with half butter.

Flour is the usual thickening agent, but you can substitute arrowroot, potato flour or cornstarch.

For the liquid use plain or flavoured milk, wine, light or heavy cream, water, tomato juice, beef consommé, home-made or canned chicken or veal stock.

A *béchamel* can be made in two ways, either by mixing the thickening agent and fat into a *roux* and then adding the liquid, or by simmering the liquid with the flavoring ingredients first, then adding *beurre manié.* The following recipe describes the second method:

Sauce Béchamel

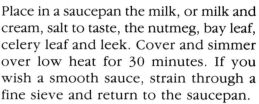

2 cups (500 ml) milk or 1 cup (250 ml) milk and 1 cup (250 ml) light cream

Salt

⅛ tsp (0.5 ml) grated nutmeg

1 bay leaf

1 piece of celery leaf

1 or 2 inches (2.5 to 5 cm) leek (optional)

2 tbsp (30 ml) salad oil and 2 tbsp (30 ml) butter or 4 tbsp (60 ml) butter

4 tbsp (60 ml) flour

Place in a saucepan the milk, or milk and cream, salt to taste, the nutmeg, bay leaf, celery leaf and leek. Cover and simmer over low heat for 30 minutes. If you wish a smooth sauce, strain through a fine sieve and return to the saucepan.

Make a *beurre manié,* using the mixture of salad oil and butter with the flour, or the butter only with the flour. Add it to the hot flavoured milk, and beat with a wire whisk over medium heat until smooth and creamy. Taste for seasoning, adding more salt if necessary.

When ready to serve, remove the sauce from the heat, add a piece of cold butter — 1 to 3 teaspoons (5 to 15 ml), depending on taste — and stir it in until melted; or fold in a few spoonfuls of whipped cream. Makes about 2 cups (500 ml).

VARIATIONS

There are many possible variations on *sauce béchamel.* Here are just a few. The extra ingredients listed are just enough for the quantity of sauce in the basic recipe. If you want to make a larger amount, all the ingredients must be increased proportionally.

Instead of making *beurre manié* with the fat and flour, use the mixture to make a *roux.* When it is cooked, add the strained flavoured milk. Cook and stir over low heat until the sauce is thickened and hot.

Sauce Aurore *(for eggs and all poultry dishes)*
Add 1 tablespoon (15 ml) tomato paste or paprika to the finished sauce.

Sauce Mornay *(for fish, eggs, vegetables or gratiné topping)*
Use only 3 tablespoons (50 ml) flour when making the roux. The sauce will seem thin until the eggs and cheese are added. Beat 2 egg yolks with ½ cup (125 ml) grated cheese and 1 tablespoon (15 ml) water. Stir the mixture into the slightly thickened milk and stir over very low heat until the sauce is quite thick and very hot. Do not boil.

Sauce soubise *(for eggs, roast pork, chicken and pasta casseroles)*
Slice 4 large onions. Sauté the slices in 1 tablespoon (15 ml) butter and 2 tablespoons (30 ml) salad oil in a large frying pan.
Cook over low heat until the onions are soft, but do not let them brown. This should take about 25 minutes.

For the classic sauce, purée the onions in a food mill or blender. Omit this step if you want the onions to be apparent in the sauce.

Make a basic *sauce béchamel,* starting with a roux. Use chicken or veal stock as the liquid instead of milk, and use only nutmeg to flavour. When the sauce is smooth and creamy, add the onions. Taste for seasoning, and adjust if necessary.

Sauce suprême

Make the basic béchamel with 2 cups (500 ml) light cream instead of milk. When ready to serve, add 3 tablespoons (50 ml) heavy cream, whipped until very thick.

Dill sauce *(for boiled or poached fish or meat)*

Make the sauce with butter and flour, and for the liquid use veal, chicken or fish stock instead of milk. When ready, add 1 tablespoon (15 ml) chopped fresh dill mixed with 2 tablespoons (30 ml) cider or wine vinegar, and ½ teaspoon (2 ml) sugar. Season to taste.

Caper sauce

Add 3 tablespoons (50 ml) capers to basic *béchamel* made with 1 cup (250 ml) consommé instead of 2 cups (500 ml) milk. When ready to serve, add the juice of ½ lemon.

Curry sauce

This is a basic curry sauce to serve with soufflés, vegetables or poulty. It can be used for a simple or an elaborate dish.

Stir 2 to 3 teaspoons (10 to 15 ml) of a good curry powder with 3 tablespoons (50 ml) brandy or whisky. Add 1 teaspoon (5 ml) ground turmeric and the grated rind of ½ lemon. Add this mixture to the basic *béchamel* made with milk or chicken broth.

Egg sauce *(for boiled or poached fish or other seafood)*

When the *sauce béchamel* is ready to serve, add to it 2 hard-cooked eggs, chopped, and 3 to 4 tablespoons (50 to 60 ml) minced parsley.

Mushroom sauce

Finely chop 2 green onions and enough mushrooms to make 1 cup (250 ml). Melt 1 tablespoon (15 ml) butter in a frying pan, add the mushrooms and onions, and stir over medium heat for 10 minutes. Add to the basic *béchamel* made with milk. Season with salt and pepper to taste.

Mustard sauce *(for fish, egg dishes, boiled meats, ham)*

Add to the flavoured milk 2 tablespoons (30 ml) prepared mustard, 1 teaspoon (5 ml) dry mustard, and a 1-inch (2.5 cm) strip of lemon rind. Beat with a wire whisk until the mustard is well incorporated. Different varieties of mustard will produce subtle changes in the colour and flavour of the sauce. Strain the milk into the *roux* and finish the sauce in the usual way.

White-wine sauce

Use 1 cup (250 ml) light cream and 1 cup (250 ml) dry white wine instead of 2 cups (500 ml) milk in the basic *béchamel* recipe. Follow the usual procedure. When ready to serve, add 3 tablespoons (50 ml) heavy cream whipped until very thick.

Sauce fines herbes

Add to the white-wine sauce (above) ¼ cup (60 ml) minced fresh parsley, ¼ teaspoon (1 ml) crumbled dried tarragon, and 1 minced shallot.

Sauce velouté

One difference between *velouté* and *béchamel* is that in velouté the liquid from the cooked food to be served is used in the sauce. Another is that *velouté* is finished off with egg yolk and cream to make it "velvety," which is what the name means.

There are two basic types of *velouté* — meat *velouté,* for chicken and veal, and fish *velouté,* for deep-water fish or other seafood.

The cooking liquid, called a fumet, must be well flavoured. When 2 cups (500 ml) of liquid are required and the liquid from the cooked food falls short of that amount, make up the difference with milk, cream, white wine or consommé; for fish *velouté,* you can make up the difference with fish stock or clam juice.

Sauce velouté

3 to 4 tbsp (50 to 60 ml) butter

3 to 4 tbsp (50 to 60 ml) flour

2 cups (500 ml) liquid from cooking

1 egg yolk

¼ cup (60 ml) light cream

Make a *roux* with the butter and flour. Add the liquid. Cook and stir over low heat until smooth and thickened.

To finish a *velouté*, blend together the egg yolk and the cream. Add to the finished sauce and bring to a rolling boil, beating constantly with a wire whisk. The moment the sauce reaches the boiling point, remove the saucepan from the heat and continue to whisk it for a few seconds longer. **0—** For a perfectly velvety sauce, do not stop beating as the sauce is brought to the boil, and keep stirring for a few minutes when you take it off the heat. Makes about 2½ cups (625 ml).

VARIATIONS

The number of possible variations is enormous, since the fumet can be made with so many foods — meats, fish and shellfish, vegetables — and there is a wide choice of herbs or other flavourings.

Sauce Bercy *(for fish and meat)*
Mince 3 shallots and cook them in the butter required for the sauce until they are "melted" but not browned. Add the flour, cook it, then add 1 tablespoon (15 ml) minced parsley and the cooking liquid. When the sauce is to be used with seafood, use fish stock or clam juice to make up any deficiency in the liquid; when it is to be used with meat, use white wine or chicken stock.

Sauce bretonne *(for eggs, fish, white meats, poultry)*
Mince 2 celery ribs, the white part of 1 leek, 1 small onion and 6 mushrooms. Melt the butter needed for the sauce and add the vegetables. Stir until well covered with the melted butter. Cover the saucepan and simmer over low heat until well softened, but do not brown. Add the flour and cook. Then add the cooking liquid of the fish, meat or poultry. Add white wine if necessary to bring the quantity to 2 cups (500 ml). Simmer, covered, for 20 minutes.
Stir in a tablespoon (15 ml) of butter, seasoning, and serve.

Sauce diplomate *(for fish and other seafood)*
Make velouté with part seafood cooking liquid and part clam juice. Flavour with brandy and cayenne to taste. You can also add about ¼ cup (50 ml) of diced lobster or chopped truffle.

Sauce poulette *(for braised white meat, vegetables or seafood)*
Melt the butter needed for the sauce and add ¼ pound (125 gr) mushrooms, minced. Cook until they just start to brown. Then add the flour, cook. Add the cooking liquid. If there is too little cooking liquid to make up the 2 cups (500 ml) make up the difference with light cream.
Beat the egg yolk with only 2 tablespoons (30 ml) cream and the juice of ½ lemon. When the sauce is ready, add the egg, lemon and cream mixture and simmer for 2 minutes, stirring constantly. Taste for seasoning, adding salt if necessary, and serve.

Velouté Chantilly *(for eggs, poultry, sweetbreads, brains)*
This sauce should be thick, so add 1 more tablespoon (15 ml) of flour to the basic recipe. When ready to serve, stir in ½ cup (125 ml) heavy cream whipped until very thick, or 1 cup (250 ml) commercial sour cream. Beat with a wire whisk while warming, and serve immediately.

½ cup (125 ml) chopped celery

½ cup (125 ml) chopped carrot

½ cup (125 ml) chopped onion

¼ tsp (1 ml) dried thyme

1 bay leaf

¼ tsp (1 ml) dried marjoram, savory or tarragon

3 tbsp (50 ml) fat

4 tbsp (60 ml) flour

2 cups (500 ml) liquid (stock, red wine, etc.)

First prepare the vegetables. Then add the herbs. The choice of fat is important; my own favorites are pure turkey fat or unsalted fresh pork fatback. Melt the fat of your choice and then stir in the vegetables with a wooden spoon. Cook over low heat, uncovered, until they are soft and translucent. Stir frequently. Let them take on a light golden colour, but not brown.

Make the *roux;* sprinkle the softened vegetables with the flour and stir over medium heat until the flour completely disappears. Keep stirring until the whole mixture takes on a light brown colour. **०➤** It is this operation that gives the colour to the sauce, but make sure that nothing sticks or burns, for this would give the sauce a bitter taste. Lower the heat if the vegetables or the flour appear to be overcooking.

The next step is to add the liquid. While the classic choice is brown stock, the sauce is particularly good if the liquid is made in part from the juices of a roast with red wine added. Measure the liquid you wish to use and let it cool. **०➤** Add only a cold liquid to a hot *roux.* Or, if you prefer, a hot liquid can be added to a cold *roux.* The important thing is the difference in the temperature of the two — one hot, the other cold. Stir the mixture of *roux* and liquid over medium heat until smooth and creamy. Cover and simmer in a 200°F (95°C) oven for 1 hour.

Strain through a very fine sieve, or through a sieve lined with cheesecloth. Only then season to taste. This makes an excellent brown sauce that keeps well and can be used for any number of dishes. Makes about 2 cups (500 ml).

Brown sauce

०➤ To save time and trouble, prepare 12 cups (3 L) of a good stock. Then make a *roux* with enough vegetables for 6 recipes. When this is ready, pour it into a large casserole, cover it tightly, and cook the sauce in a 200°F (95°C) oven for 3 hours. Strain the finished sauce, then pour it into small containers. Store 1 or 2 containers in the refrigerator; the sauce will keep for 3 weeks. Freeze the rest for later use. It will keep frozen for 6 months.

VARIATIONS

Sauce Madère or **Madeira sauce** *(for all roasted meats and for boiled tongue and ham)*
Add ¼ cup (60 ml) of Madeira wine to the 2 cups (500 ml) liquid, or substitute ½ cup (125 ml) Madeira for ½ cup (125 ml) of the liquid.

Sauce espagnole
Add 2 garlic cloves, minced, with a generous amount of freshly ground pepper to the vegetables. When the vegetables are soft and translucent, add 2 tablespoons (30 ml) of tomato paste. Finish the sauce in the usual fashion.

Sauce Robert *(for roasted pork, or to warm up beef and root vegetables)*
Instead of the 3 vegetables, use only 4 chopped onions. Flavour with ¼ teaspoon (1 ml) dried thyme and the grated rind of 1 lemon. Use ½ cup (125 ml) white wine to replace that much of the liquid. When the sauce is finished, flavour it with 1 teaspoon (5 ml) of Dijon mustard.

Sauce piquante *(for roasted veal, all pork dishes and all chops)*
Use onions only instead of the vegetables, as in sauce Robert. Flavour with 1 bay leaf and ¼ teaspoon (1 ml) salt. Replace ¼ cup (60 ml) of the liquid with ¼ cup (60 ml) cider vinegar, and add 1 teaspoon (5 ml) sugar. When the sauce is finished, add 4 tablespoons (60 ml) thin slices of baby gherkins.

Sauce diable *(for meat and poultry)*
Chop 2 shallots or 1 small onion and place them in a saucepan with ½ cup (125 ml) wine or cider vinegar, 8 crushed peppercorns, 1 bay leaf, ½ teaspoon (2 ml) dry mustard, ½ teaspoon (2 ml) paprika, and ½ teaspoon (2 ml) salt. Simmer until the mixture is reduced by half. Strain and add to cooked brown sauce.

EMULSIFIED SAUCES

An emulsion is a combination of two basically incompatible liquids, such as oil and water. In order to combine them, an emulsifying agent such as an egg yolk is needed. When making a hot emulsified sauce like hollandaise, the egg yolk binds together the melted butter (oil) with the lemon juice (water). As the oil is beaten, it breaks down into tiny globules that spread evenly through the water. By adding the egg yolk as an emulsifying agent, the two are combined. This principle applies to both hot and cold emulsified sauces.

An emulsified mixture separates easily without such an agent. For instance, French dressing will separate as soon as you stop stirring it, because there is nothing in it to bind the ingredients together. In a *hollandaise* or any of its variations, which contain egg yolk, the emulsion will remain in suspension if not overbeaten. If you master the art of making emulsified sauces, you will be able to serve elegantly sauced dishes for the most sophisticated menus.

HOT EMULSIFIED SAUCES

Hollandaise and its variations
Hollandaise is the basic sauce of the hot emulsified type, and it is a classic in itself. Other well-known related sauces are béarnaise, *Choron, maltaise, mousseline, muscovite* and *Bordeaux hollandaise.* Each is distinctive. These sauces are used to complement such foods as artichokes, asparagus, broccoli, chicken, eggs and fish.

The wonder of *hollandaise* lies in its simplicity. Once you have mastered a few basic techniques and understand the principle of emulsification, it is easy to make and almost never fails. The ingredients are few — egg yolks, lemon juice, butter and salt. The egg yolks contain the liquid that gives the sauce its base, the protein that acts as a thickening agent and gives the sauce its texture, and lecithin, the emulsifying agent that binds the lemon juice and the liquid of the egg yolks with the oil of the butter. The acid of the lemon juice also plays a role in blending the yolks with the butter. The combination of heat and constant stirring brings about the emulsion; very little heat is required.

There are three ways to make *hollandaise*. The chef's method, the hot-water method and the double-boiler method. Only the first two are reliable.

Only the simplest equipment is required. First, you need a heat-resistant nonmetallic bowl; the best is made of heavy crockery, glass or enameled cast iron. Aluminium or stainless steel may affect the flavour and texture of the sauce. To stir the sauce while cooking, a wire whisk is best, but almost any non-mechanical hand beater that will fit the curves of the bowl will do — a wire spoon, a Scandinavian twig beater, a wooden spoon or a plastic spatula.

If a *hollandaise* separates during cooking, too much heat has been applied. When this happens, beat the sauce vigorously while adding one of the following: an ice cube, a few drops of thick cream, or a few drops of boiling water. Any one of these should bind the sauce, but if one fails, immediately try the next, until one or all three have achieved the desired effect.

If the sauce turns out to be too thin, this means it has not been cooked enough. Return it to low heat and stir until thickened.

Don't be discouraged if you experience either of these apparent failures. It takes only a few degrees too much heat or a few minutes too little cooking. Practice.

If you need to reheat the sauce, place the sauce container over hot water or over very low heat and beat vigorously until warm. *Hollandaise* is served warm, not hot.

Hollandaise can be kept refrigerated in a covered bowl for 2 or 3 days, or in the freezer for 2 to 3 months. Before reheating a frozen sauce, thaw it in its covered freezer container.

Chef's hollandaise

This is one of the best ways to make hollandaise. It can be kept warm in a container set over warm water, or on a hot tray set at a low temperature, for up to 1 hour.

2 egg yolks

⅓ cup (80 ml) cold butter, in 3 pieces

1 to 4 tbsp (15 to 60 ml) lemon juice

½ tsp (2 ml) salt

Place the egg yolks in a bowl and break them up lightly with a fork. Top with the 3 pieces of cold butter. Pour in the lemon juice and sprinkle with the salt. Place the bowl over direct low heat and stir until all the butter has melted.

At no time should the pan containing the sauce get too hot, because excess heat will cause the sauce to curdle. To test the temperature, lift the bowl occasionally from the source of heat and touch the bottom. If it is too hot to be comfortable to the touch, remove it from the heat for a few seconds, but continue to stir constantly.

When the butter has melted, continue stirring and testing the temperature of the bowl until the sauce is smooth and creamy. Once you have removed it from the heat, continue to stir for another 40 to 50 seconds because the heat of the container will continue to cook the sauce. The entire procedure takes no more than 5 or 10 minutes. Makes 1 cup (250 ml).

Hot-water hollandaise

This recipe produces a fluffier sauce than the previous recipe. It is also more economical because the yield is greater. It is especially good served on heavier foods such as hard-cooked eggs. It can be blended with mayonnaise.

3 egg yolks

¼ cup (60 ml) hot water

1 to 3 tbsp (15 to 50 ml) lemon juice

Cayenne (added to taste), or ½ tsp (2 ml) salt

½ cup (125 ml) cold butter

Place the egg yolks in a bowl and beat vigorously over low heat, while slowly adding the hot water. When well mixed, remove from the heat and add the remaining ingredients. Return to low heat and proceed as for chef's hollandaise. Makes 1½ cups (375 ml).

Sauce béarnaise

Serve with baked or fried fish, beef tenderloin, sautéed tournedos, as well as egg dishes and cheese soufflés.

Prepare a hollandaise, but substitute the following mixture for the lemon juice.

4 tbsp (60 ml) cider or wine vinegar

1 shallot, minced

1 tsp (5 ml) minced fresh tarragon or dried tarragon

4 peppercorns, freshly ground

Reduce the vinegar, shallot, tarragon and pepper to 2 tablespoons (30 ml), then add to the *hollandaise* mixture instead of the lemon juice.

Blender hollandaise

Using the hot-water hollandaise recipe, proceed in the following manner: Rinse your blender container with hot water. Place the egg yolks, hot water, lemon juice and seasoning in the container.

Melt the butter over medium heat.

Cover the blender container and blend at high speed for 3 seconds. Keep the blender turned on as you remove the cover and pour in the hot melted butter. As soon as all the butter has been added, the hollandaise is ready.

VARIATIONS

Bordeaux hollandaise

Make a *chef's hollandaise* or hot-water hollandaise, but replace the lemon juice, or the hot water and lemon juice, with an equal amount of white wine or white-wine vinegar. Add minced fresh tarragon, chives, parsley or dill to taste immediately before serving with fish, boiled chicken or mild vegetables.

Sauce mousseline

Whip ¼ to ½ cup (60 to 125 ml) heavy cream until very thick. Immediately before serving, beat the whipped cream into 1 cup (250 ml) of chef's hollandaise. This is perfect to serve with fish, boiled vegetables, or a soufflé.

Light mousseline sauce

Beat until stiff the egg whites left over from making the *hollandaise*. Add these to the sauce immediately before serving. This mousseline can be served either hot or cold.

Sauce Choron

Add 2 tablespoons (30 ml) tomato paste to a recipe for *hollandaise* or *béarnaise*. Serve with beef tenderloin, roast veal, meat loaf and fried fish.

Sauce maltaise

Make a *hot-water hollandaise,* but replace the hot water with hot orange juice. Add 1 teaspoon (5 ml) grated orange rind to the sauce immediately before serving. This is best served with asparagus, artichokes or herring dishes.

Sauce muscovite

To *chef's hollandaise* add 2 tablespoons (30 ml) heavy cream, 2 to 3 tablespoons (30 to 50 ml) black caviar, and the grated rind of ½ lemon or lime. Serve with fresh poached salmon, Dover sole, poached eggs or fish soufflés.

Special chef's secrets

0→ Add 2 to 3 tablespoons (30 to 50 ml) of cold or hot *hollandaise* to 1 cup (250 ml) of white sauce when you want it to be smoother and richer.

0→ Add ¼ cup (60 ml) cold *hollandaise* or any of its variations to 1 cup (250 ml) whipped cream to serve over cold poached meat or fish. This goes particularly well with steamed chicken breasts or salmon steak.

0→ Immediately before serving a casserole, pour ¼ cup (60 ml) *hollandaise* over it and brown under the broiler for a few seconds.

COLD EMULSIFIED SAUCES, *mayonnaise and its variations*

Mayonnaise is the typical cold emulsified sauce. It is simple to make, and it is well worth the trouble because there is a world of difference between the mayonnaise you make yourself and the best of the commercial types.

Mayonnaise

Use the best ingredients and have them close at hand before you begin. The better the oil, the better the mayonnaise. Use a good brand at room temperature. The eggs you use should be the freshest possible; they are the strongest emulsifying agents. The mustard also contributes to the emulsifying action.

You will need a 1-quart (1 L) mixing bowl and a wire whisk.

The whole process of emulsifying a mayonnaise will take you about 25 minutes once you have your ingredients and utensils assembled.

If the oil is added too quickly, the mayonnaise will separate and no amount of beating will bind it together again. If this should happen, this is what to do: In clean bowl place 1 teaspoon (5 ml) of dry mustard and mix it into a thin cream with a few drops of water. Then, beating vigorously, start adding to this the separated mayonnaise, drop by drop, as with the oil when you began. You can speed up the process as it re-emulsifies.

If you want a mayonnaise with a tart flavour, add a spoonful or two (15 to 30 ml) of cider vinegar or fresh lemon juice once the mixture has thickened but while you are still beating.

0→ Remember, the secret of a perfect mayonnaise lies in the slow addition of the oil and the use of a wire whisk to beat it.

Store mayonnaise in a well-covered glass jar and keep it in a cool place. Do not freeze or keep in the coldest part of the refrigerator. The oil will solidify at too cold a temperature, and in all probability the emulsion will break down.

Mayonnaise

2 egg yolks

½ tsp (2 ml) dry mustard

2 to 4 tbsp (30 to 60 ml) cider vinegar, white wine or fresh lemon juice

1 cup (250 ml) olive oil or salad oil

1 tsp (5 ml) salt

Place the egg yolks in the bowl. Add the dry mustard and 2 tablespoons (30 ml) of the vinegar, wine or lemon juice. Mix well with a wire whisk. When well mixed, add the oil; *the way the oil is added is the secret of making mayon-* *naise successfully. Add it almost drop by drop, and beat vigorously and constantly with the wire whisk until the mixture is emulsified.* You will know when this takes place because the texture will become smooth and creamy. Once this happens, you can add the oil a little more quickly, but never add too much at one time. Make sure the oil has been completely beaten in before adding more. The more slowly the oil is added in the beginning, the firmer the mayonnaise will be. A perfect mayonnaise should have the consistency of thick whipped cream. Add the salt toward the end and taste to be sure the seasoning is just right.

VARIATIONS

Swedish mayonnaise *(for cold boiled ham and meat salads)*
Add to 1 cup (250 ml) mayonnaise, 1 tablespoon (15 ml) well-drained prepared horseradish, 1 tablespoon (15 ml) prepared German mustard, 3 tablespoons (50 ml) applesauce. Blend well.

Russian mayonnaise *(for cold or jellied fish or othere seafood)*
Add to 1 cup (250 ml) mayonnaise, 2 tablespoons (30 ml) black caviar, 1 teaspoon (5 ml) prepared Dijon mustard, ½ teaspoon (2 ml) crumbled dried tarragon. Blend well.

Green mayonnaise *(for cold chicken, aspics, salmon, jellied vegetables)*
Chop 1 well-packed cup (250 ml) of fresh spinach very fine. Mince ¼ cup (50 ml) parsley leaves. Place both in a bowl and add ¼ to ½ cup (60 to 125 ml) boiling water; the leaves should be covered. Let stand for 3 minutes. Strain through cheesecloth into a bowl, allowing the water to drip out for 1 hour. Reserve the liquid. Add the reserved liquid to 1 cup (250 ml) mayonnaise. The soaking and draining are necessary to give extra deep colour to the mayonnaise.

If you have a blender, place the mayonnaise mixed with the water into the blender container and add the drained chopped spinach and parsley. Cover and blend for 2 seconds. If you do not have a blender, mix well in a bowl. The mayonnaise will turn a beautiful green colour.

Horseradish mayonnaise *(for cold ham, meat and fish salads, cabbage, potato salad)*
Whip ½ cup (125 ml) heavy cream. Fold in 3 tablespoons (50 ml) well-drained prepared horseradish. Fold the mixture into 1 cup (250 ml) mayonnaise.

Tartar sauce *(for all fried fish and other seafood)*
Dice ½ cup (125 ml) sweet pickles very fine. Slice 2 small sour gherkins thin. Mince 2 tablespoons (30 ml) chives or parsley. Add all to 1 cup (250 ml) mayonnaise with 1 tablespoon (15 ml) capers. Blend well.

Watercress mayonnaise or mayonnaise cressonière *(for cold meat, mild fish, vegetables, eggs)*
Grate 1 hard-cooked egg. Chop the leaves of 1 bunch of watercress; there should be ½ to ¾ cup (125 to 190 ml)

chopped leaves. Add these to 1 cup (250 ml) mayonnaise with 1 teaspoon (5 ml) anchovy paste. Blend well.

Mustard mayonnaise or mayonnaise dijonnaise *(for hors d'oeuvres, fish, salads of all types)*

Grate 1 hard-cooked egg. Add 1 tablespoon (15 ml) prepared Dijon mustard to the grated egg and blend together until creamy. Add the mixture to 1 cup (250 ml) mayonnaise made with lemon juice rather than vinegar (or with half lemon juice and half vinegar). Blend well.

MORE TASTY SAUCES

In addition to the basic sauces that can be varied in so many different ways, here are some of the secondary sauces.

Curry mayonnaise or mayonnaise indienne *(for eggs, chicken, seafood, vegetables)*

Blend together 1 teaspoon (5 ml) curry powder, ½ teaspoon (2 ml) ground turmeric, and 1 teaspoon (5 ml) of brandy, sherry or lemon juice. When well blended, add to 1 cup (250 ml) mayonnaise with chives or parsley to taste. Blend well.

Pimiento mayonnaise or mayonnaise niçoise *(for salads, tomatoes, fish)*

Blend together 1 red pimiento chopped fine, 1 teaspoon (5 ml) tomato paste, and ½ teaspoon (2 ml) crumbled dried tarragon. When well blended, add to 1 cup (250 ml) mayonnaise. Mix well.

There is nothing quite like a well-made bread sauce to accompany roasted chicken or broiled or roasted game birds.

English bread sauce

6 whole cloves

1 medium-size onion, peeled

1½ cups (375 ml) milk

2 inch (5 cm) piece of lemon rind

¾ cup (190 ml) soft white bread crumbs, from fresh bread

2 tbsp (30 ml) butter

Salt and pepper

Stud in peeled onion with the cloves and place the onion in the top part of a double boiler with the milk and lemon rind. Heat over boiling water, covered, for 30 minutes. Do not let the milk boil. Remove and discard the onion with cloves and the lemon rind.

Add to the milk the soft bread crumbs. (All trace of crust should be removed when making the crumbs; crusts would cause discolouration of the white sauce.) Add 1 tablespoon (15 ml) of the butter. Cook, beating with a wire whisk or hand beater, until the sauce is smooth and creamy and has absorbed all the crumbs. Add salt and pepper to taste. Add the second tablespoon (15 ml) of butter and stir until it has melted. Serve immediately, as the sauce will turn yellow if kept standing. Makes about 2 cups (500 ml).

Mint sauce

Serve this popular sauce with all lamb dishes.

¾ cup (190 ml) minced fresh mint

1 tsp (5 ml) salt

¼ cup (60 ml) cider or white-wine vinegar

1 tbsp (15 ml) sugar

¼ tsp (1 ml) ground ginger

1 tsp (5 ml) lemon juice

Place all the ingredients in a screw-top jar and shake hard for a few seconds. Refrigerate for 6 to 12 hours before using. Makes about ½ cup (125 ml).

Mustard cream sauce

This excellent English sauce goes particularly well with charcoal-broiled lamb, veal kidneys and beef.

2 egg yolks

½ tsp (2 ml) dry mustard

½ tsp (2 ml) tomato paste

1 tbsp (15 ml) tarragon vinegar

Salt

Cayenne pepper

4 tbsp (60 ml) light cream

¼ pound (125 gr) butter

Place in a bowl the egg yolks, mustard, tomato paste, tarragon vinegar, and salt and cayenne to taste. Beat with a wire whisk until smooth. Add 1 tablespoon (15 ml) of the cream and mix in. Place the bowl over hot water and beat until the sauce thickens. Beat in the butter, piece by piece. Thin the sauce by adding some or all of the remaining cream, 1 teaspoon (5 ml) at a time, until you have achieved the desired consistency. makes about 1 cup (250 ml).

Scandinavian egg sauce

Use this unusual sauce with boiled poultry, white meat or poached fish.

4 hard-cooked eggs

2 tbsp (30 ml) butter

1 tbsp (15 ml) flour

2 cups (500 ml) chicken stock

⅛ tsp (0.5 ml) ground savory

¼ cup (60 ml) minced parsley

Salt and pepper

Capers (optional)

Separate the eggs. Mash the yolks with the butter and flour until well blended. Stir in the chicken stock and simmer for 5 to 7 minutes, stirring occasionally. Remove from the heat and add the savory, parsley, and salt and pepper to taste. Shred the egg whites and add them and the capers; stir. Makes about 2 cups (500 ml).

This is not a spaghetti sauce, but fresh-tasting tomato sauce to be served with meat, eggs or fish. It freezes very well. When tomatoes are in full season, make the sauce in quantity and store in the freezer for use throughout the year.

3 tbsp (50 ml) butter

1½ tbsp (25 ml) flour

½ tsp (2 ml) salt

Pinch of cayenne pepper

2 tbsp (30 ml) tomato paste

1 small garlic clove, crushed

½ tsp (2 ml) minced fresh basil

2 large tomatoes, peeled and sliced

1 tsp (5 ml) honey

1½ cups (375 ml) water

Melt 2 tablespoons (30 ml) of the butter and blend in the flour, salt, cayenne, tomato paste and crushed garlic. Stir until well blended. Add the basil, sliced tomatoes, honey and water. Stir over medium heat until sauce comes to a boil. Simmer over reduced heat for 10 to 15 minutes. Immediately before serving, add the remaining tablespoon (15 ml) of butter. Adjust seasoning. If you wish, you can add ¼ cup (60 ml) minced fresh parsley at this point. Makes about 2 cups (500 ml).

Fresh tomato sauce I

This sauce is somewhat thicker and richer and is flavoured differently from the sauce above. Since it is puréed, it has a velvety texture

5 tbsp (75 ml) unsalted butter

1 onion minced

1 tbsp (15 ml) all-purpose flour

6 large fresh tomatoes

1 tbsp (15 ml) sugar

½ tsp (2 ml) dried thyme

Pinch of grated nutmeg

Salt and pepper

1 tbsp (15 ml) tomato paste

Melt 4 tablespoons (60 ml) of the butter and add the onion. Cook together over low heat until the onion is soft but not brown. Sprinkle the flour on top and blend thoroughly.

Chop the unpeeled tomatoes into small pieces and add them to the onion with the sugar, thyme, nutmeg, and salt and pepper to taste. Bring to a boil, stirring constantly. Cover and cook over low heat for 15 minutes. Remove from heat and pass the sauce througfh a coarse strainer to get rid of seeds and peels, then purée it in a blender or food mill, or by pushing through a fine strainer. Add the tomato paste and the remaining 1 tablespoon (15 ml) butter to the purée. Stir until the butter is melted. Taste, and add more seasoning if necessary. Makes about 4 cups (1 L).

Fresh tomato sauce II

Verona spaghetti sauce

This is one of the few Italian sauces for pasta that can be prepared in 30 minutes. Not only is it delicious, but it has the added advantage of being easily digestible. Its the perfect sauce for spaghetti.

7 tbsp (100 ml) butter

1 lb (500 gr) chicken livers

2 garlic cloves, crushed

2 large onions, chopped fine

¼ lb (125 ml) mushrooms, chopped fine

Salt and pepper

Pinch of dry mustard

5 tomatoes, peeled and chopped into large pieces

1 tbsp (15 ml) flour

3 tbsp (50 ml) tomato paste

1 cup (250 ml) canned condensed consommé, undiluted

1 tsp (5 ml) dried basil

½ tsp (2 ml) dried marjoram

¼ tsp (1 ml) dried rosemary

Heat a large frying pan. Place 2 tablespoons (30 ml) of the butter in the heated pan and, just when it is about to turn brown, add the chicken livers. Cook over high heat until chicken livers are well browned. Remove the chicken livers. Place 2 more tablespoons (30 ml) of the butter in the same pan and melt. Add the crushed garlic and cook for 1 minute. Add the onions and cook quickly until they begin to brown. Add the mushrooms, lower the heat, and cook slowly for another 5 or 6 minutes. Add more butter if necessary to keep mushrooms from sticking. Season with salt and pepper along with a pinch of dry mustard. Add the 5 tomatoes and cook for 2 minutes.

Remove the pan from the heat and blend in the flour and tomato paste. When these are blended, pour on the consommé and return to the heat and stir constantly until the mixture comes to a boil. Simmer for about 10 minutes. Chop the reserved chicken livers and add to the sauce along with the basil, marjoram and rosemary. Simmer for about another 5 minutes. Stir in the remaining butter just before serving. Makes enough sauce for 1 pound (500 gr) of spaghetti.

SALAD DRESSINGS

Salad dressings are sauces too. You have already had an example of a sauce that we often use for salads — mayonnaise. While we most often use these cold sauces to dress lettuce leaves or other greens, they are also used to dress vegetables and other foods, asparagus with vinaigrette sauce for instance. The sauce the French call *sauce vinaigrette* is almost the same as the one we call French dressing. And French dressing can have endless variations.

The best-known and simplest salad dressing is prepared by mixing 1 part vinegar with 2 to 3 parts oil and adding salt and pepper to taste. The flavour and colour of this dressing will vary, however, depending on whether you use French, Italian, Spanish or Greek olive oil, or corn oil, and whether you use a white, cider or malt vinegar, or a white — or red-wine vinegar, or a vinegar flavoured with tarragon, garlic or basil. You can also use lemon juice instead of vinegar and freshly ground white pepper instead of black.

If you want to be an accomplished cook, you will vary the ingredients in your salad dressing to suit the dish it is intended to enhance. Only by constantly experimenting will you discover what combinations you like best.

0—🗝 With tomatoes, use white vinegar with basil and an Italian or Greek olive oil. 0—🗝 With cold salmon, use lemon juice with French olive oil.

0—🗝 With rice and fresh vegetables, use cider vinegar and corn oil. 0—🗝 With an everyday salad, fresh lemon juice is best, with a French or Spanish olive oil, freshly ground black pepper, and coarse salt crushed in the bottom of the bowl before the vegetables are added.

These are only a few suggestions. Experiment for yourself and you will discover all sorts of interesting combinations to suit your own taste.

French dressing, American style

2 tbsp (30 ml) fresh or bottled lemon juice

2 tbsp (30 ml) cider vinegar

¾ cup (200 ml) salad oil

1 tsp (5 ml) salt

¼ tsp (1 ml) pepper

1 tsp (5 ml) Worcestershire sauce

½ tsp (2 ml) paprika

¼ tsp (1 ml) garlic powder

½ tsp (2 ml) sugar

Mix all the ingredients in a blender, or shake in a glass jar, or beat with a rotary beater. The dressing will keep for 2 to 3 weeks. Shake well before using. Makes about 1 cup (250 ml).

Chiffonade dressing

Add to the above recipe 2 tablespoons (30 ml) minced parsley, 2 teaspoons (10 ml) each of diced green pepper and pimiento, 2 minced green onions, and 1 grated hard-cooked egg. Add salt if necessary. Blend, shake or beat, just as for the basic recipe.

Danish dressing

This can serve as a year-round recipe for those who like a piquant dressing. It is delicious on sliced or diced cucumbers, and perfect on cold broiled or barbecued chicken. It has a different flavour from Roquefort dressing, even though both are made with blue cheese.

4 oz (115 ml) Danish blue cheese

½ cup (125 ml) salad oil

1 tbsp (15 ml) Worcestershire or H.P. Sauce

1 tbsp (15 ml) lemon juice

1 tbsp (15 ml) vinegar

¼ tsp (1 ml) dried basil

Mash the cheese with a few tablespoons (30 to 50 ml) of the oil. Add the rest of the oil and the rest of the ingredients. Beat thoroughly. The dressing will keep, covered and refrigerated, for a few weeks. Shake well before using. If the oil is thick and opaque, leave at room temperature for 15 to 25 minutes. Makes about 1½ cups (375 ml).

English dressing

½ cup (125 ml) tarragon vinegar

1 cup (250 ml) olive oil

1 tsp (5 ml) dry mustard

½ tsp (2 ml) Worcestershire sauce

½ tsp (2 ml) salt

½ tsp (2 ml) pepper

¼ tsp (1 ml) celery seeds

2 ice cubes

Place the vinegar in a bowl and gradually add the oil, beating constantly as you add. Then add the dry mustard, Worcestershire sauce, salt, pepper, and celery seeds, 1 ingredient at a time, beating well after each addition. Add the ice cubes and beat for 3 to 4 seconds. Refrigerate for 30 minutes. Stir well before using.
Makes about 1⅔ cups (410 ml).

American salad dressing

1 cup (250 ml) salad oil

¼ cup (60 ml) malt vinegar

1½ tbsp (25 ml) ketchup

1 tsp (5 ml) sugar

½ tsp (2 ml) paprika

1 tsp (5 ml) salt

½ tsp (2 ml) dry mustard

1 tsp (5 ml) grated onion

1 egg white, unbeaten

Place all the ingredients in a bowl and beat with a hand beater or electric beater until well blended. Keep refrigerated. Shake well before using. Makes about 1½ cups (375 ml).

Roquefort dressing

4 oz (115 ml) Roquefort cheese

¼ tsp (1 ml) salt

¼ tsp (1 ml) paprika

6 tbsp (90 ml) cider vinegar or port wine

6 to 8 tbsp (90 to 120 ml) olive oil

Place the cheese in a bowl and crush it with a fork. Add the salt, paprika, vinegar and oil. Beat with a wire whisk until the mixture is smooth and creamy. If you prefer, force the dressing through a fine sieve. Store in a closed jar in the refrigerator. Makes about 2 cups (500 ml).

Honey dressing for fruit salads

3 tbsp (50 ml) honey

1 tbsp (15 ml) lemon juice

1 cup (250 ml) heavy cream

Pinch of salt

Mix the honey and the lemon juice together. Whip the cream and add to the mixture along with the salt, folding it in gradually. Makes 2 cups (500 ml).

⅓ cup (80 ml) heavy or light cream

½ tsp (2 ml) salt

1½ tsp (7 ml) poppy seeds

⅓ cup (80 ml) honey

⅓ cup (80 ml) lemon juice

Combine all together, place in a container with a lid and shake hard. The lemon juice will thicken the cream. Makes about 1 cup (250 ml).

Poppy-seed dressing for fruit salads

DESSERT SAUCES

Sauces are also used with desserts of all kinds. A sauce can transform something simple into a party dessert. Here are a few examples.

This superb light but rich custard sauce can be served hot or cold with fruits, cakes, puddings and soufflés.

Custard sauce

2 cups (500 ml) light cream, or
1 cup (250 ml) light cream and
1 cup (250 ml) milk

¼ cup (60 ml) sugar

½ vanilla bean

½ cup (125 ml) cold milk

4 egg yolks

1 tbsp (15 ml) cornstarch

¼ tsp (1 ml) salt

2 tbsp (30 ml) butter

In a sauce pan place the cream, or the cream and milk, the sugar and the vanilla bean. Heat slowly over low heat. Beat together the cold milk and the egg yolks. Add the cornstarch and salt. Pour into the hot cream, beating as you pour, and continue to beat with a wire whisk until blended. Add the butter. Continue to cook over low heat, stirring constantly, until the mixture coats the back of the spoon.

If the sauce is to be served hot, remove the vanilla bean at once. If it is to be served cold, remove the vanilla bean only after the sauce has cooled. Makes about 3½ cups (875 ml).

This is an uncooked creamy light sauce, good for all types of desserts.

Vanilla brandy sauce

⅓ cup (80 ml) unsalted butter

1¾ cups (440 ml) sifted icing sugar

2 eggs, separated

3 tbsp (50 ml) brandy

2 tsp (10 ml) vanilla extract

1 cup (250 ml) heavy cream

Cream the butter with the sifted sugar until fluffy and smooth. Beat the egg yolks with the brandy and vanilla. Add to the butter mixture. Beat with a rotary beater or whisk until well blended. Beat the egg whites stiff and fold in. Refrigerate until ready to serve, then whip the cream. Stir the sauce and fold in the whipped cream. Makes about 3 cups (750 ml).

Mocha chocolate sauce

Perfect for light-coloured puddings, for chocolate, coffee or vanilla soufflés and for custards or ice cream.

2 cups (500 ml) water

½ cup (125 ml) sugar

⅓ cup (80 ml) powdered cocoa (use only pure cocoa)

1 ½ tbsp (25 ml) cornstarch

Pinch of salt

2 tsp (10 ml) instant coffee powder

½ tsp (2 ml) vanilla extract

Bring 1 ½ cups (375 ml) of the water to a boil and add the sugar. Stir until the sugar is dissolved, then boil for 5 minutes. Remove from the heat.

Blend together the cocoa, cornstarch, salt and remaining ½ cup (125 ml) cold water. When smooth, add to the hot syrup. Stir over medium heat until creamy, then simmer over low heat for 3 minutes. Add the instant coffee powder and the vanilla. Stir until the coffee is blended. Serve hot or cold. This recipe makes about 2 cups (500 ml).

Whipped cream and chocolate

It is easy to whip heavy (or whipping) cream with a rotary hand beater or electric beater. But if you do not have heavy cream on hand and you want to make a sauce that calls for whipped cream, you can use powdered skim milk or evaporated milk, instead.

To whip powdered skim milk

Combine ½ cup (125 ml) of powdered skim milk and ½ cup (125 ml) ice water in a bowl. Whip 3 to 4 minutes, using an electric or hand beater, until soft peaks form. Add 2 tablespoons (30 ml) lemon juice. Continue whipping for another 3 to 4 minutes, until stiff peaks form. Gradually add ¼ cup (50 ml) icing sugar. Makes 2½ cups (625 ml).

To whip evaporated milk

Place 1 can (6 ounces/170 gr) of evaporated milk in the refrigerator until it is quite cold, or in the freezer for 1 hour. Pour the undiluted contents into a cold bowl and whip for 2 to 3 minutes. Add 2 tablespoons (30 ml) fresh lemon juice. Continue to whip for another 3 to 4 minutes until stiff peaks form. Gradually add icing sugar to taste. Makes 2 cups (500 ml).

Chocolate is another ingredient sometimes called for in dessert sauces. If you do not have any, you can replace 1 square (1 ounce/28 gr) of unsweetened chocolate with 3 tablespoons (50 ml) powdered cocoa and 1 tablespoon (15 ml) butter. To replace the same amount of semisweet chocolate, use the same amount of cocoa and butter plus ½ teaspoon (2 ml) fine granulated sugar.

CHAPTER 8

Freezing foods

WHETHER it actually pays to own a freezer is of little concern to some people who feel that convenience alone is worth whatever it costs. Buying one represents such a considerable investment, however, that for most people it must be justified economically. Here are some of the factors to consider when evaluating the economic usefulness of a freezer:

1. At first glance it would appear that buying wholesale cuts of meat, such as a quarter or half of beef, offers great savings. But it isn't that simple. You need a very large freezer to hold a wholesale cut of a large animal, and you need to know how to cut up these large sections. The only way you could really save is to use all the fat, bones and other low-cost parts. This does not mean that it is impossible to economize on the monthly meat bill through the use of a freezer. It is possible, because nearly every store runs weekly or seasonal low-price specials on retail cuts, which do not include the fat, bones and gristle present in the quarter or half of beef. **O—⚷** When you own a freezer, you can take advantage of these special prices and stock up against the time when prices will inevitably be higher. By following specials and noting when they are offered, you will know when to take advantage of the best buys.

2. O—⚷ You can save by dividing your low-cost purchases. For example, a large turkey may be too much for your family at once, but it may be a better buy than a smaller bird. Buy the turkey that costs less per pound and ask the butcher to cut it into halves. Wrap one half and freeze it for later use.

3. The freezer can help you provide greater variety in meals. It is no longer necessary to eat some particular prepared food until your family is tired of it. If you freeze part of it, it will be an appetizing new dish for another occasion instead of a boring leftover.

4. Buy large quantities when special prices warrant it. There are advantages and savings when you buy four to six frying chickens at a time when they are offered as specials. Freeze legs or wings or livers; then, when time or money are short, you can turn to the freezer for a good chicken dinner.

If you have a dozen legs in your freezer, you have uniform pieces for guests; or you can prepare attractive dishes for occasions such as a buffet.

5. It might seem that one of the main purposes of a freezer is to store commercial frozen fruits and vegetables, but this is economical only when you are able to take advantage of a real bargain. Generally speaking, it is easy to buy frozen products when you need them; they are always readily available.

Freezing fresh vegetables in the summer when their price is lowest is economical. But remember that many fruits and vegetables are available at a fair price all year long.

O━☞ So buy commercial frozen vegetables and fruits only when you can take advantage of special price offers.

O━☞ When freezing vegetables and fruits that are in full season and at lowest cost, remember these two important guidelines: Buy the freshest ingredients and freeze them as soon as they reach your kitchen. Fruits and vegetables that sit all night will not produce as good a frozen product as those frozen as quickly as possible after purchase or, better still, after being gathered fresh from a garden.

6. When preparing anything that requires long cooking, such as stews, or foods that call for use of the oven, such as cakes or pies, you can economize on fuel with the help of the freezer. Instead of making only one cake, make several and freeze the extras. Instead of making stew for one occasion, make a larger amount and freeze enough for later meals.

7. If ice cream is a favourite in your family, stock your freezer when prices are low. Also, use your freezer to make certain kinds of ice cream. The freezer makes it possible to have all sorts of special or party ice creams on hand.

8. A freezer can be a tremendous help to a family with adults who work outside the home. Individual or family-sized servings can be kept to feed the family. Small casseroles and desserts can be frozen in ovenproof dishes that can go straight from the freezer into the oven.

9. A family with a freezer can cut down the number of shopping trips, saving time and money.

10. O━☞ Some foods normally stored in packages in a cupboard will keep fresher and retain better taste and colour if stored in the freezer. Nuts and candied or glazed fruits are good examples.

11. Leftovers can be frozen for later use. Syrups from canned fruits, leftover gravy and leftover pancakes and waffles are some examples. Leftover vegetables stored in the freezer can be puréed to make nutritious soups, or can be added to stews or salads for variety. Freezing can reduce waste in your kitchen, thereby saving on food costs.

12. One wonderful aspect of a freezer is that the cupboard is never bare. Friends can appear at opportune or inopportune times, the weather may be too unpleasant to go shopping, or you may not feel up to shopping or cooking. Whatever the circumstances, you will never find yourself at a disadvantage if you have been wise enough to keep your freezer well stocked.

13. Arrange the foods in your freezer so you can find things easily. Store frozen fruits in one part, vegetables in another, baked goods in another and so on. Mark contents and the date frozen on the food packages.

Do not try to freeze too much food at one time. Usually one-tenth of the capacity of the freezer is the maximum; more than this will raise the temperature, which may spoil foods already stored there and slow the freezing of the new items. Quick freezing makes a better, more nutritious product, less likely to spoil.

14. The freezer is designed to work best at ordinary room temperature. Even though it is below freezing inside the box, on the outside it should not be below 40°F (4.4°C) or the motor lubricants will start to congeal. Therefore, place the freezer in the same sort of area as your refrigerator.

WHAT NOT TO FREEZE

Only a few foods cannot be frozen successfully. Tomatoes, cucumbers and cabbage cannot be frozen when raw. Pears do not freeze satisfactorily because they turn brown. ☛ Celery cannot be frozen whole, but it can be if it is cut into pieces. This is handy, since it is often used in cooked dishes. Mince the leaves. Dice the celery ribs. Package, uncooked, in separate bags. Add while still frozen to the dish to be cooked. The flavor will be just as good as fresh, but remember that frozen celery cannot be used in a salad, or raw in any uncooked preparations because it wilts when it defrosts.

Boiled potatoes become mealy when frozen. Remember this if you are planning to freeze a stew or casserole; leave the potatoes out.

Boiled frosting turns sticky.

Commercial sour cream separates.

Mayonnaise separates. ☛ However, if you plan to use it in sandwiches, mix it thoroughly with creamed butter; this prevents separation.

Custard and cream pies should not be frozen. They have a tendency to curdle or separate.

Stuffed poultry of all types should not be frozen, but poultry stuffing can be frozen separately.

Cured meats — bacon, ham, sausages — can be frozen, but the salt used in curing slows the freezing process and tends to cause the fat in the tissues to become rancid. Therefore, they have a short freezer life.

PLANNING THE SEASON'S FROZEN FOOD SUPPLY

It is important to be methodical when planning the food supply in a freezer for a season or for a full year. ☛ Keep an annual record of what you want to have in your freezer; what you had; what did not keep well; what was most useful or most economical; the cost or the economy realized on different items; and menus of the meals served with the foods in the freezer, ready cooked and to be cooked. This will help you eliminate items that prove too costly.

You can freeze foods you have purchased when they are at their freshest and most nutritious. However, technical discoveries have so improved the quality of commercial frozen foods that often they are better than home-frozen foods, and competition among processors has made them cheaper than ever. So it is worthwhile to process fruits and vegetables yourself only when you have an inexpensive supply of first-class produce available; when you can freeze some kind your family enjoys that is not readily available commercially, or when you do something special to it, such as turning fruits into sauces or preparing soup base from leeks. (You'll find methods for these in the following pages).

The following tables give an estimate of the number of 1-pint or 1-pound (0.5 L or 500 gr) packages a family of four might use in a year. Remove from the lists items you know your family would never use. Remember, the economical way is to buy good commercial brands on sale at special prices, unless you grow your own. Your freezer probably cannot hold these quantities at one time, so you will need to replenish periodically.

Fruits

Apples, baked	15 pounds (6.8 kg)
Apples, sliced (partly cooked)	5 packages
Applesauce	20 packages
Blueberries	25 packages
Cherries, pitted, sugared	20 packages
Grapefruit in syrup	10 packages
Peaches	25 packages
Pineapple	20 packages
Raspberries	15 packages
Rhubarb	15 to 20 packages
Strawberries, commercially frozen	15 packages
Strawberries, home frozen	20 packages

This list represents about one package of fruit or fruit products a day for the time of year when fresh counterparts are not available. The fruits can be either home-processed or commercial brands. Further on in this capter you will find details on how to do your own processing, packaging and wrapping.

Vegetables

Asparagus	20 to 25 packages
Beet greens	6 to 8 packages
Broccoli	10 packages
Carrots, diced or creamed	20 packages
Cauliflower	10 packages
Corn, cut from cobs	20 packages
Corn, on the cobs, 6 ears per package	8 to 10 packages
Leeks	10 packages
Mushrooms, blanched	12 packages
Mushrooms, buttered	10 packages
Onions	5 packages
Peas, green	25 packages
Peppers, green and red, cut into different shapes	10 packages
Pumpkin (for pies)	15 packages
Spinach	10 packages

Meats, poultry and fish

While people's eating habits vary a good deal in consumption of fruits and vegetables, they vary still more with regard to meats. This makes it quite difficult to estimate the amount of meat a family should store in the freezer. Here is the best way to make an assessment on the amount of meat each person will need for a year.

Assuming meat is served only once a day, and allowing 4 ounces (113 gr) per serving, this would add up to 90 pounds (41 kg) of meat a year for each person. Assuming that you won't eat at home every day, a fair estimate would be to allow for 75 pounds (34 kg) per person per year, or about 300 pounds (136 kg) per year for a family of four.

This estimate includes beef, lamb, pork, ham, chicken, turkey and duck. Include fish also and count on at least one meal a week at which fish is served instead of meat or poultry.

Take advantage of specials and keep your freezer stocked with the cuts of meat, poultry and fish you and your family prefer. However, the usefulness of a freezer does not stop with fruits, vegetables and meats, since you can freeze everything from soup to nuts.

Miscellaneous foods

This is a list of foods that might be found in a large family freezer. Many of the items are constantly being used, such as butter, bread, coffee, ready-cooked foods and soup.

Bread; assorted	Ice cream
Butter, unsalted and salted	Lemon and orange rinds, grated
Cake, without icing	Marshmallows
Candies and fudge	Nuts, in the shell
Coconut, fresh, grated or sliced	Nuts, shelled, assorted
Coffee in beans	Pies
Dripping, in ½-pound packages	Rolls, home baked or bought
Eggs, whole (not in shell)	Sandwich filling
Egg yolks	Soups
Egg whites	Tea and coffee
Gingerroot, fresh	Turkey or chicken dressing

FREEZING

When you come to the actual steps of freezing, some basic information is useful for all kinds of foods.

First, remember that a freezer is not a magician; it does not improve food. Its function is to preserve quality and prevent spoiling. **0—** Therefore, it is not economical to freeze anything but first-class produce and you must do it as soon after you buy it as possible.

0— Liquids expand in freezing, so allow ½-inch (1.25 cm) headspace at the top of containers holding liquids or foods that have been packed in liquids.

0— Never freeze more food in a container than you can serve at one time. This is particularly important with cooked foods. Frozen foods lose nutritional value more quickly when thawed than freshly cooked unfrozen foods.

Seasoning foods to be frozen

0— Some seasonings — pepper, cloves and curry powder, for example — tend to intensify in flavour when they are frozen. And foods such as celery, green pepper and garlic taste stronger. When preparing foods for freezing, it's a good idea to season with a light hand and to adjust the seasoning, as needed, when the food is reheated.

0— Salt tends to lose flavour when frozen. The first time you prepare baked goods, such as cakes, pies and cookies for the freezer, use the quantity of salt called for in the recipe. After your family has sampled the first batch, you can increase the amount of salt to their taste the next time you bake the same recipe for freezing. Remember to record the quantity of salt used for future reference.

Wrapping and packaging

Packages for freezing must give adequate protection against moisture and vapour losses. So the colour, flavour and texture of the food won't deteriorate. Also, the package material must be odourless and tasteless. Here is a list of possible wrappings and containers:

Laminated freezer paper
Transparent plastic wrap
Heavy-duty aluminium foil
Pie plates, pans, and containers made of aluminium foil
Polyethylene containers
Polyethylene bags
Waxed cardboard containers
Casseroles
Coffee cans

Containers are usually sold in 16 ounces/1 pint (0.5 L) and 32 ounces/1 quart (1 L) sizes. Choose the size that will hold only enough fruit or vegetable or prepared food for one meal for your family. Uniformity of package size helps to save freezer space, too. Rigid containers made of heavy aluminium foil, plastic or heavily waxed cardboard are suitable for both dry pack and liquid pack.

Two other important things to have on hand are freezer tape and a marking pencil.

0— When selecting a container or wrapping, keep in mind how the food will be handled when thawed for serving. Foods such as meat loaves, casserole dishes and pies, which require heating in the oven, should be frozen in metal, ovenproof glass or pottery containers. Breads that require reheating should be wrapped in aluminium foil. Cakes and cookies that do not require reheating or that must be unwrapped for baking, can be stored in boxes, polyethylene bags or transparent plastic wrapping. Never put a plastic-wrapped package in the oven.

Foods that will be removed from the containers to be reheated can be stored well in polyethylene containers, waxed containers or coffee cans.

0— To keep foods at the peak of freshness, they must be completely sealed to keep out all air. When the surface of a food is exposed to the air, evaporation — a form of freezer burn — takes place.

Some containers have covers that fit so tightly that further sealing is not necessary. When in doubt, seal the edge of the cover with freezer tape. When using aluminium foil, shape it around the food. To avoid freezer burn on ice cream, smooth the surface and place a sheet of foil directly over the ice cream.

Wire twists and pipe-stem cleaners are good for sealing plastic bags. Force the air out and twist the cleaner around the open end several times.

Drugstore wrap

Place the food in the centre of the wrapping material and pad any sharp or protruding edges with extra wrapping, or with a small piece of foil.

Bring the long ends of the wrapping up over the food and fold together, over and over, until they rest on the food. Press gently, molding the wrapping as tightly as possible to the food so that air pockets are removed.

Turn the corners toward the centre at both ends to form a point, then fold each one over and down gainst the food. If you use foil, no further sealing is needed. Other types of wrapping need to be securely closed with freezer tape or tied with string.

Good labels are important

After food is wrapped and sealed, it should be carefully labeled with the contents, the number of servings, and the date. The date is important because the length of time foods can be stored is important. (See charts later in this section).

The ink in some freezer marking pens is indelible, so it's a good idea to attach a piece of freezer tape in a conspicuous place on reusable containers, and print all information on the tape. Don't forget the labels; as the weeks go by, frozen-food packages begin to look alike and your memory can trick you.

STORAGE TIME

Food should be stored in the freezer only so long as it retains its full food value and flavour. After too long there will not only be a loss of value and flavour, but actual deterioration of the food itself, caused by enzymes within it. This brief chart will give you some idea of these storage times. For best taste and nutrition, use your frozen foods within the number of months listed under BEST.

NUMBER OF MONTHS FROZEN FOODS RETAIN QUALITY

	BEST	GOOD	FAIR	POOR
Apples, sliced, partly cooked	6	12		
Peaches	6	24		
Cherries, sour, fresh	12	24		
Strawberries, home frozen	4	6	12	
Most vegetables	6	12	18	
Baked goods	4	8		
Butter	3	6		12
Ice cream, sherbet	1	2	3	
Poultry, whole, dressed	6	9	12	
Poultry, cut up	3	6		
Prepared foods, homemade and leftovers	1	2	3	6

HOW TO FREEZE FRUITS

Freezing is a convenient and easy way to preserve many fruits. Freezing fruits at the peak of their seasons makes it possible to have a great variety of seasonal fruits all year round, at low cost.

The condition of fruit before freezing largely determines its quality when served. Select only fresh fruits that are at an ideal stage of maturity for good eating. Do not freeze fruit that is green, overripe, bruised or beginning to spoil.

Assemble equipment, ingredients and packages before starting to prepare fruit. Prepare fruit quickly and carefully, working with only enough to fill four containers at one time.

Freeze fruit at 0°F (-18°C) or lower, as soon as possible after packaging. Place packages to be frozen in the fastest freezing area, stacking them so that air can circulate freely. If a delay in getting the packages into the freezer is unavoidable, place them in the refrigerator as soon as they are sealed.

Label all packages with the name of the fruit and date frozen, and any other details that will be helpful.

Packing and sealing

Use any of the following containers for fruits:

- rectangular freezer cartons with polyethylene inner bags
- plastic freezer bags for dry packs
- heavily waxed, cylindrical freezer cartons with slip-over or slip-in lids
- flexible plastic containers

When freezing liquids or foods that have been packed in liquids, remember that it is essential to leave a headspace of ½-inch (1.25 cm) in containers.

Pack fruit tightly to cut down on the amount of air in the package. When fruit is packed in bags, press air out of the unfilled part of the bag. Press firmly to prevent air getting back in. Seal immediately, allowing adequate headspace.

To seal freezer bags, twist the neck of the bag, fold the twist over, and secure it with a "twister".

Common gummed paper tapes and Scotch tape are not satisfactory for sealing frozen-food packages. They tend to loosen and peel off at low temperatures. Use freezer tape (sometimes called locker tape) for sealing and labeling.

Ascorbic acid

It is advisable to treat strawberries, raspberries, cherries, apricots, peaches and plums with ascorbic acid to prevent oxidation or browning. You can buy ascorbic acid at pharmacies in powdered or tablet form. The ascorbic acid is added either to the syrup or, in the case of dry sugar pack, to the fruit before the sugar is added. There also are commercial preparations for preserving the natural colour of fruit.

Ascorbic acid for syrup pack: Use ¼ teaspoon (1 ml) powdered ascorbic acid for each 4 cups (1 L) syrup, or 800 milligrams in tablet form for each 4 cups (1 L) sugar.

Ascorbic acid for dry sugar pack: Use ⅛ teaspoon (0.5 ml) powdered ascorbic acid for each 1-pint (0.5 L) container of fruit. Dissolve the ascorbic acid in 2 tablespoons (30 ml) cold water. Sprinkle over the fruit in a bowl and mix gently; then mix in dry sugar. Or use 400 milligrams in table form for each 1-pint (0.5 L) container of fruit. Crush tablets, then dissolve in 2 tablespoons (30 ml) cold water. Sprinkle over fruit in a bowl and mix gently; then mix in dry sugar. The amount of sugar per pint (0.5 L) depends on the fruit used.

SYRUP

Make syrup just before preparing fruit. Don't make more than is immediately required. Ascorbic acid is not stable in solution, so its strength deteriorates when stored. Allow ⅔ to 1 cup (160 to 250 ml) syrup for each 16-fluid-ounce (0.5 L) container.

Add the ascorbic acid (powdered or crushed tablets) to the measured amount of water and stir until dissolved.

Add the required amount of sugar, and again stir to dissolve. Chill while preparing fruit.

TYPE OF SYRUP	SUGAR	WATER	YIELD
Thin	1 cup (250 ml)	2 cups (500 ml)	about 2½ cups (625 ml)
Moderately thin	1 cup (250 ml)	1½ cups (375 ml)	about 2 cups (500 ml)
Medium	1 cup (250 ml)	1 cup (250 ml)	about 1½ cups (375 ml)
Heavy	1 cup (250 ml)	¾ cup (200 ml)	about 1¼ cups (315 ml)

Packing fruits with sugar or syrup
Dry sugar pack: Place fruit, ascorbic acid, and sugar in a bowl and mix gently. Fill containers, seal and freeze.

Syrup pack: Use the strength of syrup that best suits the tartness of the fruit and your personal taste. Slice large fruits directly into containers that have about ⅓ to ½ cup (80 to 125 ml) syrup in them. Be sure the syrup covers the fruit and that headspace is left for expansion.

To keep fruit such as peaches under the syrup and to help prevent surface discolouration, place a crumpled piece of waxed paper on top of the fruit.

Uncooked whole apples
In the summer, you can successfully freeze whole apples for baking, or for use in pies and puddings. The tartness of a summer apple seems to give a better apple flavor throughout the winter.

Wash firm apples without blemishes, then place 6 to 10 of them in a polyethylene freezer bag and put them in the freezer.

To prepare the fruit for cooking, run cold water over each frozen apple for 3 to 5 minutes, then peel, core, slice or whatever the recipe requires. It's important to work fast; apples that thaw before peeling darken quickly. Peel, then cut. To bake them, peel, prepare according to recipe, and bake even if the apple is not completely thawed out.

Sliced apples
Put about 4 quarts (1 L) of water in a large kettle with a cover. Bring to a vigorous boil. This is for blanching, and the water must be ready when you need it.

Select firm apples and have them at room temperature. Peel, core and cut into twelfths. Work with a small amount at a time, about 5 apples, to prevent discolouration. This is enough for 1 package, which will make 1 pie.

As the apples are peeled and cut, drop them into a weak salt brine, 2 tablespoons (30 ml) salt in 1 gallon (4.5 L) water. When one lot is ready, lift apple segments from the brine and place them in a large square of cheesecloth or muslin; have a piece of cloth large enough for easy handling.

Lower the muslin square of apples into the vigorously boiling water and over the kettle. Keep heat on high so the water will quickly return to the boil. As soon as the water returns to a vigorous boil, remove the cover; using a large spoon, force the bag of apples down into the water to ensure uniform blanching. Blanch for 60 seconds, counting from the time when the water begins to boil the second time.

Immediately after blanching, plunge apple segments into cold running water, or into ice water, to chill as quickly as possible. Drain. Package dry without sugar or syrup. Place in freezer.

To use, defrost apple segments only enough to separate pieces, then make into pie in the usual way.

Note: If brown areas appear in the apples after treatment, they were insufficiently blanched.

Baked apples

Use a good baking apple, such as a Jonathan, Rome Beauty or Baldwin. Peel and core the apples. Make a syrup with 2 cups (500 ml) sugar, 1 cup (250 ml) water, 3 whole cloves, a 2-inch (5 cm) piece of cinnamon stick and 8 to 10 coriander seeds. Dip each apple into the boiling syrup for 3 minutes, then lift to a baking pan. Put a few raisins in each cavity, then 1 teaspoon (5 ml) brown sugar and 1 tablespoon (15 ml) butter. Bake in a 350°F (180°C) oven for about 35 minutes, or until the apples are soft, but not mushy or broken. Then set under a broiler for a few seconds to brown the tops. Cool.

To freeze, place the whole uncovered tray in the freezer until the apples are frozen solid. Next day, place the apples in containers, or wrap individually in foil. Label and store in the freezer.

To serve, remove the required number of apples from the container; or unfold the foil from the top of foil-wrapped apples, but leave the foil around the base. Allow them to thaw at room temperature for about 1 hour. If you prefer to serve them hot, place frozen apples in their foil bases on a baking pan and heat in a 425°F (225°C) oven for about 30 minutes, or until apples are soft.

Applesauce

This is particularly good when made from summer apples. Prepare applesauce in the usual manner, sweetening to taste. Cool quickly. Place in containers, leaving a headspace. Seal and freeze.

Pink applesauce

In a large saucepan place 2 cups (500 ml) cranberries, fresh or frozen, 2 to 4 cups (0.5 to 1 L) quartered unpeeled apples and ¾ cup (200 ml) water. Bring to a boil, then cook, uncovered, over low heat until the fruits are tender. Place 1 to 1½ cups (250 to 375 ml) sugar in a bowl. Push the hot fruits through a coarse sieve or a food mill right into the sugar. Stir until the sugar is dissolved; add the grated rind of 1 orange. Cool, package, label and freeze.

Apricots

Apricots freeze with only fair success.

A syrup pack is preferred for apricots to be served uncooked. Use a sugar pack for apricots to be used for pies or other cooked dishes.

Select firm ripe apricots. Wash. Cut apricots into halves or quarters.

Syrup pack: Pack prepared fruit directly into syrup in the containers, using moderately thin syrup. Seal and freeze.

Dry sugar pack: Combine 4 pounds/ 10 cups (1.8 kg/2.5 L) prepared fruit with ascorbic acid (p. 133) and 1 pound/2 cups (500 gr/500 ml) sugar. Pour into containers, seal and freeze.

Cherries, sweet or sour

Uncooked sweet cherries freeze with only fair success, but uncooked sour cherries freeze very well.

Syrup pack: Select well-colored fruit with sweet flavour. Sort, stem, wash and drain. Remove pits if desired; they tend to give an almond like flavour to the fruit. Pack cherries into containers with medium syrup. Seal and freeze.

Dry sugar pack: Not recommended for sweet cherries.

Stewed cherries freeze well, and have excellent flavour. See recipe for stewed prune plums (p. 137), which is especially good for sweet cherries.

Cranberries, raw

These are very nice to freeze since little work is required. Buy the cranberries during the Christmas season when their price is at its lowest. Wrap and label each box as bought, and freeze. To use, no thawing is necessary, even if only a small quantity is needed, since they do not stick to each other. Frozen cranberries will keep in perfect condition for 12 months.

Cranberry relish

The well-known raw-cranberry relish will freeze to perfection and keep for 8 to 12 months. To make, pass 4 cups (1 L) raw cranberries and 2 whole oranges, rind and pulp, through a food chopper together. Stir with 1 ½ cups (375 ml) sugar.

Grapes and cantaloupe

When seedless green grapes are sweet and plentiful, mix them with cantaloupe balls in the proportions you prefer. Divide them into ½-pint (8 ounces/225 gr) boxes, then cover the whole with reconstituted frozen lemon or orange juice, or pink lemonade. Cover, label and freeze. In the winter, serve as is or add to canned fruits for a salad, or serve with a scoop of sherbet.

Peaches

Choose firm ripe peaches. Dip them into boiling water for 30 to 45 seconds, then into cold water. Peel. Work with a small quantity of fruit at a time.

Syrup pack: Slice peaches directly into syrup in the containers, using moderately thin syrup.

Dry sugar pack: Combine 4 pounds/ 10 cups (1.8 kg/2.5 L) sliced peaches with ascorbic acid and 1 pound/2 cups (500 gr/500 ml) sugar. Pour into containers, seal and freeze.

Ripe peaches, sliced and frozen when they are plentiful, can be used in the winter for breakfast, as a dessert or as a sauce over ice cream. Their flavour and colour are splendid.

3 cups (750 ml) fresh orange juice

¼ cup (60 ml) sugar

Juice of 1 lemon

12 to 14 peaches

Remove pits from the orange juice but do not strain it. Mix juice with the sugar and lemon juice. Stir until the sugar is dissolved. Fill ½-pint (250 ml) freezer containers one-third full with the mixture.

Pour boiling water over the peaches, let them stand for 3 minutes, then drain and place in cold water. Peel, and slice directly into the containers. Leave a good headspace, then add enough of the orange-juice mixture to cover the peaches. Place a crumpled piece of freezer paper over the peaches; this will keep them submerged. Seal and freeze. To use, thaw and serve. Makes 6 to 8 cups (1.5 to 2 L).

These small blue plums, sometimes called Italian prunes, are dried to make prunes. Other varieties of plums freeze with only fair success.

4 pounds (1.8 kg) prepared plums

2¼ cups (560 ml) water

1¾ cups (440 ml) sugar

Cut washed prune plums into halves; remove pits; weigh. Bring water to a boil and add prepared fruit. Continue cooking over high heat. Stir in sugar and bring again to a boil. Boil gently, stirring constantly, until fruit is heated through, 5 to 8 minutes. Remove from heat; cool. Fill containers, seal and freeze.

This recipe can also be used for stewed sweet cherries. To prepare them, wash and remove stems; then weigh, and proceed with the recipe.

Uncooked prune plums
While stewed prune plums retain maximum colour and flavour, you can also freeze them uncooked.

Choose firm ripe fruit. Wash, halve and pit.

Syrup pack: Add fruit to thin syrup in freezer containers. Seal and freeze.

Dry syrup pack: Combine 5 pounds/ 13 cups (2.3 kg/3.125 L) prepared fruit with ascorbic acid and 1 pound (500 gr) sugar. Fill containers, seal and freeze.

Rhubarb
There are two simple ways to deal with rhubarb.

First: Wash and trim the rhubarb and cut it into pieces. Then simply place in freezer bags, label and freeze.

In the winter, add very little water to a bagful of frozen rhubarb and simmer over low heat until cooked. Remove from heat and add sugar to taste.

The other way is to make the rhubarb into a sauce before freezing. Cool, package and freeze.

Apricot purée

Select fully ripe fruit. Wash, cut into halves, remove pits. Mash fruit a little to start the juice. Add a little water to prevent scorching, 1 cup (250 ml) water to each 5 pounds (2.3 kg) fruit. Bring quickly to the boil, stirring occasionally. Boil for 1 minute.

Put fruit through food mill or sieve. Sweeten extracted pulp with 1 pound (500 gr) sugar to each 5 pounds (2.3 kg) extracted pulp. Measure ¼ teaspoon (1 ml) ascorbic acid for each 4 cups (1 L) sweetened pulp. Dissolve ascorbic acid in a small amount of cold water, then add to the mixture.

As soon as sugar is dissolved, cool quickly, then fill freezer containers. Seal and freeze.

If preferred, the fruit pulp or purée can be left unsweetened and dissolved ascorbic acid added (¼ teaspoon/1 ml for each 4 cups/1 L). Fill containers, seal and freeze.

Banana purée

Often bananas become too ripe before we have an opportunity to use them. When this happens, peel the bananas and push them through a food mill. Add 1 teaspoon (5 ml) fresh lemon juice, or ¼ teaspoon (1 ml) ascorbic acid, for each 2 cups (500 ml) puréed bananas. Then package and freeze.

To make banana bread or cake, simply thaw the frozen banana purée for 15 to 20 minutes.

Peach purée

Choose ripe peaches, cut and crush them with a potato masher. Add ½ to 1 cup (125 to 250 ml) sugar and ¼ teaspoon (1 ml) ascorbic acid to each 4 cups (1 L) crushed fruit. Combine well. Fill containers, seal and freeze.

Another method is to use a food mill or sieve; this makes a smoother purée. Peel, pit and cut peaches into pieces. Mash fruit a little to start juice. Bring quickly to a boil, stirring constantly.

Remove from heat, and press through a food mill or sieve. Add sugar if desired. Add ascorbic acid (¼ teaspoon/1 ml to 4 cups/1 L fruit pulp). Cool quickly. Fill containers, seal and freeze.

Frozen fruit sauces

Fruit sauces can be made of apricots, peaches or prune plums. Use the sauces as toppings for desserts and ice cream, or in baking. Fruit sauce is also delicious by itself.

Do not attempt to handle too large a batch at one time, as quick preparation and quick cooking are necessary to preserve colour and flavour. A batch no bigger than 4 pounds (1.8 kg) of prepared fruit is recommended.

Choose fruit that is ripe but sound. Wash. Pit apricots and prunes. Scald peaches to remove skins and then remove pits.

Weigh 4 pounds (1.8 kg) of prepared fruit. Put fruit through food chopper, using coarse blade; work quickly.

Use the following table for proportion of fruit, sugar and quick-cooking tapioca.

FRUIT	QUANTITY	SUGAR	QUICK-COOKING TAPIOCA
Apricots	4 lbs (1.8 kg)	¾ lb (340 gr)	2 tbsp (30 ml)
Peaches	4 lbs (1.8 kg)	¾ lb (340 gr)	2½ tbsp (38 ml)
Prunes	4 lbs (1.8 kg)	¾ lb (340 gr)	2 tbsp (30 ml)

Mix the tapioca with ½ cup (125 ml) of the sugar. Add remaining sugar to the ground fruit. Place in a heavy saucepan over high heat. Bring to a boil, stirring constantly. Stir in sugar-tapioca mixture. Boil hard, stirring constantly, for 1½ minutes.

Remove from heat. Cool quickly. Fill freezer containers, leaving headspace. Seal and freeze.

Frozen fruit pie fillings

It is not wise to handle too large a batch at one time, as quick cooking is desirable. About 4 pounds (1.8 kg) of prepared fruit for each batch can be handled easily with the equipment found in most homes.

Choose fruit that is ripe but sound: Wash. Pit cherries. Halve apricots and prunes and remove pits. Scald peaches to remove skins, remove pits, then cut into ½-inch (1.25 cm) segments.

Use the following table for proportion of fruit, sugar, and quick-cooking tapioca.

oca. Return to a full rolling boil. Boil again for 1 minute, stirring constantly.

Remove from heat. Cool as quickly as possible.

This filling may now be made into pies. Or it can be stored in the refrigerator in jars; it will about fill two 1-quart (1 L) jars. Or the filling may be put into freezer containers, sealed and frozen to be used at a later date for such dishes as pies and tarts.

Or you can freeze the fruit pie filling in the following manner. Line an 8- or 9-inch (20 or 23 cm) pie plate with heavy foil or with a double thickness of light foil, making sure the foil extends at least 6 inches (15 cm) above the rim. Prepare your pie filling as usual. Pour into the plate and bring foil over the top to cover loosely. Freeze until firm. Then remove filling from pie plate, label and store in the freezer until ready to use.

To use, unwrap,, place frozen mixture on a pastry-lined pie plate of the same size you used to freeze in, dot with butter, and cover as your recipe directs.

FRUIT	QUANTITY	SUGAR	QUICK-COOKING TAPIOCA
Apricots	4 lbs (1.8 kg)	1 lb (500 gr)	4 tbsp (60 ml)
Cherries (Sweet)*	4 lbs (1.8 kg)	1 lb (500 gr)	5 tbsp (75 ml)
Peaches	4 lbs (1.8 kg)	1 lb (500 gr)	5 tbsp (75 ml)
Prunes	4 lbs (1.8 kg)	1 lb (500 gr)	4 tbsp (60 ml)

* If using sour cherries, use 1⅓ pounds (670 ml) sugar and 6 tablespoons (90 ml) quick-cooking tapioca.

Place prepared fruit in a heavy saucepan with three-quarters of the sugar. Combine well to start the juice flowing. If necessary, add about ⅓ cup (80 ml) water to prevent burning. Place over high heat and bring to a boil. Boil for 1 minute, stirring constantly.

Add remaining sugar which has been combined with the quick-cooking tapi-

Place in a preheated 425°F (225°C) oven for 45 to 50 minutes, or until crust is golden brown. Keeps for 6 to 8 months.

STORAGE OF FROZEN FRUITS

In general, frozen fruits can be stored for up to one year, but there are some exceptions. See the chart on page 132 and information with specific recipes. Avoid longer storage, as fruits will not remain at top quality indefinitely.

THAWING AND SERVING FRUITS FROM FREEZER

Thaw fruit just before serving. Defrost in the original sealed package, turning container over several times to distribute syrup evenly. Thaw only as much as you can use at one time. Cook any leftover thawed fruit.

For thawing a pint (0.5 L) container of fruit, allow 6 to 8 hours in the refrigerator, about 3 hours at room temperature, about 1½ hours if the air current of a fan is directed on the container, about 1 hour if the container is placed in a pan under cold running water.

Serve the fruit while it is still cold. Do not allow it to stand at room temperature after thawing, for the flavor, appearance and texture will deteriorate.

It is not necessary to thaw completely fruit to be used for pies, baked puddings or stewed fruit. For pies or puddings, thaw fruit sufficiently to separate the pieces, then proceed as with fresh fruit. Fruits such as sour cherries, used for pies and tarts, are softened by the freezing process, so they cook in much less time than fresh sour cherries.

To serve unsweetened purées, defrost and use like fresh-fruit purées in various desserts.

To serve sweetened puréed apricots or prune plums as a fruit juice, defrost, measure, then add to an equal amount of water. Stir well. Serve.

Golden glazed carrots

When you thin out the first baby carrots from your garden, glaze some to serve at New Year's dinner. Of course, any fresh carrots can be used.

**1½ lb (750 gr) baby carrots, or
1½ lb (750 gr) standard carrots, cut into strips**

2 tbsp (30 ml) all-purpose flour

¼ cup (60 ml) light brown sugar or maple sugar

½ tsp (2 ml) salt

¼ tsp (1 ml) ground thyme

1 tbsp (15 ml) cider vinegar

1 tbsp (15 ml) fresh lemon juice

½ tsp (125 ml) orange juice

Grated rind of 1 orange

2 tbsp (30 ml) butter

Place the carrots in a saucepan. Pour boiling water over them and boil 5 minutes. Drain thoroughly.

Blend the flour, sugar, salt and thyme. Add vinegar, juices and orange rind. Bring to a boil, while stirring, and continue stirring until creamy. Add the butter and cook over very low heat for 5 minutes. Line a casserole with foil, leaving enough around the edge to cover. Put in the blanched carrots and pour the sauce over. Freeze uncovered.

When frozen, cover completely with the foil. Remove the foil-wrapped carrots from the casserole and put them back in the freezer. To serve, unwrap the frozen block of carrots and put back in the same casserole. Bake, covered, in a 350°F (180°C) oven for about 40 minutes. Uncover for the last 15 minutes. Makes 6 servings.

HOW TO FREEZE VEGETABLES

It is not economical to freeze vegetables when commercially frozen produce is available all year long and often at sale prices. But it does make sense to freeze certain favorites or specialties that your family enjoys. Here are some examples of vegetable dishes that you can adapt to your own taste.

Whole kernel corn

Freezing is the best way to preserve corn — no other drying nor canning give as fresh-tasting a vegetable. However, this method does require some effort, so freeze corn only if your family really enjoys it.

Use the freshest corn possible; husk, remove the silk, and place the ears in a saucepan. Sprinkle with 1 teaspoon (5 ml) sugar for each 12 ears of corn. Pour on rapidly boiling water to cover completely. Boil fast for 4 minutes. Remove the ears from the water with tongs and place them, one by one, in a large bowl of ice water. Leave them in the ice water for 4 minutes. Then take an ear from the water, wipe it, cut the kernels from the cob, package, label and freeze. A 1-quart (1 L) plastic freezer usually holds the kernels from three ears of corn.

Cucumber purée

Cucumbers, like tomatoes, have a way of flooding the market or the garden all at once. They are not good frozen except as a purée that can be added to a French dressing or to a cream of potato soup, or used as a cold meat sauce with the addition of a little lemon juice and ground cloves or dill. The purée also makes a beautiful aspic.

12 cucumbers

2 tsp (10 ml) salt

½ cup (125 ml) boiling water

Peel cucumbers, taking off the thinnest possible layer of peel. Cut lengthwise, remove the seeds, and slice thin. Sprinkle with the salt. Place in a heavy metal saucepan and add the boiling water. Let come to a boil, then cook, uncovered, for 10 minutes. Pass through a food mill or a sieve. Package in ½-pint (8-ounce/ 250 gr) containers and freeze. Enough for 4 containers.

Leeks

In September and October leeks are plentiful and low in cost. Clean and slice them and package them in 1- or 2-cup (125 or 250 ml) portions to use for soups, casseroles and many other dishes. They freeze well and thaw very quickly. Melt some of the leeks in butter to use later for vichyssoise.

Leek base for vichissoise

Make this in the autumn, too, and you will be able to prepare a gourmet soup in 20 minutes, all year round.

12 medium-sized leeks

4 large mild onions

1½ cups (375 ml) butter

Remove top coarse leaves from leeks. Make a long split from the white part to the end of the green part. Wash carefully under cold running water, then shake off surplus water. Cut into thin slices, starting at the white base. Peel the onions and slice as thinly as possible. Melt the butter in a saucepan, add the leeks and onions, and stir well for a few seconds. Cover and cook over very low heat for 25 minutes, stirring a few times. The mixture must soften completely but must not brown. It will reduce quite a bit as it cooks. Divide by cupfuls into containers and freeze. Makes 6 cups (1.5 L).

To make the soup: Bring 3 to 4 cups (750 ml to 1 L) chicken broth to a boil and add 1 cup (250 ml) of the frozen leek mixture. Simmer fror 20 minutes. Stir ½ cup (125 ml) cold milk into 1 cup (250 ml) instant mashed potatoes, then beat into the soup mixture. Simmer together for a few minutes. Add 1 cup (250 ml) cream. When the soup is creamy, adjust seasoning. Serve as is or refrigerate and serve cold. The soup can be strained if you prefer.

Mushrooms

Choose perfect, fresh, button mushrooms. Rinse them very fast in a quart (1 L) of ice-cold water to which is added 1 tablespoon (15 ml) lemon juice. Then roll the mushrooms in absorbent paper and immediately package in a small plastic bag, or in several bags. Then label and put into the freezer. No thawing is needed to cook them. Brown some butter; then, keeping the pan over high heat, add the frozen mushrooms and stir constantly for 2 to 3 minutes. Remove from heat, season to taste, and serve.

When using mushrooms in a sauce, simply add them as they come from the bag, or slice them while frozen.

Fresh mushrooms can also be frozen after cooking. Cook quickly in butter, for no more than 3 to 4 minutes. They can be whole or sliced. Cool, package, label and freeze.

Onions

When small white (silverskin) onions or the large sweet red onions are plentiful and cheap, it is time to make the winter provision. Simply peel the onions and place them whole in good plastic containers, then freeze. When you need them, open the container and take out what is required; they do not stick together. It is much easier to slice or chop onions when they are still partly frozen. If you plan to boil the onions, you do not need to thaw them before cooking.

Parsley and other fresh herbs

If you grow your own herbs, gather some when they are at their prime. The best time is after a soft rainfall, when they are clean. Place small portions, whole or minced, in plastic bags. Label and freeze. To use them whole, cut with kitchen shears while crisply frozen. They will taste just like fresh herbs and retain their full green colour.

Green peppers

When green peppers are plentiful, chop, slice or halve them. Wrap the pieces and freeze them. They will keep for 3 to 4 months. Like celery, peppers become limp when they thaw but they are wonderful to use in cooked preparations. Simply add them still frozen to the recipe. When you are ready to use them, just separate as much pepper as you need and return the rest to the freezer.

Baked potatoes

Rub the skin of each potato before baking with a bit of butter, then roll it in coarse salt. A few crystals stick to the potatoes, giving a crisped tasty baked potato. French chefs call them *pommes de terre grêlées*.

Cool the baked potatoes as quickly as possible and wrap each one in heavy-duty foil. Freeze. Reheat by placing the wrapped package in a 350°F (180°C) oven for 1 hour. They will be perfect if the package is opened as soon as the potatoes are hot.

French fried potatoes

If your family loves french fried potatoes, you can save a lot of time by making many and freezing them in packages large enough for one meal. Making fries from six to eight potatoes at a time is quick and easy. Use peanut oil if possible.

Cut the potatoes into long strips about ½ inch (1.25 cm) thick, or into much smaller strips for matchstick (allumette) potatoes, or into thin round slices. Place the pieces in a bowl and cover with cold water. Let stand for 1 hour. Drain and dry thoroughly in a towel. Heat enough oil to have 3 inches (7.5 cm) in the saucepan. When hot (360°F (185°C) on a frying thermometer), fry a few slices at a time for about 5 minutes, or just to a light beige colour. Drain on absorbent paper and repeat with remaining potatoes.

Cool to room temperature. Do not salt before freezing. Package in convenient portions, seal, label, date and freeze. They will keep for 1 month.

To serve, place frozen potatoes on a greased baking sheet. Preheat oven to 450°F (230°C). Put in potatoes and brown for 10 to 15 minutes, turning once. Sprinkle with salt and serve.

COOKING FROZEN VEGETABLES
These notes apply to both home-frozen and commercial products.

Cook all vegetables, except corn on the cob, without thawing. When they are frozen in a solid block, as is the case with spinach, thaw for 20 to 25 minutes at the most, or enough to be able to separate the block into a few pieces.

Place the frozen vegetables in a saucepan and sprinkle with a pinch of sugar and ¼ teaspoon (1 ml) monosodium glutamate (MSG). Pour boiling water on top, bring back to a fast rolling boil, cover, and lower heat to medium. Cook for 4 to 15 minutes. The time depends on the vegetable, the variety, maturity, size of pieces. What is most important with frozen vegetables is not to overcook them; they are already partly cooked. Freezing breaks down fibres and makes the vegetables softer. And in most cases they have also undergone another breaking-down process, actually a cooking process — blanching — which reduces the necessary cooking time, generally by 25 to 75 per cent. Some vegetables are frozen after being completely cooked; for these only reheating is necessary. Taste a small piece of vegetable after 4 or 5 minutes; then decide how much longer it needs to cook to your taste.

Use the minimum amount of water to cook frozen vegetables. Generally, ½ cup (125 ml) water is adequate for 1 pint (500 ml) of vegetables.

A cooked frozen vegetable does not stand without losing much of its colour and flavour, so serve them as soon as they are cooked.

Corn on the cob, because of its heavy starch and sugar content, is an exception to the rule of cooking without thawing. Partially thaw corn, then place it in a saucepan and pour boiling water on top. Cover and cook for only 3 to 6 minutes. A longer time will make the corn mealy and hard. Serve as soon as ready.

Cook frozen spinach, pumpkin and squash unthawed, without water, on the top part of a double boiler. Add a piece of butter when the vegetable is partly thawed. Keep the water in the bottom part boiling rapidly, and break up and stir the vegetable often. It takes a little longer, but the final result is excellent.

HOW TO FREEZE EGGS

Eggs are more plentiful and as a result cheaper at certain times of the year. You can store them frozen in several ways, but dont expect to be able to make poached or fried eggs with them afterward, as they are not frozen in their shells. Frozen eggs can be kept in storage for four months.

Uncooked eggs

WHOLE EGGS. Beat the eggs with a fork just enough to break the yolks and blend them into the whites. Add 1 teaspoon (5 ml) salt or 1 tablespoon (15 ml) sugar, honey or corn syrup for each 2 cups (500 ml) of beaten eggs. Freeze in an ice-cube tray with the divider in place. When frozen, remove the cubes from the tray and store them in a plastic bag. In 1 large frozen cube you will have about 3 tablespoons (50 ml), or slightly less than 1 medium-sized egg. Measure your own ice cube so that you will know how much liquid it contains.

With whole eggs you may want to package the number required for a specific recipe you make often. For example, a cake may call for 8 whole eggs. Beat, season with salt, and freeze the required eggs, then package after freezing and label "8 eggs for cake".

Some recipes call for whites or yolks alone. Instead of mixing the parts together, separate the eggs carefully, then measure and freeze.

EGG YOLKS. Beat the egg yolks lightly with a fork. Stir in 1 teaspoon (5 ml) salt or 1 tablespoon (15 ml) sugar, honey or corn syrup to each 1 cup (250 ml) yolks. Freeze in an ice-cube tray with the dividers in place. When frozen, remove the cubes from the tray and store them in a plastic bag. Label as to quantity of yolks and salt or sugar. About 14 egg yolks of medium-sized eggs equal 1 cup (250 ml). A large frozen cube usually equals 3 tablespoons (50 ml) egg yolk, or 2 or 3 egg yolks.

EGG WHITES. Egg whites can be packaged without the addition of either salt or sugar; they need no mixing. Freeze in an ice-cube tray with the divider in place. Store the frozen cubes in bags. Label and freeze just as for egg yolks. About 8 egg whites of medium-sized eggs equal 1 cup (250 ml). A large cube usually equals 3 tablespoons (50 ml) egg white, or 1½ egg whites.

Thaw at room temperature or in the refrigerator before beating.

When thawing uncooked eggs, here is a good rule to follow: 6 eggs will thaw, in an unopened container in the refrigerator in 2 to 3 hours, or at room temperature in 30 to 45 minutes. Waterproof containers can be placed unopened in a bowl of cold water for even faster thawing.

Cooked eggs

Hard-cooked eggs freeze nicely when finely grated. Thaw to use in salads, sandwich fillings, soup garnishes and to garnish vegetables such as spinach.

HOW TO FREEZE MEAT

First let us consider buying meat in wholesale portions. Although there are disadvantages to this, you might find that it results in substantial savings because of the size of your family or its preferences. For instance, if beef is your favourite, you have a 15-to 20-cubic-foot freezer and your family consists of four or more persons, it can be a long-run economy to buy a half of beef. A half usually runs from 215 to 250 pounds (96 to 113 kg) untrimmed, so you will have a supply of beef for several months. Of course, you will have a variety of cuts, and you will get approximately 30 pounds (14 kg) that can be ground or cut for stew. Ask the butcher to leave any ground meat unfrozen so you can shape it and wrap it yourself.

If your family is fond of steaks and not interested in pot roasts or soups, then a hindquarter might be a good buy, though it will cost more per unit of weight than the half. The roasts in this cut will be rump and sirloin tips. The hindquarter runs slightly smaller than the forequarter.

When the pieces have been cut by the butcher, he may freeze them for you. Be sure the meat is cut into pieces of an appropriate size to cook or it will be difficult for you to manage. Then wrap it and store it for future use.

If the meat is not frozen for you, this is the general procedure to follow: Chill the meat thoroughly. Pad all projecting bones with freezer paper or foil so they will not pierce the wrapping. Then wrap in suitable freezer wrapping. Press the wrapping close to the meat to exclude air. If you are packing steaks or chops, separate individual pieces with sheets of waxed paper or freezer paper. Hearts, kidneys and livers can be frozen uncooked, but brains, sweet-breads and tripe should be cooked before freezing. Put the wrapped packages close to the walls of your freezer for rapid freezing.

It is particularly important to label each meat package with date and contents, as different cuts can be stored for different lengths of time. See the chart later in this chapter for some of these times.

Frozen ground meats

Ground meat is very difficult to manage if it is frozen loose in a large package. Not only is it necessary to thaw it out almost completely before it can be used, but after thawing it will not stick together to form a compact patty. It is better to make the patties before freezing, seasoning as you usually do, except for salt, which should be added only when the meat is cooking. This is important because salt in meat that is frozen causes oxidation by preventing quick freezing of the water in the meat.

Shape the ground meat into patties of a size to fit the bread or bun you usually use. Place a square of waxed paper between each 2 patties. Then wrap 6 to 8 per package in moistureproof freezer paper. Place in the freezer. When you are ready to serve, separate the number you need and rewrap the rest and return them to the freezer. Thaw the patties you are using just enough so that you can get the paper off. Then season each with salt, and other seasonings if you have not already done this before freezing. Cook quickly over medium-high heat. When browned on one side, turn and brown the other side. The whole process should take from 8 to 10 minutes.

When you are too rushed to season and blend before freezing, just shape the meat into patties, wrap and freeze. At cooking time, separate the frozen patties and sprinkle them with salt and MSG. Then blend in a bowl the thyme, parsley, pepper or Worcestershire sauce and consommé. Soak each patty in the liquid for 5 minutes. Then fry them in melted beef suet (delicious!), or broil them 3 inches (7.5 cm) from the source of heat for 4 to 6 minutes on each side.

My favourite hamburger mixture ⚬⇥

1 lb (500 gr) ground beef

1 tsp (5 ml) MSG (monosodium glutamate)

¼ tsp (1 ml) dried thyme

1 tsp (5 ml) minced fresh parsley

⅛ tsp (0.5 ml) pepper or 1 tbsp (15 ml) Worcestershire sauce

¼ cup (60 ml) undiluted condensed consommé.

To the ground beef add the MSG, dried thyme, minced fresh parsley, pepper **or** Worcestershire sauce, undiluted condensed consommé. Blend the whole thoroughly, shape patties, wrap and freeze. They keep in the freezer 4 to 6 weeks.

Meat storage time

Although some frozen meats will store satisfactorily for several months if properly wrapped, it is not practical to fill up limited storage space with them for long periods of time. Large or thick cuts can be stored frozen considerably longer than small pieces, for the small bits tend to dry out and develop off-flavours. It is necessary to label all packages of frozen food, but it is especially important with meats to mark on each package the kind of meat, name of cut, weight and date so that none will be kept longer than the storage time that has been recommended.

The maximum storage times at 0°F (-18°C) according to Agriculture Canada are:

MEATS	MAX. STORAGE TIMES
Bacon	1 to 2 months
Beef, roasts, steaks	10 to 12 months
Cooked meats, stews, loaves, etc.	1 to 2 months
Cooked roasts	2 to 3 months
Gravy, unthickened	3 to 4 months
Lamb chops	4 to 5 months
Lamb roasts	6 to 8 months
Minced or ground meat, raw	2 to 3 months
Pork chops, fresh	3 to 4 months
Pork, cured, smoked	1 to 2 months
Pork roasts, fresh	4 to 5 months
Sausages, wieners	2 to 3 months
Variety meats, liver, heart, kidneys, etc.	3 to 4 months
Veal roasts, chops	4 to 5 months

COOKING FROZEN MEATS

Years ago it was a must to thaw meat completely before cooking, but experience has shown that completely frozen meat can be cooked with excellent results.

To thaw meat, place it, still wrapped, in the bottom of the refrigerator for 6 to 8 hours. Often it does not completely thaw out, but the thawing process is started. Or leave it at room temperature for 2 to 3 hours. Thawing times vary, of course, with the weight of the piece of meat, its shape and thickness. To thaw meat completely in the refrigerator, you must allow from 10 to 12 hours per pound (500 gr). At room temperature, meat will thaw in 2 to 3 hours per pound (500 gr). Be sure to keep it wrapped while thawing to prevent evaporation of the juices.

Thawing meat in a bowl of cold water, even when still wrapped, is not recommended.

Leftovers and sliced cooked meat are at their best when thawed, still wrapped, over boiling water, or by steaming. This prevents any dryness when it is reheated. Never thaw frozen food by placing it in a slow oven; this will dry it out.

Cooking meat in its frozen state does not in any way change its quality, but of course it must be properly cooked. There is only one disadvantage: it takes longer, and consequently uses a larger amount of fuel.

0➔ A very important secret for success in cooking frozen meat is to use a meat thermometre. Timing is absolutely unreliable when dealing with frozen, partially frozen, or even totally defrosted meat; their texture varies too much. In general, completely frozen roasts take from half again to twice as long to cook as completely thawed-out roasts. But the safest way to determine doneness is by the internal temperature; the meat thermometre should read the same as for unfrozen meats. Of course a thermometre cannot be inserted into a solidly frozen roast or steak, so wait until the meat has cooked for a time and has started to soften before you try inserting a metal skewer. If the skewer will go in, you can insert the thermometre.

As to the cooking and seasoning of frozen meat, you can follow any of the recipes and methods given in the sections that describe ways to cook meat in Vol. II. Here are a few examples of how to cook solidly frozen meat.

When you have an emergency and a roast or steak must be started while still frozen, first preheat oven to 450°F (230°C); allow 20 minutes for this temperature to be reached. Set the unwrapped and prepared roast in it and sear for 25 minutes. Lower the heat to 350°F, (180°C), then cook as you would an ordinary meat roast.

For a steak, use a heavy metal frying pan, heat the pan, and sear the steak on both sides, in the minimum of fat, over high heat; then finish cooking the steak as usual.

HOW TO FREEZE POULTRY

In general, the rules that apply to meat are useful for poultry. It may be frozen whole, in halves, or in pieces. All birds should be eviscerated, cleaned of feather or hairs, and carefully washed and well dried. If you buy it eviscerated, be sure to examine inside the carcass to remove any forgotten bits. Remove all extra fat, for this can become rancid. If the bird is to be frozen whole, truss it to give it a more compact form. Do not stuff it, for this can encourage the growth of bacteria. Chill the poultry thoroughly, then wrap it, remembering to be sure to cover any projecting bones. Separate individual pieces if you are freezing cut-up poultry.

Poultry will thaw in about five hours in the refrigerator, in about 1½ hours at room temperature. It should be thawed still in its wrapping. Just as with meat, it is not recommended to defrost poultry by placing it in a bowl of cold water.

Cook frozen raw poultry as soon as thawed, and use frozen cooked poultry as soon as thawed.

Leftover cooked poultry that is to be frozen is usually most successful when cut from the bones, which saves space. However, even when well wrapped, such poultry tends to dry and lose flavour in the freezer. It is better to pack it with poultry gravy or other appropriate sauce.

Cook frozen poultry by any of the methods described for fresh poultry, but remember that the freezing process affects the food just like partial cooking does by helping to break down the tissues of the food and make them softer; with a chicken, the ice crystals formed in the muscle fibres help to break them apart and make the meat easier to cut and chew, even though the flavour is unaffected. Therefore, the cooking time for completely thawed poultry may be less than for unfrozen poultry. It is better to thaw or partially thaw poultry before cooking it.

HOW TO FREEZE FISH

Fish can be frozen, but the frozen product is very different from freshly caught fish. There is a loss of juice and flavour, particularly with fillets or slices. Clean all fish as quickly as possible, and keep them cold until placed in the freezer. Remove any streaks of fat on fish to be frozen; it is apt to become rancid. This applies especially to salmon and mackerel.

There are three methods for freezing fish:

Glazing method: Clean the fish and place it on a tray in the freezer until frozen solid. Then dip it into very cold water for 2 minutes and freeze it again. Repeat this soaking a second time, freeze again, then wrap carefully and store.

Brine method: Clean the fish. Make a brine with 1 cup (250 ml) coarse salt and 4 quarts (4.5 L) cold water. Soak the fish in this for 10 minutes. Drain, wrap carefully and freeze.

Ice-block method: Brook or lake trout or any other fisherman's catch can be frozen this way. Clean the whole fish and place it in a long pan, like a loaf pan, appropriate to the size of the fish. Cover the fish with ice-cold water. To get water of the right temperature, place ice cubes in a bowl of water for 10 to 15 minutes ahead of time. Finnish housewives sometimes add a few sprigs of fresh dill to the water. Place the fish in the freezer. When frozen solid, unmould from the pan. This will be easy if you let hot water run on the underside of the pan for 2 or 3 seconds. Wrap the block of ice containing the fish in heavy-duty foil. Then return to the freezer.

To thaw out a whole fish frozen in this fashion, break up whatever ice you can without touching the fish, then place the fish in a large bowl in the refrigerator. It may take 4 to 8 hours to thaw, depending on its size.

In addition to freezing whole small fish, steaks or fillets can be frozen.

Frozen fish cakes

All cooked and canned fish apart from cod can be mixed, formed into cakes and balls, wrapped and frozen. **0—** *This recipe for fish cakes gives good results regardless of what fish is used.*

3 cups (750 ml) cooked fish or drained canned fish

3 cups (750 ml) mashed potatoes

2 eggs

2 tbsp (30 ml) melted margarine

½ tsp (2 ml) salt

¼ tsp (1 ml) pepper

½ tsp (2 ml) celery seeds or curry powder

½ tsp (2 ml) MSG (monosodium glutamate)

½ tsp (2 ml) dry mustard

1 tsp (5 ml) grated onion

Grated rind of ½ lemon

2 tsp (10 ml) lemon juice

Place in a large bowl the cooked fish or drained canned fish and plain, unseasoned mashed potatoes. Add well beaten eggs, melted margarine, salt, pepper, celery seeds or curry powder, MSG, dry mustard, grated onion, grated lemon rind and lemon juice. Mix thoroughly with your hands until smooth. Form into cakes, wrap with 2 pieces of freezer paper between cakes and freeze.

To cook, sauté, while still unthawed, in vegetable oil, bacon fat or melted suet over medium-high heat until brown on both sides. Makes 16 cakes.

Separate individual pieces with 2 pieces of freezer paper, wrap and freeze. Cut-up chunks of fish can be frozen also; for these the brine method is best.

Shelled clams, oysters, scallops and shrimps can be frozen raw. Pack in cartons and fill spaces with the shellfish's own liquid or with a light brine — 1 tablespoon (15 ml) salt to 4 cups (1 L) water. Crabmeat and lobster meat should be cooked before freezing, then cooled and packed in airtight containers.

Thawing and cooking frozen fish and shellfish

For best flavour do not store frozen fish for more than 4 months, although it probably is safe for up to 6 months. Oily or fatty fishes should be stored for shorter times because of the possibility of the fat in the tissues becoming rancid. Fish can be cooked without thawing.

As for shellfish, frozen shrimps should be used within 6 weeks; clams, oysters, and scallops within 3 months. Cooked crabmeat and lobster meat can be stored longer, but after 6 weeks the meat tends to toughen, so it is better to use it within that time. Shellfish should be thawed before cooking or serving.

HOW TO FREEZE BREAD

Freeze breads and baked products in heavy kraft-paper bags, plastic bags or aluminum foil. Write the date on the packages so they are used in proper rotation. Most baked products will keep for 3 to 4 months.

Bread for toast
Simply wrap sliced fresh bread in foil. It will go straight from the freezer to your toaster without defrosting. Keeps for 3 to 4 months.

Bread for poultry dressing
Cut dry bread into small cubes, package and store in the freezer for a soft poultry stuffing. Add fresh herbs if you like; they freeze well together. Keeps for 8 to 12 months.

Buttered croutons
Cut bread into croutons. If the bread is not dry, place the croutons on a baking sheet and set in a 300°F (150°C) oven for 5 minutes. When the croutons are dry, brown slowly in butter in a large skillet. Drain on absorbent paper. Package in small plastic bags. Freeze.

To serve, set the frozen croutons on a baking sheet and reheat in a 300°F (150°C) oven until crisp. Add to soup while they are hot or to salads when they cool.

Pancakes
0—🍴 Make your favorite pancake recipe. Let the cakes cool completely in a single layer on a wire rack. Then place a double thickness of waxed paper between the pancakes. Wrap in foil and freeze. To serve, preheat oven to 425°F (225°C). Remove as many pancakes as you wish to serve and rewrap the rest. Bake on a baking sheet for 15 to 18 minutes. They taste just as though they had been freshly made.

Doughnuts
Doughnuts, frozen, then warmed up in 300°F (150°C) oven, are delicious.

HOW TO FREEZE CAKES

Cakes with frostings and fillings

It is simple to freeze cakes without frosting. Just cool the cake, wrap and freeze. In addition, some cakes with frosting can be frozen. Frostings made with butter or margarine and icing sugar store best. Boiled or fudge-type frostings also freeze well. Never try to freeze a frosting made with egg whites; it becomes very spongy.

The best fillings are fudge and nut-fruit types. Cream and custard fillings are not satisfactory for freezing.

When a cake is frosted, first freeze it uncovered. As soon as it is frozen, wrap, and then return it to the freezer immediately.

Fruitcakes

Wrap these in a cloth soaked in orange juice, lemon juice or brandy and then in heavy-duty foil. You can freeze the cake sliced, with pieces of waxed paper between slices. This makes for quick defrosting when only a few slices are needed. Keeps for 12 months.

DAIRY PRODUCTS

HOW TO FREEZE DAIRY PRODUCTS

Butter

Salted butter will keep under ordinary refrigeration for a very long time. However, if you buy it in quantity, it is better to store it in the freezer because there is some flavor loss during refrigeration. Unsalted or sweet butter, on the other hand, is definitely perishable. It is best to keep out only what you plan to use within a week.

Wrap butter in heavy-duty foil. To use, thaw it in the refrigerator for 3 hours, or at room temperature for 1 to 2 hours. Keeps for up to 6 months.

Light and heavy cream

0━┳ It is useful to know that you can freeze cream, because fresh cream sours easily. Freeze in unopened cartons or in small plastic containers.

Use frozen light cream for cooking only in hot sauces; no need to thaw before adding to the sauce.

Use heavy cream for whipping after thawing in refrigerator.

Grated cheese

Freeze grated cheese of one type, or small leftover pieces grated and mixed. Simply package in small plastic bags, label and freeze. No need to thaw to use.

HOW TO FREEZE MISCELLANEOUS ITEMS

Nutmeats and whole nuts

Freeze these in plastic ice-cream containers or in heavy plastic bags. They keep for 12 to 14 months.

Marshmallows

If you store marshmallows in the freezer, they do not dry out. When they need to be cut for a recipe, your shears will not stick if you cut them while they are still frozen. Keep for 8 to 12 months.

Lemon and orange rinds

These lose none of their colour and flavour when frozen and do not have to be thawed before using. Before squeezing lemons or oranges for juice, grate the rinds and put in small jars. Keep for 6 to 9 months.

Mixed fruit peels and glacéed fruits

Stock up with these at Christmas, when they are fresh and plentiful. Place the fruits or peels, still in their original containers, in plastic freezer bags and freeze. They will retain their moisture and freshness for one year.

Syrup from canned or stewed fruits

0—➤ Freeze leftover syrup from canned or stewed fruits in individual ice-cube sections. When frozen, remove cubes to plastic bags. Use the defrosted syrup to poach fruits or to make dessert sauces or custards. The syrups from different fruits can be mixed. They also make delicious cold drinks in summer.

Fresh gingerroots

If you are an ardent user of fresh gingerroot, you will be pleased to know that it freezes very well. Scrub the roots thoroughly and dry them. Then wrap them or place them in a container; freeze. When a recipe calls for ginger, simply grate the frozen root. Keeps for 12 to 18 months.

Ready-cooked casseroles

When preparing a casserole for eventual freezing, line the baking dish with heavy-duty foil, allowing enough to fold over the top of the dish. Cook it, cool it, then place it in the freezer. When it is frozen solid, lift the foil-wrapped food from the casserole and wrap it again with extra foil. This saves freezer space. Make a label stating which casserole dish was used and reheat in the same dish. Keeps for 2 to 3 months.

Leftover gravy

Freeze leftover gravy in small containers, or in an ice-cube tray. Remove from the tray, package, label and store. Very useful for hot meat sandwiches and emergency gravy.

Coffee, tea

Whether in beans or ground, coffee can be frozen in the bag in which it was purchased. If you have a coffee mill, the beans can be freshly ground straight from the freezer. Frozen coffee never loses its flavour, as it may do if kept on the kitchen shelf. Keeps for 3 to 5 months.

Tea can be stored in the freezer in the same way and does not lose flavour.

Sandwich fillings

Keep some of these fillings in your freezer, plus packages of different types of sliced breads. It will be easy to prepare sandwiches for your lunch box, picnic or unexpected company. Each recipe makes a filling for 5 to 6 sandwiches.

PEANUT BUTTER FAVOURITE: Cream together 1 cup (250 ml) peanut butter and ½ cup (125 ml) each of orange marmalade and honey. Add the grated rind of 1 orange. Freeze.

HUSBAND'S PREFERENCE: Mix ½ pound (250 gr) bacon, cooked crisp and crumbled, with 1 cup (250 ml) peanut butter. Blend in ½ cup (125 ml) relish. Freeze.

SARDINE BRITTANY: Empty into a bowl 1 can (about 4 ounces (113 gr) smoked small sardines with their oil; add 2 or 3 hard-cooked eggs chopped fine, the juice of ½ lemon and ½ teaspoon (2 ml) curry powder. Blend thoroughly; freeze.

B.C. SPECIAL: Empty a 1-pound (500 gr) can of salmon into a bowl; when possible use red sockeye. Remove the skin but not the bones or the juice. Mash the fish and crush the bones with a fork. Then add the juice and grated rind of 1 lemon, ½ cup (125 ml) chutney, 1 teaspoon (5 ml) curry powder, 3 green onions chopped fine, and ¼ cup (60 ml) minced fresh parsley. Mix thoroughly. Freeze.

FROZEN PIES

HOW TO FREEZE PIES

Fruit pies and mince pies are better when they are frozen before baking. Sprinkle a little ascorbic acid solution or lemon juice over fresh apples and peaches to prevent the fruit from darkening.

You may find it helpful to add about one-third more flour or cornstarch to the fruit than the recipe calls for. This prevents the lower crust from becoming soggy. It is also better not to make steam vents in the top crust. If the pie has a fancy fluted edge, freeze the pie before wrapping. This helps protect the edge.

Unbaked pies keep well for 3 to 6 months. To bake them, remove wrappings, cut a steam vent in the top crust and place in a 450°F (230°C oven for 15 minutes. Then reduce heat to 375°F (190°C) and continue baking for an additional 45 minutes, or until browned evenly all over.

To freeze baked fruit pies, cool the pies; place a paper pie plate over each; wrap, seal and freeze. To thaw, place in a 375°F (190°C) oven for 25 to 30 minutes, or let them stand at room temperature for about 3 hours.

Chiffon pies also freeze well for about 3 months. To thaw, let stand at room temperature for about 2½ hours.

Crumb topping for fruit pies
0➤ Do not throw away cake crumbs. Freeze them and use them later to make a crunchy topping for a fruit pie.

Mix the frozen cake crumbs with a bit of brown sugar and a sprinkling of cinnamon, or another spice of your choice.

HOW TO DEFROST YOUR FREEZER

If you do not have a frost-free freezer, it is necessary to defrost and wash your freezer. Choose months when the food content is low, which usually happens between seasons.

First, place frozen foods in cartons and top with a good layer of newspaper. This helps to keep the cold in.

Then spread a large bath towel or a thick layer of newspaper in the bottom of the empty freezer. This makes it easy to remove ice and water. Turn off the electricity. Then start to scrape off the frost with a wooden or plastic scraper. Do not use metal.

Place in the bottom of the freezer 2 pails of boiling water. Close the freezer and let stand for 20 to 30 minutes. Then scrape whatever stubborn ice remains. It will slide right off the side of the freezer.

Remove the pails of water. Have a large bowl or box at hand into which you can put the towel or paper lifted from the bottom with as much as possible of the ice moisture it has absorbed.

Wash the whole inside with a solution of 3 tablespoons (50 ml) baking soda to 1 quart (1 L) hot water. Rinse and wipe. Turn on the electricity. Return the food, inspecting each parcel before putting it in to be sure no crack or broken paper is left uncovered. This may sound involved, but it is comparatively easy to do and the food has no time to defrost.

All the information in this chapter relates to a freezer whose temperature is a constant 0°F (-18°C) or lower, which is rarely the case with a small freezer compartment in a refrigerator. Small refrigerator freezing areas are best used for making and storing ice cubes and for short-term storage of items in regular use so that they are replaced fairly often.

Table of Contents

Lithographié au Canada
sur les presses de
Métropole Litho Inc.